# Modern Bride®
## Guide to Etiquette

Also available from Wiley's *Modern Bride®* Library:

## Modern Bride® Wedding Celebrations
*The Complete Wedding Planner for Today's Bride*
by Cele Goldsmith Lalli and Stephanie H. Dahl

# Modern Bride
## Guide to Etiquette

Answers to the questions today's
couples *really* ask

**CELE GOLDSMITH LALLI**
Editor-in-Chief of *Modern Bride*

**JOHN WILEY & SONS, INC.**
NEW YORK · CHICHESTER · BRISBANE · TORONTO · SINGAPORE

Interior Design and Composition: Impressions, a division of Edwards Brothers, Inc.
Cover Photography: © 1993, Comstock, Inc.
Interior Illustration: Luann Roberts
MODERN BRIDE is a registered trademark of Reed Properties Inc. used under
license by Cahners Publishing Company.

This text is printed on acid-free paper.

*Library of Congress Cataloging-in-Publication Data*

Lalli, Cele Goldsmith, 1933–
    Modern bride guide to etiquette: answers to the questions today's
couples *really* ask / Cele Goldsmith Lalli.
        p.  cm.
    Includes index.
    ISBN 0-471-58299-9 (pbk.)
    1. Wedding etiquette. 2. Weddings—Planning.   I. Title.
BJ2051.L349   1993
395'.22—dc20                                                              92-42166

Printed in the United States of America
10  9  8  7  6  5

*To Viola W. Goldsmith,*
*my extraordinary mother*
*and role model.*

*To Michael, Francesca, and Erica Lalli,*
*my husband and daughters,*
*for their unconditional love and encouragement.*

*To Stephanie H. Dahl,*
*my colleague and dear friend,*
*who is always there for me.*

# *Acknowledgments*

I extend my thanks to the thousands of readers of *Modern Bride* who have looked to me for advice throughout the years. This book is the result of that correspondence. In addition, I am grateful for the cooperation and support given to me by the following: Howard Friedberg, Joel Ehrlich, Mike Tucker, Gail Altsher Jasne, Mary Ann Cavlin, Nancy Davis, Martine Aerts-Niddam, Linda Magloire Wolfe, Elyse Salman Spiewak, Carolyn Bartel, Margaret Schell, Linda Hirst, Geri Bain, Laurel Cardone, Debbra Gill, Lisa Moore Cusick, Jihan Kim, Michele Aurora, Suzanne Oppenheimer, Paul Rodina, Kristen O'Rourke, Melanie Kubat Rush, Lisa Marmorato, Kim Lanciloti, Allan Dexheimer, and Drew Reid Kerr.

A special note of appreciation goes to my editor, Judith N. McCarthy, for her very constructive suggestions based on her own recent wedding and those of so many of her colleagues and friends.

# Preface

Wedding planning today is more complicated than it was when our parents were at this happy point in their lives. Currently, greater mobility; higher levels of education; relocation away from where the bride- and groom-to-be grew up; stress in the work place; economic restraints; limited leisure time; divorce and remarriage among parents; interfaith, intercultural, interracial marriage; as well as remarriage for the bride and/or groom, have all contributed to a need for individualization and greater personalization of each couple's arrangements. The result is that there are no absolute criteria for "the" perfect wedding; the goal is rather to plan "your" perfect wedding.

Every day letters arrive with questions about how to deal with complications that used to be the exception, but now have become the rule. This book addresses the commonality of pressures faced by today's engaged couples. It covers the gamut from ordinary confusion because the bride-to-be has never read an etiquette book to outright hysteria because nothing is going right. It is intended to provide practical solutions to help the couple and those they love come to realistic and constructive compromises that will get them all to the wedding in the spirit of joyful celebration, which is what this rite of passage is all about.

I hope that you will find the answers to all of your questions between these covers, so that when the big day arrives you will be able to savor every precious moment. With that end in mind, you and your fiancé should commit yourselves to making certain that your wedding is the best wedding you will ever attend!

Congratulations and good luck.


Cele Goldsmith Lalli
Editor-in-Chief
*Modern Bride*

# Contents

## 1 — Engagement 1
Telling Family and Friends  1
The Ring  2
Length of Engagement  3
Newspaper Announcements  4
Parties and Presents  5
Postponed or Broken Engagements  8
Quick Tips for the Modern Bride:
Engagement Guidelines  10

## 2 — Budgeting 11
Who Pays for What?  11
Allocating Expenses  12
How to Stretch Your Wedding Dollars  14
Hiring a Wedding Consultant  15
How Much Should You Spend on Your Dress?  16
Quick Tips for the Modern Bride:
Budgeting Guidelines  18

## 3 — Taking Control 19
Selecting the Date  19
Choosing a Wedding Style  20
Handling "Buttinskies"  21
Determining Who Does What  22
Quick Tips for the Modern Bride:
Ways to Keep It *Your* Wedding  24

## 4 — Invitations & Announcements 25
Compiling the Guest List  25
Choosing the Invitations  28
Bride's Parents Hosting  29
Divorced and Remarried Parents Hosting  31
Divorced but Not Remarried Parents Hosting  31
Parents Co-Hosting  32
The Couple Hosting  33
Addressing Invitations  33
Invitation to Ceremony or Reception Only  35
Sending Announcements  36

Quick Tips for the Modern Bride:
Hints on Invitations and Announcements  *38*

## 5 — *Attendants* *39*

The Bride's Attendants  *39*
Bridesmaids' Attire  *44*
Mom as Honor Attendant  *46*
Bride's Attendants' Duties  *46*
The Groom's Attendants  *47*
Groom's Attendants' Duties  *48*
Children in the Wedding  *49*
Pregnant Attendants  *51*
Quick Tips for the Modern Bride:
Attendant Etiquette  *53*

## 6 — *What to Wear* *55*

The Bride's Attire  *55*
Headpiece, Veil, and Accessories  *59*
Full-Figured Styles  *62*
Petite Bride  *63*
Wedding Dress Rental  *63*
Preserving Your Gown  *64*
The Groom's Attire  *64*
Mothers' Dresses  *66*
Fathers' Attire  *67*
Guests' Attire  *67*
What to Wear  *68*

## 7 — *Choosing Resources* *71*

Choosing the Photographer and Videographer  *71*
Choosing Ceremony Musicians  *73*
Choosing the Reception Musicians  *74*
Choosing the Florist  *76*
Transportation  *78*
Dealing with Legal Issues  *79*
Quick Tips for the Modern Bride:
Hints on Choosing Resources  *81*

## 8 — *Guest Accommodations* *83*

Arrangements for Out-of-Towners  *83*
Parking and Other Amenities  *85*

Quick Tips for the Modern Bride:
Ways to Accommodate Your Guests  *87*

## 9 — *The Ceremony* *89*

Finding an Officiant  *89*
Personalizing Your Service  *91*
Wedding Rings  *92*
Seating  *92*
Escorting the Bride  *93*
Order of Processional and Recessional  *95*
Interfaith Accommodations  *97*
Candlelight and Candle-Lighting  *99*
Quick Tips for the Modern Bride:
Planning the Ceremony of Your Dreams  *101*

## 10 — *The Reception* *103*

Choosing the Location  *103*
Choosing the Caterer  *105*
Menu Options  *107*
Receiving Line  *108*
Seating Options  *108*
Schedule of Events  *110*
Wedding Cake  *111*
Smoking and Allergies  *112*
Other Quandaries  *112*
Quick Tips for the Modern Bride:
Making the Reception Worry Free  *116*

## 11 — *Specialty Weddings* *117*

Destination Weddings  *117*
Remarriage  *119*
Military Weddings  *121*
Long-Distance Weddings  *122*
Garden or At-Home Weddings  *123*
Marrying Abroad  *124*
Double Weddings  *124*
Holiday and Theme Weddings  *126*
Reaffirmation  *128*
Quick Tips for the Modern Bride:
HInts on Specialty Weddings  *131*

## 12 — *Related Parties* 133
Showers *133*
Bridal Luncheon *136*
Bachelor Bash *137*
Rehearsal Festivities *138*
Pre- and Post-Wedding Receptions *140*
Quick Tips for the Modern Bride:
Party Etiquette *142*

## 13 — *All About Gifts* 143
The Bridal Gift Registry *143*
Displaying Gifts *144*
Cash and Other Alternatives *145*
Gifts for Attendants *146*
Gifts for Each Other and Parents *148*
Thank-You Notes *149*
Quick Tips for the Modern Bride:
Handling Gifts *151*

## 14 — *Special Situations* 153
Dealing with Divorced Parents *153*
Parents Who Object to the Wedding *156*
The Pregnant Bride *158*
Teen Marriage *159*
Different Cultures *159*
Ethnic Traditions and Customs *162*
Participation of Loved Ones with a Disability *164*
Combining Another Family Milestone with Your Wedding *165*
Conflicting Wedding Dates *166*
Remembering Deceased Relatives *167*
Alcoholism *168*
Other Quandaries *169*
Quick Tips for the Modern Bride:
Handling Special Situations *171*

## 15 — *Your Honeymoon* 173
Where to Go *173*
How to Plan *174*
Quick Tips for the Modern Bride:
Honeymoon Hints *179*

## 16 — *Wedding Stress* 181

When Enough Is Enough! *181*
Give Yourselves a Break *182*
Quick Tips for the Modern Bride:
Keeping Stress to a Minimum *184*

## 17 — *Your New Life* 185

The Name Question *185*
Premarital Agreement *187*
Living with Parents *187*
Money: Mine, Yours, Ours! *188*
You Work, He Works, Who Does the Housework? *188*
Quick Tips for the Modern Bride:
Your New Life Together *190*

## 18 — *Groom's Questions* 191

Taking the Initiative *191*
Not Just a Prop *192*
Quick Tips for the Modern Bride:
Hints for the Groom *195*

## *Resources* 197

## *Index* 205

# Modern Bride®
## Guide to Etiquette

# CHAPTER 1
# Engagement

## Telling Family and Friends

*I became engaged a week ago and plan to be married in 20 months. When should we put the engagement announcement in the newspaper? Do I submit it just to our local paper or to newspapers where other friends and relatives will see it?*

You may announce your engagement as soon as you and your fiancé are officially engaged and start making plans for the wedding. The announcement indicates the month in which the wedding will take place, however far in the future that may be. Send the information to your hometown newspaper and to your fiancé's local paper. If you and your fiancé are living and working elsewhere, you may want it to appear in that newspaper as well.

*If there is no engagement party, should I send engagement announcements to relatives and friends?*

Telling family and friends either in person or by phone and announcing it in the newspaper is sufficient to make those who should be informed aware of your good news. For out-of-towners, a personal note or a telephone call is more appropriate than a printed announcement.

*My boyfriend proposed in an unusual way, and I considered us engaged. When my sister heard how he had proposed, she told me it is not an acceptable proposal and the engagement is not valid. Is there a certain procedure that must be followed?*

The manner in which your fiancé proposed may be untraditional by your sister's standards, but that does not affect the validity of his intent to ask you to be his wife. If you accepted, you are officially engaged regardless of what your sister says.

# The Ring

***My boyfriend and I have been talking a lot recently about becoming engaged. I know he is planning to buy a diamond engagement ring for me, and I would like to have something to say about the choice. I also realize there is a lot to know about diamonds before making a purchase. Is it all right for me to mention that to him?***

There is no harm in letting your boyfriend know that you would like to do some window shopping with him to see the different styles of engagement rings available. Some fellows are delighted to have an idea of what will please their future fiancée. He might be relieved to know you want to help make the selection, or he might prefer to get an idea of what you want and then surprise you with the final choice. (See *Resources* for more information on how to select a quality diamond.)

***I do not want an engagement ring because I want a very expensive wedding band and prefer that my fiancé put the money towards that. He is afraid that people will not take our engagement seriously if he does not present me with a ring. Is it really necessary to do this?***

Although not in the majority, some women do not want an engagement ring. Some are not comfortable wearing rings in general and would rather limit their wear to the wedding band. Others, like yourself, want something very special for their wedding ring and feel that an engagement ring would detract from that. Tell your fiancé he can rest easy now and go for broke when you two select your wedding ring.

***Diamonds may be a girl's best friend, but I prefer something different for my engagement ring. Is there any reason I cannot ask for another gem?***

None whatsoever. An emerald, sapphire, ruby, or whatever else you have in mind is equally appropriate. It may look perfect with your wedding band, or you may want to wear it on the other hand after your marriage.

***When I received my engagement ring, my mother said I should give an equivalent symbol to my fiancé. Have you ever heard of that?***

It is not usual, but it is a lovely gesture. Today, jewelers have engagement rings designed for men, and a woman may be happy to have the choice of reciprocating in kind. Some cultures expect that the man will be given an engagement ring. For example, in Holland it is an accepted tradition. A young Dutchman I know became engaged to an American woman and told me he was disappointed when she did not give him a ring as well. If your fiancé comes from such a background, do consider honoring that tradition. Often, a newly engaged woman gives her fiancé a gift as a memento of the proposal. Nothing could be more perfect than presenting him with his own engagement ring.

# Length of Engagement

*We have been dating for one year and just became engaged. The date is set for 22 months from now. Whenever we tell this to anyone, their response is, "Why wait so long?" We do not like having to explain and wonder why they find this time frame so incredible. Are we unusual?*

Hardly. The average length of engagement today is 15 months. Those questioning your timing may not understand the many reasons for this. First, often couples must save money to pay for the wedding. Second, obtaining the best wedding services requires considerable research, time to interview, and advance booking. That is because there are only 52 weekends annually, and the good ones are reserved years ahead. Third, frequently couples do not live where the wedding will take place, and long distance planning involves extra time. Finally, and perhaps most important, an extended engagement period gives couples an opportunity to thoroughly explore their relationship in marriage planning programs or even with professional marriage and family therapists to be sure that they are well suited to a lifetime of sharing responsibilities and working toward mutual goals. If there are any doubts, this is the time to explore them. If there are family conflicts or other problems, this is the time to identify them, acknowledge their influence on your lives, and develop strategies for constructive communication. (For a list of marriage preparation programs, see *Resources*.)

*I am having problems planning my wedding. We moved in together last month and would very much like to get married next month, on the first anniversary date of when my fiancé proposed to me. We do not have the time or money now for a church wedding and reception, so we are thinking of a civil ceremony now. Then, we would like a renewal celebration with all the trimmings next year. I would want to have a shower then, wear a traditional gown, send formal invitations, etc. Does this make sense?*

It is not wise to marry so hastily just for the sake of a date on the calendar. It would be much more practical to take the year or whatever more time is required to plan the wedding you ultimately want to have. As you can see from the answer to the previous question, a two-year engagement is not uncommon and, for all of the reasons explained, you would be smart to postpone the wedding until you can afford the time and money.

*We just announced our engagement. Because of job relocation, we must move in six months. We would like to have our wedding before that. Is there enough time to pull it off?*

Yes, as long as you move fast and are flexible. Resources are not booked as heavily during the months of January through March, so if that fits in with your calendar, you will be quite successful. If not, think of a midweek evening celebration, or one that is held in the morning or at noon on the weekend. (See "Choosing the Location" on page 103, and "Choosing the Caterer" on page 105.)

# Newspaper Announcements

*Is there any standard procedure for submitting an engagement announcement to the newspaper?*

Most newspapers print instructions for submitting your announcement in the section where announcements appear. They tell you where to obtain forms that you fill out and return. If there are no instructions in your paper, phone the paper's society or features department for information on how to proceed.

*I want to include a photograph of my fiancé and myself with our engagement announcement. My mother thinks this is trendy and prefers that I follow the more traditional approach by submitting only my photograph. Is this in better taste?*

Inclusion of both the future bride and groom in the photograph accompanying the engagement announcement (and the wedding announcement) is a trend that is here to stay. If that is your preference, it is no less tasteful than a photo of you alone.

*My father passed away years ago, but I want him acknowledged in the engagement announcement. How is that done?*

Examples of the wording are: "Mrs. David Hampton announces the engagement of her daughter Mary Jane Hampton to Mr. John Masterson. Miss Hampton is also the daughter of the late David Hampton." If the bride's mother has remarried, she uses her married name: "Mrs. Thomas Remington announces the engagement of her daughter Mary Jane Hampton," followed by acknowledgment of the bride's father's name. If the bride's mother has passed away, it would be handled in the same manner with her father announcing the engagement and the notation that "the bride is also the daughter of the late Roseann Smith Hampton."

***My parents are divorced and remarried. How do I handle that in the wording of the engagement announcement?***

The bride's mother and father make the announcement as follows: Mrs. Robert Andrews and Mr. Thomas Bouton announce the engagement of their daughter Heather Bouton. If the bride's mother has not remarried, she would use her given name: Ruth Smith Bouton. If the bride is close to her mother and estranged from her father, wording may be: Ruth Smith Bouton announces the engagement of her daughter Heather Bouton to.... Miss Bouton is also the daughter of Mr. Thomas Bouton of (his city, state, if different).

***My parents are divorced and my father is remarried. Although I have lived with my mother, my father has kept in touch, and I have spent considerable time with him and his wife. She is a good friend, and I would like to acknowledge her importance in our family. Is it possible to include her name in the engagement announcement?***

Noting my response to the previous question, take it a step further and after "Miss Bouton is also the daughter of Mr. Thomas Bouton," you may add, "and the stepdaughter of Bernice Bouton." Or: "Her stepmother is Bernice Bouton."

***I have been on my own for a very long time and am not on good terms with either of my parents. May I announce my own engagement?***

Yes. The wording is: Announcement is made of the engagement of Miss Anne Marie Longley to Mr. Jason Lee Daniels . . .

# Parties and Presents

***My mother thinks an engagement party should be held shortly after I receive my ring and before anything appears in the newspaper. I say the announcement can be published and the party can be held anytime thereafter. Who is right?***

It is not who is right or wrong. Rather, it is a matter of traditional practice and contemporary adaptation. Years ago, the bride's parents held an engagement party at which her father presented the good news to those present, most of whom would be hearing it for the first time. Following that formal announcement, the information was submitted for publication in the newspaper. The question of gifts brought to the party did not come up then because, theoretically, no one knew about the engagement prior to the event. They might have chosen to send a gift to the bride's home subsequently, but that was not required.

Some families still prefer to handle the engagement announcement in this manner. Others schedule an engagement party after the newspaper announcement appears. It may be hosted by the bride's parents, the groom's parents, or any other member of the family—even a friend—who would like to have this party for the couple.

***Is it necessary to have a dinner or some other formal get-together for our parents to meet each other? If so, who is responsible for arranging it?***

It is thoughtful for the groom's parents to phone the bride's parents shortly after learning of her engagement. They only need to congratulate them and indicate how happy they are to have the bride become a part of their family. If they live near one another, it is nice to invite the bride's parents to their home or to meet them elsewhere for lunch, tea, cocktails, or dinner. Of course, the couple should be included. If the groom's parents do not make the overture, the bride's parents should not stand on ceremony. They may arrange a get-together. Or the couple may take the initiative. Nothing fancy is required, just a relaxed, convivial opportunity to get to know each other. That might also be a good time to talk about wedding expectations and what roles each person will play in planning and paying for the event. On the other hand, it might be wise to keep this simply social and set up another meeting to discuss the logistics. Each couple and their parents must determine the approach that best suits their circumstances.

***What is the appropriate wording for invitations to an engagement party?***

Invitations may be formally printed, handwritten, or even issued by phone. Written options are:

Please join us for
_____ (it could be brunch, cocktails, or dinner)
*in honor of Sarah Smith and John Jones*
or
*You are invited for* _____
*in honor of Sarah Smith and John Jones.*

***My parents feel that hosting a wedding is sufficient and do not want to be responsible for an engagement party. My fiancé's family has expressed a desire to host a party. Is that all right?***

As long as your parents have opted out of hosting an engagement party, his parents may certainly carry on with their plans to do so.

*Does an engagement party have to be fairly formal, or may we have an informal event, which my fiancé and I much prefer?*

A picnic-type party, barbecue, or any other less formal celebration is a fine way to celebrate your engagement with those who are close to you.

*Much as we appreciate my parents' desire to give us an engagement party, my fiancé and I are concerned about guests feeling they have to bring gifts. Is there any way we can discourage gift giving?*

You will note that the suggested wording for the invitation mentioned earlier does not indicate it is an engagement party; therefore, guests will not automatically think they need to bring a gift. Although you prefer they not do so and gifts should not necessarily be expected for this occasion, many who are invited will want to bring or send you something, and there is nothing you can or should do about it.

*For the engagement party, my parents are planning to invite a considerable number of people who will not be invited to the wedding. This troubles me. Am I worrying for nothing?*

You have good reason to question this. In general, guests invited to the engagement party should also be on the wedding guest list. The only exception is when the wedding is very small and private.

*Our families live in different parts of the country. His family and close friends will not be able to attend the engagement party my parents are hosting. Is it all right for his parents to give us another one in his hometown?*

That is an excellent idea and a good way for each of you to meet the important people in each other's life before the wedding day.

*Some people tell me that gifts should be opened at the engagement party and others say absolutely not. What should I do?*

Gifts brought to the party should be set aside and opened in private at another time. There are two reasons for this: You should be mingling and visiting with guests throughout the party; and guests who did not bring a gift will not be embarrassed. A thank-you note should be written for each gift and mailed promptly. A note and/or a token gift to the hosts (yes, even if it is your parents) is a thoughtful gesture.

# Postponed or Broken Engagements

***Because of circumstances beyond our control, my fiancé and I have had to postpone our wedding. Invitations have already been mailed. How do I handle this?***

You must notify all guests. When time allows, it is done by having cards printed by a stationer in a rush order. If a new date is set, the card reads:

*Mr. and Mrs. Thomas Jones*
*announce that the marriage of*
*their daughter*
*Elizabeth*
*to*
*Robert Brown*
*has been postponed from*
*day, date*
*time*
*place*
*to (the new) day, date*
*time*
*place.*

If the date is not set, simply end after "postponed." When the date is determined, send cards following the aforementioned wording, but after the groom's name, say:

*will take place*
*day, date, etc.*

If time is too short to print and mail postponement cards, notification may be done with personal notes, telegrams, faxes, or telephone calls.

***What must be done when an engagement is broken?***

Here, as above, everyone must be notified. Information should be submitted to the newspapers that carried your engagement announcement. It is short and simple: "The engagement of Julia Montgomery and Bruce Wolf has been canceled by mutual consent." If invitations have not been mailed, personal notes and telephone calls from you and members of your immediate family will suffice to let people know that you are no longer engaged. If the decision is last minute, follow the procedures mentioned above. It is not necessary to explain why the engagement has been broken. The engagement ring must be returned to the former fiancé unless it was an heirloom from the bride's family, whether he had it reset or not. The other exception would be if he does not want the ring returned and insists that she keep it. Any engagement gifts received should also be returned. (Note: Couples who are sharing a household may be tempted to put engagement gifts to use as they are received. Think twice about doing this. In the unfortunate event that wedding plans are aborted, it is impossible to return used items. There should be no embarrassment if it is necessary to cancel a wedding, but there is plenty associated with not being able to return the gifts intended for use after marriage.)

*My fiancé and I had a lot of conflicts during our engagement and decided to break it. But we continued to see each other and now, a year later, we have worked through most of the problems and plan to marry. Only this time we do not want a wedding anything like the large formal affair we originally planned. My relationships with some of the friends I had asked to be attendants have changed considerably. I am not even in touch with some of them. Do you think they will still expect to be in the wedding? Also, many of the people on the original guest list are not on the new one. Do I have to explain this to anyone?*

No, that was a different time and a different set of circumstances, all of which have changed except for the groom-to-be. You are starting off fresh, and the plans you make now have nothing to do with what went on then. Be certain to explain this to your immediate families so that they do not have any erroneous expectations; then make the arrangements that reflect what you and your fiancé want.

⊰❊⊱ Quick Tips for the Modern Bride ⊰❊⊱
# Engagement Guidelines

- Your engagement can be as long as you need or want it to be. There is no "right" length of time.

- You are officially engaged once you have both agreed to marry. No ring or party is necessary, though both are favored by most couples.

- Formal announcements should not be sent out for an engagement. Phone or write informal notes to family and friends, or announce the good news at a party and/or in the newspaper.

- The groom's parents traditionally contact the bride's parents once the news is spread, but neither should stand on ceremony. What is important is that the families begin to communicate.

- Once your families are informed, an announcement can be submitted to your newspaper if you wish.

- Many people will give you engagement gifts, although they are not obligatory. Do not open gifts in front of party guests, but respond promptly with a written thank-you note.

- Discuss all decisions with your fiancé—use the time you are engaged to establish a solid relationship based on trust and cooperation.

# CHAPTER 2
# Budgeting

## Who Pays for What?

*My mother and father say it is ridiculous to expect the bride's parents to pay for the wedding today. Is this true?*

Some parents of the bride still undertake the traditional expenses because it is part of their cultural background and they would be embarrassed not to pay for their daughter's wedding. Other parents of the bride who have the financial wherewithal and a particular vision of how the wedding should be also prefer to handle everything. If their daughter and her fiancé share this vision, everyone is happy. *But,* today, these circumstances are often the exception rather than the rule. Large, formal weddings are by far the preference of most engaged couples. The average number of guests is 200, and many of the receptions take place in the evening. Such events are expensive, and the cost is frequently shared by the bride's and groom's parents and the couple. In fact, it is not unusual for the couple to contribute the bulk of the costs and in some cases pay for it all themselves.

*My fiancé and I are paying for some of our wedding. (He is also paying for our furniture and new home.) We both want a fun reception with either a DJ and dancing or a piano player for background music. My mother has nixed this, saying she and my father plan on giving us a pleasant, quiet reception. Is it wrong for me to want to have the kind of wedding that will please me and my fiancé and expect my mother and father to pay for it?*

It is not wrong for you to accept financial assistance from your parents to pay for your wedding reception, if they are willing to do that. However, by doing so, you and your fiancé must respect their guidelines. If you and your fiancé have different ideas about the kind of reception you want to have, that's certainly your prerogative, but the two of you would be wise to save up until you can afford to handle the entire celebration yourselves. Then, whatever you want is appropriate because you are the hosts. (For more on this, see *Selecting Your Resources* and *The Reception*.)

*My parents have both passed away. My fiancé and I are paying for our wedding, but could use some help. In this case, is it appropriate for the groom's parents to undertake some of the wedding expenses usually handled by the bride's family? They know about my circumstances and have been like second parents to me. How can we ask them for financial assistance without putting them on the spot?*

As you can see from the previous questions, help from the groom's family is welcome under any circumstances and in yours even more so. You and your fiancé should spend time with his parents talking about the wedding plans. If they indicate a willingness to share cost, determine what they can afford, combine that with what you can handle, establish a budget, and stick to it. If they do not offer financial assistance, plan only what you two can afford.

# Allocating Expenses

*We are having a real problem determining how to allocate what we have to spend on the wedding. My dress is very important to me; my fiancé thinks the band is the key to a good reception; and my parents are most concerned about what is served. Are there any guidelines to help us work this out?*

There certainly are. Costs should be allocated in order of priority determined by what is most important to you and your fiancé. Usually, the reception food and drink represents 50 percent of the total budget. In general, the other expenses break out as follows: invitations 4 percent; bride's attire (includes headpiece, undergarments, shoes, accessories) 10 percent; flowers 10 percent; photography 10 percent; music 10 percent; gifts, favors, fees, transportation, unexpected taxes and tips, 6 percent (see the following diagram). You may want to spend more on photography and less on flowers, or omit favors, or hire only one limousine and apply the money saved there elsewhere. Your fiancé is right about the importance of music, so that will be one of your priorities. At the very beginning of your planning, you should meet with your parents and your fiancé's parents to discuss the type of wedding you want. If some of them are unable to contribute for financial or other reasons, you will need to develop a budget that reflects the money you can count on, not what you wish you had. Once you know that, you can divide expenses in a number of ways: assign specific items to your parents, his parents, and yourselves, each to be billed and paid directly, or establish a wedding bank account to which the agreed upon monies are deposited with one person assigned to handling payments as they are due.

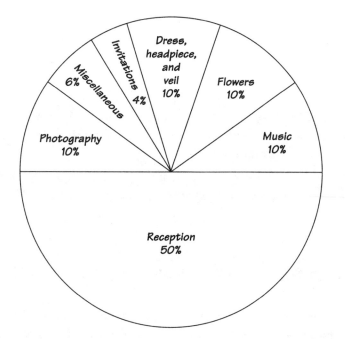

*Our wedding will take place in my fiancé's hometown. My family and close friends must travel to be there. Our list numbers only 50, while he and his family will have 175 guests. Should my parents have to assume the traditional expenses in these circumstances?*

This is a perfect example of the importance of discussing up front realistic expectations about who will pay for what with both sets of parents. It seems reasonable to suggest that the costs be divided according to the number of people coming from each side. If the bride's parents and guests must incur travel expenses for a wedding held where the groom's family resides, his parents should be willing to undertake as much expense as possible.

*Our son, a resident of St. Louis, is being married in Chicago. He is going to have eight groomsmen, five of whom are married. None of these groomsmen lives in Chicago. We have several conflicting opinions about who should pay for their accommodations. Are we responsible for the hotel rooms of these groomsmen and their wives?*

The groom is responsible for providing lodging for his attendants. Often, relatives and close friends offer to help provide those accommodations in their homes. If any attendant prefers to stay at a hotel rather than someone's home, he would be expected to pay for that. However, if a hotel is the only option for attendants' accommodations, the groom or his parents should pay for the rooms and tax, but no other charges. Hotels provide discount packages for weddings, so inquire about the best rates and reserve a block of rooms in advance. (The same guidelines apply to accommodations for the bride's attendants. For more on attendants' financial obligations, see *Attendants* and *Related Parties*.)

*In trying to determine the most equitable, least argumentative way to handle the expense of our wedding reception, we came up with this: My parents pay for the per person charges for their guests, his parents pay for theirs, and we pay for ours. What do you think of this solution?*

Brilliant. I wish I had thought of that, and I certainly recommend it as a logical solution to handling the most expensive part of a wedding.

# How to Stretch Your Wedding Dollars

*We have always envisioned an elaborate, elegant wedding, but our budget is very tight. What can we do to make our wedding as beautiful as possible under these circumstances?*

There is a big difference between reasonable "splurging" and reckless spending. Paying for things you neither need nor want or for products and services that do not measure up to their promise can be avoided by following these tips:

- Plan far enough ahead to permit you to compare services and prices so that you can make decisions based on what is best for you rather than on what is available.

- Consider a brunch, luncheon, afternoon finger-food reception, or evening cocktail party with hearty hors d'oeuvres as an alternative to a more costly sit-down or buffet dinner.

- Limit cocktails to one hour, then serve only champagne and/or wine thereafter. Eliminating an open bar completely in favor of only champagne and wine is in good taste and can save you considerable money.

- When hiring any service—caterer, florist, photographer, musicians, etc.— discuss in detail what they will deliver. Question each charge and *omit what is not important to you*. Be sure all expectations are listed in a contract that you read carefully before signing. Have the vendor sign as well and make a copy for your records. (More details can be found in *Choosing Resources* and *The Reception*.)

- Arrange an at-home wedding with the help of talented relatives and friends as well as some professionals to keep costs down. (To obtain a "Do Your Own Wedding" video, see *Resources*.)

# *Hiring a Wedding Consultant*

*My fiancé and I have heavy professional commitments and do not have time to do all the research for our wedding. My mother is busy, too. We would like to hire a wedding consultant, but have heard that this adds unnecessary expense. Granted, we want a pretty formal, sophisticated celebration, but we do not want to spend any more money than necessary and we do have a budgetary limit. Will hiring a consultant reduce or increase our anxiety about getting our wedding together at our price?*

Hiring a wedding consultant should definitely reduce your concerns because such an expert can help you turn your wedding planning into a worry-free, cost-effective experience. The consultant's job is to learn what kind of wedding you envision and how much you can afford to spend, then work with you to achieve your dream wedding without making expensive mistakes. When you hire a wedding consultant, he or she works within your budget and *that includes the consulting fee.* For example, if your budget is $15,000 and the consultant's fee is 15 percent, he or she will provide you with all that you expect for $12,750. The result, because of the consultant's expertise, should be a wedding worth much more than you could otherwise afford. Add in the time saved— especially important to you and your fiancé and other brides and moms who work full time—and this is the ticket for keeping your budget on track. When selecting your consultant, request client references for reassurance of the consultant's credentials and abilities. Also, rely on your instincts as you interview consultants to be sure your personalities are compatible. You will be working closely with your consultant, so the right chemistry is essential.

*My mother and I have very different ideas about what my wedding should be. We argue constantly. My parents are paying for a lot, but I am also contributing. I would like to hire a wedding consultant to end the fighting. Is this a good idea?*

Yes, because a professional planner brings objectivity along with experience to the project. When so much money is being spent on such a large social event, tempers rise. The third-party vantage point of a wedding consultant can bring order out of chaos and solve much of the conflict so that everyone feels satisfied.

*We have a considerable number of resources we know we can count on to do our wedding. But we could use some help at the beginning to organize our thoughts and give focus to what we want to accomplish. Is it possible to make this kind of arrangement with a wedding consultant?*

Many wedding consultants provide hourly consultation service and bill accordingly. You should certainly look for one who will be happy to work with you on that basis.

*It seems that the most common payment among wedding consultants is a percentage of the total wedding budget. Are there any other terms?*

Some consultants charge a flat fee based on the number of people invited to the wedding. Although that fee might be $5,000 or more, for a very large, elaborate wedding, that is probably most cost-effective. (Remember, the fee is built into the total budget, not added on.) For a much smaller wedding, the flat fee would have to be considerably less to be practical. Other wedding consultants may not charge the client, but rather receive payment from the vendors with whom he or she works. This sounds good and might actually be, but it does limit the wedding resources that the consultant is able to use.

# How Much Should You Spend on Your Dress?

*Ever since I was a little girl, I have dreamed of a very elaborate wedding dress, one totally covered with exquisite beading. My mother and I went shopping, and she was stunned at the price of the ones that I tried on. My father is familiar with my taste and has indulged me plenty through the years, but he has given us a budget. I can just hear him saying, "One day, that's all, you'll wear this just one day!" How am I going to get him to pay for the kind of dress I want?*

Earlier in this chapter, you read the approximate percentage of your total budget that is usually allocated to your wedding attire. The average price of a wedding gown today is $800 plus $150 for a headpiece/veil and another $200 to $500 for undergarments and accessories. (This includes shoes, gloves, and jewelry.) If you want the finest natural fabrics, hand beading, and customization on your wedding dress, you are going to pay thousands of dollars because creating such a garment is labor intensive. On the other hand, if you are happy with a wedding gown made from synthetic fabric or a blend of natural with synthetic and machine-applied beading, you will be able to find a dream dress that gives the same effect for much, much less. The following tips will help you find the wedding gown you love at a price you can afford:

- Go to a bridal salon that has been recommended to you by friends or relatives who had a pleasant experience shopping there. Tell the bridal consultant what your budget is and ask that she honor that when showing you samples.

- Ask the consultant to use a vinyl tape measure to determine measurements of your bust, waist, and hips, and from the base of your throat to the hemline. (The vinyl tape is more accurate and will prevent the need for excessive alterations when the dress is delivered.) Each manufacturer has its own sizing chart, which the consultant should show you. Select the size closest to your largest measurements. Alterations can be made to take in the dress but not to enlarge it.

- Look for sample sales in a full-service bridal shop because you can save money and still get the special attention every bride-to-be deserves.

- Be cautious about having a relative or friend make your wedding dress. An accomplished seamstress with experience in making such a lavish garment will probably save you money. *But* such talent is rare, and you could find it more expensive and/or disappointing to pursue that course.

❧❧ QUICK TIPS FOR THE MODERN BRIDE ❧❧
# Budgeting Guidelines

**Traditional**

The bride's family pays for invitations/announcements, the reception, the bride's clothing, flowers, music, sexton fees, bridal party transportation, accommodation for bride's attendants, photographs, gifts for the bride's attendants, gift for groom.

The groom and/or his family pays for engagement and wedding rings; gift for the bride; gifts for the groom's attendants; boutonnieres for the groom, his father, and his attendants; clergy fee; marriage license; honeymoon; rehearsal dinner.

**Contemporary**

The bride's family still pays for the full reception in many cases, but more and more couples are splitting costs between their families, and many are paying for their own receptions. Whatever works best for your situation is acceptable.

One way to split costs is to have the bride's family pay for the food at the reception and the flowers; the groom's family pays for the alcohol at the reception and the photography; the couple handles the music; and the bride may pay for her own gown.

# CHAPTER 3
# Taking Control

## Selecting the Date

*My fiancé and I have been talking about a Christmas holiday wedding ever since we decided we were meant for each other. Now we are engaged, and that is still what we want. Our parents are against it because they feel many of the family and friends we want to attend will have other commitments. I am sure they are right, but I would like to find a compromise solution. Do you have any suggestions?*

The key to making a holiday wedding work is to plan very far in advance. While celebrating one Christmas, folks are often making their arrangements for the next. Immediately phone or write everyone you want to come to see if they are still open to make plans to be with you or can change what they are already thinking about doing. That way you will know what percentage of your preferred list will be available. With luck, you will have enough positive responses to reassure your parents that your holiday wedding can be done. (For more information, see "Holiday and Theme Weddings" on page 126.)

*We both are busy professionals with heavy responsibilities and killer travel schedules. Trying to set a wedding date that works for both of us is difficult, mostly because we cannot get the same time off for a honeymoon in the near future. We want to marry soon, take a long weekend, then plan the honeymoon at a later date when we can get away without so much hassle. My mother does not understand this. She says you only get married once (hopefully!), and after all the work that is going into the preparations for the wedding, we should be able to have a honeymoon immediately following. I wish we could, but we cannot. Is this unusual?*

Postponing the honeymoon is not common, but neither is it unusual. Couples with professional commitments such as yours certainly do it. Sometimes couples who need more time to save the money to have the honeymoon of their dreams also postpone theirs. Nowhere is it written in stone that you must honeymoon immediately following the wedding, though 98 percent of newlyweds cannot wait to throw the bouquet and head off to paradise! (For more on this, see *Your Honeymoon.*)

*We have chosen a date that has significance in our relationship. It is not in a season that pleases my mother. She is relentless about trying to make us change it. We do need some help from her and my father to pay for the wedding. Should I capitulate or hang tough?*

Life is full of compromises, and weddings, in particular, demand them. You have to decide which means more to you—the date or the financial help. If it is the former, plan a less expensive wedding or postpone it until you and your fiancé can pay for everything. If your mother did not specifically threaten to withhold her financial support, you may be allowing yourself to be unnecessarily intimidated. Perhaps she just keeps at it in the hope that you will give in. If you tell her once and for all that it is your day and that date is it, she is likely to be ready to get on with the planning.

## Choosing a Wedding Style

*We are planning a small morning wedding followed by a champagne brunch reception. There will be 50 guests. My parents are hosting, and the theme is quiet elegance. There will be a string quartet. My fiancé and I have chosen mimosas and several fresh juices to accompany our meal, which features an omelette bar. My fiancé's mother questions our choice of beverages, insisting that we should also serve hard liquor. Recently, at her older son's wedding, her husband and younger son and their friends became drunk and unruly. We do not want a repeat performance. How can I make that clear to her without causing a rift?*

Enlist your fiancé's help in explaining to his parents that an open bar is not appropriate for the wedding brunch you plan. Your parents, who are hosting, do not want it and you two, whose wishes are most important, do not either. His parents may complain, but you do not have to pay attention because it is they who are impolite to discuss it any further. (See "Alcoholism" on page 168.)

*I have selected a simple, informal wedding dress. My mother insists that I wear a traditional, formal gown with a very long train. My parents are paying for the wedding. Does that mean I should go with her choice?*

Does your mother ordinarily select your clothing? As an adult, I hope you do this independently. The same should be true of *your* wedding dress. It should reflect your taste and style, not your mother's definition of that. However, the size of the wedding and overall degree of formality should influence the design you select. Sounds like a compromise between simple informal and very traditional is something to consider. (For more on this, see *What to Wear.*)

*Since we announced our engagement, we have run into so many kinks we think it might be best to elope. The biggest problems are the conflicts with my mother. She does not like the invitations we have chosen. We want to keep the guest list to 80; she says I have to invite aunt-so-and-so along with the cousin and her new husband and many other people neither I nor my fiancé knows. Finally, we want the marriage and reception at a hotel. She says it is inconsiderate because of the people in my church who will not be invited to the reception, but who can at least see the wedding. I do not care about having those people present at the ceremony, and I do not want to waste money on a limousine to transport me to and from the church. Who should make these decisions?*

At the risk of being repetitive, I say it is your wedding, and your mother should defer to you as much as possible. Here are some guidelines to present to her: Those invited to a wedding should be family and friends the bride and groom know and keep in touch with, not relatives who hardly ever or never have contact with the couple. If numbers must be limited, the couple's preference takes priority. The bride and groom choose the style of invitation. If a church wedding means nothing to you and your fiancé, it is inappropriate to have one just so the church membership at large can attend. The type of wedding and reception you both want is much better held at a hotel. Hope that your mother will realize that your strong stance will not tolerate any more bickering. If not, there is always the possibility of holding your wedding at your honeymoon destination. (For more information on this, see "Destination Weddings" on page 117.)

# Handling "Buttinskies"

*When my sister got married, she was a wreck because everyone had something to say about what she should do. I said I would never let that happen to me. Well, guess what, it is a repeat performance. This is supposed to be a happy time, and I find myself being pulled in every direction. What can I do to turn off all these self-professed "experts"?*

To help you have the wedding *you* want and to help you enjoy your planning, always remember that you cannot please everyone and will only create unnecessary anxiety if you try. To be sure, *everyone* has an opinion concerning weddings. Those who are underwriting the cost frequently believe that their wishes should be fulfilled in direct proportion to their contribution. Of course, their preferences should be taken into consideration and, if possible, honored. But not at the expense of the couple's friends or taste in terms of wedding style. When someone tells you, "the book says," or "we always did this," or "I never heard of that," listen politely, then carry on with your plans. Today, there are acceptable alternatives to the traditional guidelines and practical solutions to every problem. The most important thing is to feel confident about what you are doing and not to let any advice, whether well-meaning or not, undermine your resolve to have the wedding that is important to you and your fiancé. (The *Modern Bride Wedding Celebrations* book tells you how to do this. See *Resources* under "Deciding on Wedding Style.")

## Determining Who Does What

*I know that it is best to leave the wedding elements to the specialists who do this professionally. But we have some very creative people among our families and friends. Some have offered their services as a wedding gift. Is it possible to engage some professionals and have other things done by talented "amateurs"?*

Sure, as long as you communicate this to the professionals you engage. It is also important to arrange a planning session with everyone present so that you can discuss the timetable and organize everyone's area of expertise. Someone among the group who has volunteered to help should be selected to take charge of coordinating everything, and that person should check in with you regularly.

*My mother does not work, and she is very excited about having the time to plan my wedding. I am delighted that she is able to do this and so is my fiancé. My father and mother are paying for the wedding, and we have discussed our expectations with them and my fiancé's parents in great detail. We are all in synch. But I want to be sure that my mother's enthusiasm does not lead to her making on-the-spot decisions without first discussing everything with me and my fiancé. Am I creating a problem that does not exist?*

Yours is such an ideal situation that I can see why you think it is too good to be true. But it does not sound that way from my vantage point. It is nice to know that, though many couples find their wedding planning fraught with conflicts, there are still couples whose parents do everything possible to make it the wonderful family experience it is meant to be. However, it is wise to make it clear to your mother that, though her help is most welcome, no plans should be finalized without consultation and approval from you and your fiancé.

*My fiancé is a gourmand. He enjoys good food and knows a great deal about it. I cannot think of anyone better qualified to take charge of finding the caterer for our wedding. He has not asked to be involved in that, and I am wondering if he feels it would offend my parents. Do you think I should bring it up?*

I do think you should ask him if this is something he would enjoy doing for the wedding. It is easy to understand why he might be reticent to bring it up, but if he has the time and the inclination to take charge of this important part of the day, he should definitely be encouraged to do so.

*Our parents have agreed to share expenses and planning responsibilities. Can you give me some idea of how to divide the things they have to do?*

Get together with all of them and make a list of the things they each feel most comfortable handling. For example, if your mother or his is terrific with flowers, that is who should work with the florist; one of the dads might prefer to handle the liquor, another, the band and/or limousines. Remember, they will not be doing anything in isolation because you and your fiancé will be joining them in making final decisions. The point is, there is plenty of research and leg work to be done, and it is a big help to have family (including siblings) and friends (including attendants) who are ready, willing, and able to phone and run around gathering information for you to review. (See "Who Pays for What" on page 11.)

---

### ❧ QUICK TIPS FOR THE MODERN BRIDE ❧
# *Ways to Keep It Your Wedding*

- Spend plenty of time discussing the type of ceremony and reception that is most important to you both.

- Listen to your family's and friend's concerns and ideas, but make sure the final decisions are made by the two of you.

- Realize that you cannot please everyone—you should have the wedding that both of *you* want.

- Set a budget based on your financial resources and the kind of wedding you want, and *stick to it.*

- Consider waiting until you can afford to pay for the reception yourselves if there are arguments over the style.

- Divide tasks among those who want to and can handle them, but do not let anyone else make final decisions.

- Consider all legal issues before committing yourselves to anything.

- Discuss your ceremony ideas with your officiant well in advance—especially if you want to do something "different."

# CHAPTER 4

# *Invitations*
# *& Announcements*

## Compiling the Guest List

*The number of people we can invite to our wedding is limited both by budget and by the size of the reception location. We come from pretty large families. Our parents have lived in the same town for a long time and have lots of friends they would like to invite. We have many friends who are important to us and definitely should be invited to our wedding. Where do we draw the line?*

Without doubt, this is one of the most difficult parts of wedding planning. Just about every couple is faced with this dilemma. You should all compile your lists, then spend plenty of time together going over them to determine who are the absolutes and who can be eliminated. The couple's close friends and relatives—the ones they truly care about—have priority. Distant relatives (those hardly ever in touch) and children are often the first to go. Parents' friends who have little to do with the couple are also in the first cut. Be careful about inviting people you think will not accept; they might fool you.

*My daughter's future mother-in-law has given us a list of 183 people to invite to the wedding—on a budget that will accommodate only 125 guests. When we told her we could not possibly work with that number, she said we would have to **hope** that some who are invited will not attend. I was appalled. I have never sent an invitation to anyone **hoping** the person would not come. As a compromise, I offered to send announcements to those who live too far away to make the trip and to those who are elderly and unlikely to be able to come, as we are doing with our* *list. She bristled at this, saying an announcement does not necessitate a gift and she wants the couple to receive as many gifts as possible. My daughter and I are not inviting guests for the gifts they bring, but because we want close relatives and friends to witness and share this joyous occasion. Part of the reason she is making these demands has to do with her coming from a state where I am told it is customary to invite everyone who has extended invitations to her and her husband during the last few years. My husband and I do not want our daughter and their son to start marriage with friction between parents. What can we do?*

Unless your daughter's future mother-in-law would like to share the cost of the wedding with you, it is inconsiderate of her to expect to invite so many guests. Your daughter's fiancé should sit down with his mother and explain the financial limitations, as well as the fact that, in general, etiquette guidelines discourage inviting guests to a wedding to repay social or business obligations. He should also tell her that he does not want gifts from people he does not know and insist that her list be limited to the family and friends *he* wants to attend. Where your future son-in-law's mother lives, social obligations may be repaid with wedding invitations, but it is unreasonable for her to expect to do this at your expense. She can solve that problem by hosting her own reception for the couple when they return from their honeymoon.

*I have a dear friend from high school whom I want to invite to our wedding. She is engaged, but I do not know her fiancé. May I just invite her?*

No, you must invite her fiancé as well. It is also necessary to invite husband and wife even if you do not know the spouse, and the same guidelines apply to live-in couples. However, you need not invite a stranger who is simply dating a person on your guest list.

*I am close to a few people in my office and would like to invite them, but worry about hurting the feelings of the other people who work with me. I am not terribly fond of my boss and wonder if I am expected to invite him. Are there some guidelines to help me with this?*

Wedding guests should not be casual acquaintances, which is the relationship you have with the majority of coworkers. By all means invite those with whom you have social contact beyond the day-to-day office routine. If you felt more kindly toward your boss, it would be appropriate to extend an invitation, but it is not necessary under the circumstances. In fact, when you do not have a personal rapport with someone, it is more of an imposition than a favor for that person to receive an invitation to your wedding.

*We want to invite considerably more people than we can accommodate. Some of my engaged friends have handled this by creating an A and a B list. They mail invitations to the A list 10 to 12 weeks before the wedding. When they receive regrets, they mail invitations to the people on the B list. Is it all right to do this?*

Yes, as long as the invitations going to those on your B list are received no less than four weeks before your wedding.

*My fiancé and I want a small wedding with only immediate family because we would rather spend the money on quality over quantity. However, we are concerned that our friends will feel neglected if they are not invited. Do you have suggestions on how we could please our friends and still follow our plan?*

If you inform your friends that only close family will be attending the wedding, they will have no reason to feel left out. After you return from your honeymoon, you might want to hold a casual reception for your friends to celebrate with you. If you have a videotape of the wedding, you can show it then and share your honeymoon photos as well.

*I have a first cousin whom I would classify as my worst enemy (and that is putting it mildly). Throughout grammar school and high school, she did everything possible to make my life difficult. We have not spoken for six years. I do not want her at my wedding. My parents have recently reconciled with her parents and feel, because they are hosting the wedding, they must invite her to avoid hurting her parents' feelings. I do not feel my wedding day should be a time for reconciliation, especially because my past attempts at that have always been rebuffed. What is your advice?*

If you are that upset at the prospect of seeing your cousin at the wedding, do not invite her. Explain to your parents that, though they have reconciled with your aunt and uncle, it is not the case between you and your cousin. However awkward that may be for them, it does not warrant making you miserable at *your* wedding.

*I will be marrying for the second time and am not quite sure if I should invite my son's father out of common courtesy. My ex-husband's family and I are very close. They were a great support to me during the breakup. I think of his parents as my own and they, as well as his brother, will be invited. Should I be concerned that my ex will feel slighted if not included?*

In general, an ex-spouse is not invited. Let your former in-laws know that you are not comfortable about extending the invitation to their son. Chances are he will be more relieved than anything else.

*My fiancé and I do not want any children at our wedding and reception. Even if we convey this verbally to our friends and relatives, some will think they are the exception and bring youngsters. We feel it is necessary to state our preference in writing. Is there a tactful way to do this?*

When an invitation does not indicate "and family" or specify children by name, guests should never assume it is all right to bring them to a wedding. Because so many people are either unaware of this or choose to ignore it, couples have found it necessary to have printed on the invitation a line of corner copy that states: "Adult Reception." (There may be an additional printing charge.)

# Choosing the Invitations

*My fiancé and I would like to choose invitations that are more original than the traditional style. My mother says this is tacky. Is there anything wrong with what we want?*

The choice of invitation style is a matter of personal preference. There is an extensive selection of designs available today from which you will undoubtedly be able to find something that pleases you both. Although your choice is non-traditional, it will be no less tasteful.

*We want to include the reception information on the wedding invitation and omit the reception enclosure card as well as the return envelope. The stationer tells us that is not a wise thing to do. Is he right?*

Your preference is the traditional way of extending a wedding invitation, but it requires that the recipients respond by writing their own note of acceptance or regret.

The written response can read:

> *Mr. and Mrs. Michael Johnson*
> *accept with pleasure*
> *the kind invitation of Mr. and Mrs. Brian Dunleavy*
> *for Saturday, the third of June*
> *at two o'clock.*

If unable to attend, the wording is:

> *Mr. and Mrs. Michael Johnson*
> *regret they are unable to accept*
> *the kind invitation of*
> *Mr. and Mrs. Brian Dunleavy*

It is also possible to send a less formal note:

*Dear Diane and Brian,*

*Michael and I are delighted to accept your kind invitation to Eileen and Donald's wedding.*

Unfortunately, very few people today are familiar with this procedure. Most will probably think that the enclosure is erroneously missing and do nothing about responding. Therefore, someone will have to do a lot of telephoning to ascertain the number who will actually be attending. Bear this in mind when you decide whether or not to eliminate the reception enclosure.

**Many of the guests we plan to invite only know me by my nickname. May I print that name on the wedding invitations?**

No nicknames should be used on a formal invitation. Anyone who knows you well enough to be invited to your wedding must be familiar with your last name and will figure out that the invitation is from you.

**We are having a very formal wedding, but are thinking of sending invitations with the script in a color. Our parents are against this. Is it worth arguing about?**

The style of your invitation does set the tone for your wedding. If yours is formal and elegant, black ink on a white or cream-colored paper is the way to go. Save your energy to argue about something else!

**I would like my wedding invitations done by a calligrapher, but I cannot afford one. I have heard it is possible to get the same effect for much less money using a computer. If I can find someone with that software program, is it all right to have the invitations printed in this manner?**

If the result simulates the real thing closely enough, there is no reason not to use a computer. Some greeting card and party supply stores have a calligraphy printer to do this at reasonable cost. (For other options, see *Resources* under "Deciding on Wedding Style.")

# Bride's Parents Hosting

**My parents are paying for everything and want the invitations to come just from them. What is the wording?**

You are referring to the traditional form:

> *Mr. and Mrs. Robert Anthony Smith*
> *request the honour of your presence*
> *at the marriage of their daughter*
> *Lorraine Ann*
> *to*
> *Mr. Franklin Andrew Jones*
> *Saturday, the fifteenth of May,*
> *nineteen hundred and ninety-_____*
> *at three o'clock*
> *location*
> *address, city, state.*

Numbers for the date and the year must be written out. Even when the invitation is extended only by the bride's parents, mention of the groom's parents is possible following his name:

> *Mr. Franklin Andrew Jones*
> *son of*
> *Mr. and Mrs. Michael Thomas Jones, etc.*

This is a departure from the strictly traditional format, but for some families it is a thoughtful gesture.

**My daughter is an M.D. and her fiancé is a D.D.S. My husband is also an M.D. How can we include this on the wedding invitation without appearing pretentious?**

Traditionally, the invitation reads:

> *Dr. and Mrs. Wayne Perry Dalton*
> *request the honour of your presence*
> *at the marriage of their daughter*
> *Jane Elizabeth*
> *to*
> *Dr. Thomas Henry Reilly, etc.*

Then, the newspaper announcement carries all of your daughter's professional credentials. However, if it is important to your daughter to have her name on the invitation as Dr. Jane Elizabeth Dalton, that is certainly her prerogative and there is nothing pretentious about it.

**Both of my parents are general medical practitioners in a small town. They are known by their first names, Dr. Cara and Dr. Roger. May we use those names on the invitation?**

Yes, you may print Dr. Cara and Dr. Roger Acosta on the first line.

# Divorced and Remarried Parents Hosting

*My parents are divorced and remarried, and we are all on good terms. Although I lived with my mother and stepfather, my father is paying for the wedding. How should the invitation be worded?*

You have some choices:

*Mrs. Walter Johnson*
*and*
*Mr. Robert Jones*
*request the honour of your presence*
*at the marriage of their daughter*
*Heidi Marie, etc.*

Because your father and his wife are hosting the reception, the reception enclosure may indicate:

*Mr. and Mrs. Robert Jones*
*request the pleasure of your company*
*at a reception immediately following, etc.*

Or your remarried parents may wish to have both sets of names appear on the invitation:

*Mr. and Mrs. Walter Johnson*
*and*
*Mr. and Mrs. Robert Jones*
*request the honour of your presence*
*at the marriage of their daughter*
*Heidi Marie Jones, etc.*

# Divorced but Not Remarried Parents Hosting

*My divorced parents are each contributing something to the wedding, and I want both their names on the invitation. Who should be first?*

Your mother's name is first. Wording is:

*Mrs. Mary Ann Smith (or Mrs. Mary Morgan Smith, if she prefers)*
*and*
*Mr. John Smith*
*request the honour of your presence*
*at the marriage of their daughter, etc.*

**Both sets of parents are divorced, and I am confused about how to word the invitation using all four parents' names. My parents have not remarried; my fiancé's father has. How do I handle this?**

Your fiancé's parents' names need not appear on the invitation unless you want them to. If you choose to include their names, the wording is:

*Mrs. Amy Smith*

*and*

*Mr. John Smith*

*request the honour of your presence*

*at the marriage of their daughter*

*Laura Jean*

*to*

*Mr. Robert Jones*

*son of Mrs. Ellie Jones*

*and*

*Mr. Stephen Jones, etc.*

# Parents Co-Hosting

**My parents and my fiancé's parents are equally involved in the financing and planning of the wedding. We want their names together on the invitation. How do we do that?**

Both names appear at the top:

*Mr. and Mrs. Robert Anthony Smith*

*and*

*Mr. and Mrs. Michael Thomas Jones*

*request the honour of your presence*

*at the marriage of their children*

*Lorraine Ann*

*and*

*Franklin Andrew, etc.*

You and your fiancé might prefer to omit "their children" and simply use your full names:

*Lorraine Ann Smith*

*to*

*Franklin Andrew Jones, etc.*

# *The Couple Hosting*

*We live and work quite a distance from where our families live. They will be traveling here for the wedding, which we are underwriting ourselves. How should the invitations be worded?*

Invitations will be extended in your names:

*Miss Lorraine Ann Smith*

*and*

*Mr. Franklin Andrew Jones*
*request the honour of your presence*
*at their marriage, etc.,*

or

*The honour of your presence*
*is requested at the marriage of*
*Lorraine Ann Smith*

*to*

*Franklin Andrew Jones.*

If the marriage is taking place at a location other than a church or synagogue, "the honour of your presence" is replaced by "the pleasure of your company."

# *Addressing Invitations*

*What are the rules about abbreviations and the use of titles on the outside and inner envelopes?*

Guests' names should never be abbreviated except when using Dr., Mr., Mrs., and Ms. If you are inviting two physicians with the same last name, you address the invitation to: "Dr. Joan Smith and Dr. Allan Smith." A judge's name is prefaced by "The Honorable" and clergy by "The Reverend" or "The Rabbi." Military titles for men and women officers above captain in the army and lieutenant senior grade in the navy precede their name, and the branch of service appears on the line below. Address junior officers with their name on the first line, title and branch on the second line. Enlisted people and noncommissioned officers have their branch of service underneath their name: "James Andrew Thompson, United States Navy." Inner envelopes are always left unsealed and do not include first names or addresses. Simply list your guests as "Mr. and Mrs. Smith," or "The Doctors Smith," or "Dr. Jones and Dr. Smith."

(When the wife has retained her name, it appears first.) It is also "The Honorable and Mrs. _____," or "The Reverend and Mrs. _____," etc. If youngsters under 18 are invited, their first names are mentioned on a separate line beneath their parents:

*Mr. and Mrs. Jones*
*Julie, John, and Thomas.*

### Some of our guests have Ph.D's. Should they be addressed as "Dr." on the envelope?

A Ph.D. does not usually use the title socially. If you know the individuals prefer to be addressed as "Dr.," follow the form given for addressing a medical doctor.

### We are inviting a woman who is separated, but not divorced, from her husband. Should we send the invitation in her given name or in the name of her husband?

Use her given name, for example, "Mrs. Regina Ann Berry." On the other hand, if a woman is widowed, she should be addressed with her husband's name: "Mrs. Waldo Donaldson."

### I do not know whether to send individual invitations to a couple living together or to send only one. If one, how should it be addressed?

Send one invitation placing the names in alphabetical order. The outside envelope should read:

*Mr. John Alan Jones*
*Ms. Mary Ann Smith*

On the inside envelope: *Mr. Jones and Ms. Smith.*

### My mother thinks the bridal party should receive invitations, and I do not believe it is necessary. Should they and, if so, what about their guests? Also, how about grandparents?

Wedding invitations should be mailed to all of your attendants. If you know the name of their guest, that person should be sent his or her own invitation. If not, write "(your attendant's name) and guest" on the inside envelope. Your grandparents should also receive an invitation either in the mail or in person.

### I know that the inside envelope should be addressed to "Mr. and Mrs. Jones," but that seems so formal for friends we would never address that way. What about close relatives?

A formal wedding invitation should have the inner envelopes addressed formally to all friends and extended family. But for close relatives, you may write: "Aunt Betsy and Uncle Jim," or "Grandma and Grandpa."

# *Invitation to Ceremony or Reception Only*

***We have a lot of neighbors and friends we would like to have at the wedding ceremony, but we are unable to include them in the reception. Should we send invitations to only the wedding service?***

No. People receiving just the invitation to the wedding might think that the reception enclosure was inadvertently omitted or simply be confused because there is nothing about the reception. They might even just go along with those invited to the reception, a potential embarrassment for them and for you. Also, receiving a formal invitation might make the person feel obligated to give a gift, which is certainly not necessary. It is much more considerate to tell those neighbors and friends in person or with a short note that you hope they will be able to stop by the church for the wedding ceremony.

***Our wedding ceremony will be very private, limited to immediate families and closest friends. But we are having a large reception later that day. How do we handle the invitations?***

In this case, invitations to the reception are mailed to everyone. Wording is:

*The pleasure of your company*
*is requested at the wedding reception of*
*Miss Ilissa Marie Smith*
*and*
*Mr. John Lee Franklin*
*on Saturday, the fifteenth of August*
*at four o'clock*
*The Key Club*
*Cincinnati, Ohio*

For those also invited to the ceremony, enclose a ceremony card worded:

*The honour of your presence*
*is requested at the marriage ceremony*
*at two o'clock*
*St. Mary's Church*
*Cincinnati.*

# Sending Announcements

✦ *We would like to send wedding announcements to the family and friends we were not able to invite to the wedding, but are concerned that they will feel obligated to send a gift. Is that likely to happen?*

Most people know that receipt of a wedding announcement carries no obligation to send a gift, so you need not worry about that. Sending formal announcements is a nice way to inform those who could not be on the guest list, as well as professional contacts, of your marriage.

*What is the proper wording for announcements, and when should they be mailed?*

The announcement may be issued by your parents, his parents, or the two of you. Wording is similar to the wedding invitation:

> *Mr. and Mrs. John Smith*
> *have the honour of announcing*
> *the marriage of their daughter*
> *Ilissa Marie*
> *and*
> *Mr. John Lee Franklin*
> *on Saturday, the twelfth of June*
> *one thousand nine hundred and _____*
> *St. Andrews Church*
> *San Francisco, California.*

If you prefer, you may leave out the place of the ceremony and just indicate the city, state, or country. Should the announcement come from the couple it is:

> *Ilissa Marie Smith*
> *and*
> *John Lee Franklin*
> *announce their marriage, etc.*

The announcements should be mailed the day of the wedding or very shortly thereafter. You may want to enclose "at home" cards with your announcements to indicate your new address and the date you will be there. If you plan to retain your name, this is an ideal way to inform people. In that case the "at home" card wording is:

> *Ilissa Smith and John Franklin*
> *at home after July 1st*
> *street*
> *city, state*
> *phone number.*

*Our wedding will take place 400 miles away from where my fiancé's family lives. Many of his relatives and family friends will not be able to travel to the celebration. His parents plan to host a reception for us in their hometown when we return from our honeymoon. Would it be appropriate to send announcements to those people and enclose an invitation to the second reception? If so, how should the reception invitation be worded?*

Mailing announcements that include your new in-law's reception invitation is a good way to solve the problem of distance in this case. Wording is:

> *Mr. and Mrs. (your groom's parents)*
> *request the pleasure of your company*
> *at a reception*
> *day, date*
> *time*
> *place.*

The fact that it is enclosed with the announcement indicates that the party is in your honor. If you have photos or a video of the wedding, bring them along to share with the guests.

### ❧ QUICK TIPS FOR THE MODERN BRIDE ❧
# *Hints on Invitations and Announcements*

- Agree on the guest list before ordering invitations.

- Order extra envelopes in case you make mistakes in addressing.

- Be sure that both sets of parents provide full names, titles, and addresses of all guests on their lists.

- Consider the wording you want to use in special circumstances and think about any inserts you may need *before* you go to the printer.

- If you wish to have announcements, be sure that they are ready to be mailed out on or shortly after the wedding day.

- The degree of formality of the invitation usually matches that of the wedding.

- Send invitations six to eight weeks prior to the wedding, unless you have an A and B list, which requires earlier mailing.

# CHAPTER 5
# Attendants

## The Bride's Attendants

*I would like to have both a maid and a matron of honor. Is this possible? If so, how can I make them both feel important?*

You may have two honor attendants. One can hold your bouquet, and the other can take charge of the ring, if it is a double-ring ceremony. If not, she can be the "official" witness signature on the marriage certificate. Another possibility is to assign a scriptural passage or other reading for one or both to read during the service. One can be responsible for assisting with your veil and/or train. At the rehearsal, the officiant will advise where each should stand during the ceremony. (Note: Often brides-to-be want to have two single or two married relatives and/or friends as honor attendants. That is fine. Duties are shared as described previously.)

*I have three very good friends who will be in my wedding. One will be my maid of honor and the other two will be bridesmaids. I feel equally close to all of them. How do I choose the one to be maid of honor?*

Gather the three together for lunch or supper. Tell them because they are all your dear friends, you do not want to make the choice of honor attendant. Instead, you are putting their names into a hat and leaving the determination to chance. The name you draw will be maid of honor, and the others will be the bridesmaids. That is a fair and fun way to handle it.

*I have invited six friends to be attendants, but my fiancé has only five attendants. Is it all right to have an uneven number of attendants? How do they exit?*

You need not have equal numbers of attendants. After the service, one bridesmaid leaves single file behind the honor attendant and best man; then the balance pair up in the recessional.

*My best friend is a male. I would like him to be my honor attendant. He is willing, and my fiancé has no objection. To be traditional, I would have to ask a girlfriend who has not kept in touch. She would be surprised and probably not receptive. May I adapt the usual guidelines in this case?*

If the person closest to you is a male and that is who you want to be your special attendant, you may do so. He should dress as the other men in the wedding. There are two alternatives for his entrance: He could come in with the groom and best man to take his place on your side of the altar, waiting there for you, or he could walk in the processional just after the ushers and wait for you at the altar in the same place. Determine which is preferable at the rehearsal. Also, be sure your officiant knows in advance about this departure from the usual.

*Our bridal party includes a flower girl, a ring bearer, a junior bridesmaid, a junior usher, two maids of honor, a best man, eight bridesmaids, and eight ushers. With the bride and groom it totals 25 people. Is such a large bridal party appropriate?*

Such an extensive wedding party is normally associated with a very big, very formal wedding—a minimum of 300 guests and an elaborate reception. If your plans do not fit that, it is an excessively large wedding party and I suggest cutting back. A good rule of thumb to follow is one usher for every 50 guests and a similar number of bridesmaids.

*I do not have a special friend whom I would like to have as my honor attendant. Is it essential to have a maid of honor and a best man?*

It is not necessary to have either. All of your guests are witnesses to your marriage, and any two you choose may sign the marriage certificate. Explain this to your officiant when you are arranging for the ceremony. (Your mother or another caring relative is an option to consider before writing off having someone close to you stand in as honor attendant.)

*Three of my six attendants are coming from out of town. Who pays for their travel expenses and hotel bills?*

Wedding participants pay their own travel expenses. You should, however, provide them with lodging, either in your own home, with relatives or friends, or at a hotel. If you want them to stay in a hotel, you are responsible for their room and taxes, but no other charges. But, if you have other places for them to stay and they prefer to go to a hotel, they must pay for those accommodations.

*I accepted my friend's invitation to be one of her bridesmaids. A designer friend of her mother made the dresses and we have all had our final fitting. I did not inquire about the price of the dress when she extended the invitation. I just assumed it would be in the $140 to $175 range. I was stunned when told that the price is $300. I cannot afford that much for the dress, and that amount does not include the shoes that I am expected to buy as well. What can I do?*

Unfortunately, there is nothing you can do now but pay for the dress. However, you should not be embarrassed to tell the bride that the cost is considerably more than you had anticipated and that you will pay what you can now, with the balance to come as soon as cash flow permits. There is a lesson in this experience for all brides and their attendants reading this book. First, every bride should be sensitive to the expense incurred by those who agree to take part in the wedding party. She should discuss with her attendants her preferences for dresses and whatever other accessories they are expected to purchase before a decision is made. She should also understand that the expense might be prohibitive for some of her friends and allow them to gracefully regret without any hard feelings. Potential attendants should not hesitate to ask about the projected expense if it is not mentioned by the bride and, if it presents an unrealistic hardship, they should be able to decline in favor of attending the wedding as one of the guests. If the bride and her friends (and perhaps even some relatives) are unable to communicate such realistic concerns, the sincerity of the relationship is questionable. Being invited to take part in a wedding is an honor. Accepting the invitation should be a pleasure. If it becomes a burden for whatever reason—financial or emotional—the purpose is lost.

*I have selected my bridesmaids, but would also like to include my two young sisters, who will be 10 and 13, and my fiancé's sister, who will be 8. They all are too old to be flower girls, and some are not old enough to be junior bridesmaids. What can they do?*

Junior bridesmaids are usually between 10 and 14, so your sisters are perfect in that role. If your fiancé's sister is small, she may be a flower girl. If not, she may be a junior bridesmaid, too.

*When I became engaged, I immediately asked my good friends to be in the wedding party. I have just learned from my fiancé that he cannot stand one of the girls, and he wants me to eliminate her from the wedding and sever any contact with her. How can I do this when she has been nothing but nice to me and I really care for her?*

If you are fond of someone and have a long-standing friendship, you should not be expected to abandon her because your fiancé does not care for her. You should be free to maintain the relationship independent of his involvement. He need not be required to like her, but neither has he the right to demand you exclude her from your life. It would be rude and insensitive to tell your friend that you no longer want her in your wedding. I hope your fiancé realizes how heartless it is for him to ask you to do such a thing. (If not, and he wants to exercise that kind of control over your friendships, you ought to consider consulting a marital therapist before the wedding.)

*I have six bridesmaids and four ushers. How should I handle the pairing in the recessional?*

You may have each usher escort two bridesmaids at a time, one on each arm, or have two bridesmaids pair up and walk down the aisle together.

*I am considering inviting my future sister-in-law to be in my wedding party, but she is very overweight. She and I are not close, but I do not want to hurt her feelings by excluding her. On the other hand, I do not want her to be a bridesmaid unless she loses considerable weight. How do you suggest I handle this quandary?*

If your future sister-in-law's weight is the only reason you would not invite her to be an attendant, put that consideration aside. I am sure she has enough problems with that without the additional stress your demands to lose weight would place on her. Meet with her privately to see if she wants to be a bridesmaid. If her response is affirmative, that settles it. You must accept her as she is. If she shows any reticence, you could offer her the opportunity to take part by doing a special reading during the service or taking charge of the guest book. Keep her informed about your plans as they progress and invite her to all the pre-wedding events.

*I want only three close friends to be my attendants. My fiancé has two sisters and two brothers, and his mother expects them to be in the wedding party. He will include his brothers and has cut down his groomsmen from eight to three, so there will be no problem with pairing. No one from my family will be in the wedding party, and I did not anticipate any conflict because I was not asked to participate in either of his sisters' weddings. But they are implying that I should have them in mine. This makes me feel guilty. My fiancé will be happy with whatever I decide. Am I obligated to have his sisters as my attendants?*

Absolutely not. With no one from your family in the wedding party, there should be no hard feelings or further discussions. His sisters are out of order in making such an assumption and putting that pressure on you. Ignore their presumption.

*When I first became engaged, I asked a friend to be one of my bridesmaids. That was a year and a half before the wedding date. In subsequent months, she has complained about the cost of the dresses and has shown no interest at all in my plans. I no longer feel close to her and want to replace her with someone currently more involved in my life. Her parents and mine are friends. How can I handle this without causing ill will?*

Once you have invited someone to be in your wedding party, it would be very impolite to withdraw that invitation. However, because your friend expressed concern about the expense, you can tell her that you understand it might be a financial burden she does not want to incur. With the change in your relationship, she might welcome an overture from you that allows her to exit gracefully. Let her know that you will be just as happy to have her as a guest at your wedding. However, if she does not volunteer to withdraw, you must include her. (Readers note: As you can see from this experience, it is not wise to invite friends or relatives to take part in your wedding too far in advance unless you are absolutely sure the relationship is rock solid. Give yourself time to be certain of the size of the wedding—large may change to small for many reasons—and be sure to think carefully about who really will appreciate the invitation and be happy to make the investment in time as well as money.)

*I want to invite two friends who live 3,000 miles away to be bridesmaids. However, I have no idea whether they will be able to make the trip. Is there a way I can ask them to be in the wedding party and include estimated costs of the dress, plane ticket, etc.? Also, is it appropriate to ask someone to be an alternate bridesmaid in case the first choice does not accept?*

This is best done with a phone call to your friends. Tell them you would love to have them in the bridal party and give them the information about approximate costs. Assure them that if the cost is a deterrent, you will be happy to have them as honored guests. (They could be readers or take charge of the guest book.) If they regret the invitation to be an attendant, you are free to ask someone else, but do not attempt the alternative approach. You want whomever you invite to think that she is your first choice.

*My fiancé is very much influenced by his mother. She wants us to have a flower girl; therefore so does he. I want our wedding to be very sophisticated, which precludes the inclusion of a "frilly" flower girl. What is more, I do not know the child. In fact, she is the daughter of his parents' neighbors. The flower girl should be a friend or relative of the bride, should she not?*

A flower girl should be a child close to the bride or groom. She certainly should not be an acquaintance selected by the groom's mother. Your fiancé needs to make that clear to his mother.

*I have a half dozen really dear friends whom I would love to have in our wedding, but it is really not that formal an affair. We have decided to limit our attendants to our siblings, which means an honor attendant and two bridesmaids for me. Is there something I can do to make my friends feel a part of the celebration even though they will not have the traditional roles?*

You may tell them that they are honorary bridesmaids and acknowledge that by having a corsage for each on the day of the wedding and seating them up front in a reserved section. Of course, keep them posted on your plans as they evolve, and invite them to all wedding related parties including the rehearsal festivities.

# Bridesmaids' Attire

*I have three attendants who are very different in body size and coloring. One is a petite, size 4, another is size 10, and the third is 180 pounds at 5'4". How do I find a dress that is becoming to all three?*

One solution is to choose the degree of formality, color, and length of the dresses you want the bridesmaids to wear, then let them each select a style that is most becoming. Another alternative is to select a dropped waist design that looks good on heavier as well as average figures. Two-piece ensembles are a possibility, too. They can be altered easily for the various sizes.

*I want my attendants to wear black and white, but I am told that is not done. Why?*

Whoever told you that is not familiar with the wonderful selection of bridesmaids dresses in all black, or a combination of black and white, and even in all white. I believe that some bride originated the myth of attendants' not wearing white in her own best interest, so that no one else would compete for attention. Black is associated with mourning; therefore, many assume that it should never be worn by women in a wedding. (Historical note: In the nineteen century and even early in this century, brides commonly wore black or gray, as that was their one, and only, best dress.) Today, there are beautiful all-white weddings and those combining black and white. They are usually quite formal. If that is what you envision, do not let any old bride's tale deter you from it.

*I would like my maid of honor to wear something that distinguishes her from the other attendants. What do you suggest?*

She may wear a different shade dress from the bridesmaids as long as it is complementary to the overall color scheme. It could be darker or lighter than their dresses. If the bridesmaids are wearing prints, the maid of honor could wear a solid color picked up from the print or vice versa. Another way to distinguish her is to have her carry a different floral arrangement and wear a slightly different headpiece.

*I have four attendants. Each has a favorite color that looks best on her. The colors are all pastels that I think are very pretty. The girls would look wonderful in these colors, and that is what I want—for everyone to look terrific. I know this rainbow style was popular in the 1970s. Does that mean I cannot use that color scheme now?*

Of course not. That is your preference and this is *your* wedding; you may do whatever pleases you. What you are doing for your attendants is very considerate and practical. In this case, your pleasure is theirs as well!

*My wedding will be in June, and I want the bridesmaids to wear black dresses with just a touch of white on the sleeves. Most of what I read indicates that lighter colors are expected in the summer. Do I have to change my choice because of the season?*

There are no longer rigid rules for seasonal colors or fabrics. Some brides-to-be prefer pastel colors for the spring and darker colors for the fall, but it is truly a matter of personal preference. What you have in mind will be lovely, especially if the bridesmaids carry colorful bouquets. Trends and experience also indicate that the brighter tones of red, green, teal, royal, etc., are favorites year round.

*My daughter is being married in March, and I found a plum velvet bridesmaid's dress that she loves. Is velvet appropriate for that time of year?*

Absolutely. Velvet can be worn very comfortably from November through April.

*How can bridesmaids who live out of town be fitted for their dresses?*

The consultant at the bridal salon can tell you the precise measurements required to order a bridesmaid's dress to the closest size. There are two alternatives to the final fitting: You may ask the store to send the dresses directly to the individual bridesmaids for fittings in their own community. (Alterations are an additional cost in any case.) Or you may see if the bridal salon can accommodate a last-minute fitting when the attendants arrive a day or two before the wedding. If there are only one or two who require this, it may not be a problem.

*I am not keen on my bridesmaids wearing headpieces. Is that necessary?*

It is attractive to have them wear some coordinated hair ornament, but not a requirement. Ask your bridal shop consultant to show you some other hair accessories. A fresh flower, band, or cluster are also possibilities you might want to discuss with your florist.

*I would prefer not to ask my bridesmaids to purchase satin or silk pumps that must be dyed to match. Are there other alternatives?*

They may wear leather pumps or sandals in white, ivory, or even black, if they look attractive with the dresses. That is a practical alternative enabling the attendants to wear the shoes in the future.

# Mom as Honor Attendant

*My mother is my best friend, and I would like her to be my matron of honor. She wants to do it, but feels this might be awkward. What do you think?*

Inviting your mother to be your honor attendant is a wonderful idea. In fact, with such a strong relationship, no other choice is so appropriate. Your mother may be concerned about the logistics, so here are some tips to assure that all will go smoothly: She may wear a dress that is in keeping with the formality of yours and one that is becoming to her with regard to style, fabric, and color. It does not have to resemble those worn by the bridesmaids as long as the color combinations are complementary. She need not carry a bouquet; a wrist or regular corsage is fine. Nor does she have to walk in the processional as your matron of honor would ordinarily do. As in all formal weddings, your mother is the last person ushered down the aisle before the processional begins. She is seated in the first pew, left side. When the last bridesmaid has reached her position for the ceremony, your mother steps up to her place to stand at your left side. Then you and your father begin the walk down the aisle. In the recessional, your mother is escorted by the best man just behind you and your groom. Your father may step out as they pass the first pew and take your mother's other arm in the recessional. Or he may wait and walk out directly after the wedding party.

# Bride's Attendants' Duties

*My best friend of 21 years has invited me to be her maid of honor. I am excited, but not quite sure of everything the role involves. I want her to have fun during the planning and especially that day without having to worry about lots of little things. What can I do to ensure that?*

Your friend is very lucky to have such an enthusiastic maid of honor. Planning a wedding requires a great deal of work, so you should offer to help the bride-to-be with anything that needs to be done. This may mean running errands, checking out competitive prices and packages for services she is considering, addressing wedding invitations, stuffing envelopes, shopping together for your dress and those for the bridesmaids and the bride's trousseau. You should plan a bridal shower. Often attendants give the bride a group gift in addition to their independent wedding gifts. In that case, you take up the collection and purchase the gift that all have agreed upon. On the wedding day, arrive early to help the bride with any last-minute details. During the service, hold her bouquet and adjust her veil and train. Then, sign the marriage certificate and stand next to the groom in the receiving line. Bustle the bride's train for the reception, mingle with guests, and offer a toast to the couple. Finally, help the bride change into her going-away outfit and be sure the best man places all her luggage in the getaway car.

*Many of my bridesmaids live out of town. Is that going to be a problem when there are things they should be doing because of their role in the wedding?*

The bridesmaids' duties are not that crucial, especially if the honor attendant is handy, reliable, and eager to help. If possible, bridesmaids should be willing to do whatever errands the bride may require, and they assist in addressing wedding invitations, if called upon. They pay for their own attire, attend fittings, and participate in showers and pre-wedding parties. Any one of the bridesmaids may host a shower, or they may do it collectively. If the honor attendant is not a local resident, one or more of the bridesmaids who are should offer to assist the bride with any of the responsibilities usually handled by the maid or matron of honor.

# The Groom's Attendants

*I live in Oregon and my fiancé lives in Pennsylvania. Our wedding will be in my hometown. I am concerned that there will not be enough male attendants to complement my maid of honor and two bridesmaids. It would be very expensive for his friends to travel to Oregon, stay in a hotel, and rent the formalwear. I have not discussed this with my fiancé yet, but I am wondering if I should ask my brothers or some of my male friends to be in the wedding if his friends cannot come.*

You should certainly discuss this with your fiancé, and *you* should definitely not ask anyone to be his attendant. Your fiancé should make the decision on how to handle the choice of male attendants. Your brothers are a possibility, but your fiancé must agree with that. It is also likely that he will have at least one very good friend who is willing to make the trip. Do not overlook his father as the best man. It is not unusual for a groom-to-be to make that choice. Once he has considered the options, he will probably have his three attendants.

*Are the ties and cummerbunds that the groom's attendants wear supposed to match the colors the bride's attendants wear?*

No. Some couples want that, but it is definitely not a universal preference.

*My mother has told me that my brother should be an usher in our wedding even though my fiancé barely knows him. My fiancé and I believe that he should be free to choose only persons close to him. Are we misinformed about this?*

Not at all. I am sure your mother does not expect your fiancé to omit one of his close family or friends in order to include your brother. But, if it is possible to add one more attendant, it is thoughtful to include your brother out of consideration for your family and the long-term relationship. If that poses an insurmountable problem, your brother could dress as the ushers do, be assigned to escort your mother to her place in the first pew, be seated with her, and even be called upon to do a reading during the service. Finding a way to give your brother an active role in the wedding is not difficult and well worth the effort.

*My ushers live in various parts of the country. How can they be measured in advance for the wedding formalwear we are selecting at our local rental specialist?*

The formalwear stores that are part of a national franchise have measurement charts that they will gladly give to your ushers. The stores offer reciprocal services, so the guys can go into a local shop that is part of the same franchise and have their measurements taken free of charge, then mail them to you to give to the store where you are making your rental arrangements.

### Is there a difference between ushers and groomsmen?

Usually the terms are interchangeable. But some couples have groomsmen who walk only in the processional and recessional. The ushers seat guests, then take their own seats during the service. This enables couples to include a greater number of men in the wedding party.

# Groom's Attendants' Duties

*Before I ask any of my friends to be in my wedding, I want to be sure I know what is expected of them. What exactly do the best man and ushers do?*

The best man makes arrangements for the bachelor dinner and selects the gift for the groom given by all of his attendants. He might also help with honeymoon and travel arrangements. He coordinates the pick-up of the men's formal wear with the groom and the ushers and is responsible for getting it all back following the wedding. He proposes a toast to the couple at the rehearsal dinner and may plan some funny things to say, if the celebration is more relaxed and casual than formal. On the wedding day, he arrives early to help the groom dress, to offer support and friendship, and to take care of any last-minute details. At the ceremony, he holds the bride's ring. Afterwards, he signs the marriage certificate as a witness and gives the payment to the officiant. At the reception, he offers the first toast to the couple; dances with the bride, her mother, and her attendants; and reads any telegrams or special messages that the couple receive. Ushers offer any assistance they can to the groom, are fitted for their attire, help with the bachelor party, and review any preferred seating lists. On the wedding day, they arrive at the ceremony site about 45 minutes early to be ready to escort the guests to their seats: usually, the left side for the bride, right side for the groom. (How the couple wants their guests seated is determined at the rehearsal.) At the reception, ushers dance with the bridesmaids and mingle with the guests.

# Children in the Wedding

*We have three children in our wedding party, ages nine, seven, and four. Their parents will be present. Should the children be seated at the head table, with their parents, or at a separate table with adult supervision?*

If other children also attend, seat the youngsters with them, but have an adult seated at that table. Otherwise seat the children at the tables with their own parents.

*There are three-year-old twins in my family whom I would like to have as ring bearers. However, I have been advised by photographers and others who have had small children in their wedding party to be very cautious because youngsters have a short attention span, and I may find myself babysitting on my wedding day. These two little guys are quite active. What are the pros and cons of including them?*

Although these tykes are very endearing, the fact that they are three years old and act their age is reason for concern. They are too young to understand what is happening, and their participation could be a disruptive factor at the ceremony. Do you want to take that risk? If you do, employ a babysitter to sit with them during the service even if they are also sitting next to their parents. Thus, if they become restless and cause any distraction, the sitter can take them out or even home without their parents having to leave the wedding. As long as they are in some of the photos, which can be accomplished before the wedding, it is not necessary to prolong their presence at an adult celebration.

*I do not want any young children at my wedding. Crying babies and restless youngsters knocking things over is not my idea of an enjoyable wedding. The only problem is that I do want a flower girl and a ring bearer. Is it okay to make an exception in this case?*

You need not invite other children to the wedding because you are having two in your wedding party. As I have mentioned, it is wise to have a sitter on hand to supervise the flower girl and ring bearer so that their youthful behavior does not give you cause for worry.

*I just recently became an aunt to a beautiful little girl. By the time of my wedding, she will be 15 months old. Both of her parents will be in the wedding. I know she is too young to be a flower girl, but I would like to include her in the wedding activities. Do you have any suggestions?*

A 15-month-old baby is too young to participate in your wedding in any role. The most considerate thing you can do for her, her parents, and yourselves is to leave her with a sitter at home where she can play and sleep. This enables her mom and dad to enjoy the wedding and reception without worrying about the baby's restlessness or possible disruptive behavior. To include your niece in some photos, you might have her brought to your home before you leave for the wedding to take some pre-wedding family pictures. (In general, it is not wise to invite children under five to a wedding. If you do, you should have a sitter on hand with a special place to take the tots and some activity or games planned for them.)

*There are a few children in our families whom we want to include in the wedding party, but we are not sure what ages are best for the flower girl, ring bearer, junior bridesmaid, and junior usher. What are the guidelines? Also, what do junior bridesmaids wear?*

A flower girl and ring bearer range in age from four to seven or eight years old. From that age to fourteen, they may be junior attendants. A junior bridesmaid's dress should complement the bridesmaids' dresses in color and style, but should be adapted for a more youthful figure.

*Our 14-year-old nephew will be a junior usher. How does he dress and what does he do?*

Your nephew dresses as the other ushers do, helps escort guests to their seats, and walks in the processional and recessional with the ushers. If there is an odd number of ushers, he may walk single file following the other ushers.

# Pregnant Attendants

*My best friend, who is to be my matron of honor, will be five-and-one-half months pregnant on my wedding day. Her husband is socially prominent and is concerned that it is inappropriate for her to be in the wedding party under those circumstances. We have been close for years, and it means everything to me to have her as my honor attendant. She feels the same. What should I do?*

At five-and-one-half months, your friend's pregnancy will hardly be visible. But even if it is, that need not prevent her from being your matron of honor. The consultant at your bridal shop will help you select a very becoming dress that complements those worn by the bridesmaids, but certainly does not have to be identical to theirs. (An empire style adapts well.) You should both be able to enjoy sharing this special day as you have so much else in your lives.

*Our wedding is at the end of September. My best friend is the maid of honor, but she just learned that she is pregnant and her baby is due at the beginning of September. My fiancé asked her husband to be in the bridal party because we are close to both of them. I am having the bridesmaids' dresses made and do not want the tailor to have to make one at the last minute. Also, everyone knows who we have chosen for the wedding party, and if I have to ask someone to replace the maid of honor, it might seem like she is second best. What should I do?*

Under the circumstances, your pregnant friend may want to decline from being your matron of honor. You should discuss it with her and give her the option. If she decides she wants out, you can still have her husband be a groomsman and have her read a poem or scriptural passage during the ceremony. It is also possible that she will be able to be your honor attendant, if she delivers on time. Her dress will have to be specially tailored because she will still need a full fit, so you can make those arrangements in advance. My suggestion is not to make any changes, except to choose one of the bridesmaids to step in as honor attendant if needed at the last minute. That should eliminate concern about second best. It is like having an understudy in a play. The number of male and female attendants does not have to be equal, so do not worry about that if a bridesmaid has to step into the other role.

*Our wedding is eight days before my future sister-in-law is due to deliver her baby. She is a bridesmaid. I have found my bridesmaids' dresses, but have not ordered them yet. They are form fitted to the hips. Does this mean I have to change the style of the dress? I have no idea what size to order for her, and the order must be placed soon because it takes three months for delivery. I have always dreamed of a picture-perfect wedding. Will everyone snicker at my bridesmaid? What about the wedding photographs? What if she has the baby before the wedding?*

It is possible that your future sister-in-law will not want to be a bridesmaid so close to her due date. Discuss her feelings with her. If she has no qualms about it, you may order the dress you like for your bridesmaids, but have your fiancé's sister select a maternity dress in the same color and length. Ask advice from the bridal consultant at the shop where you are ordering the other dresses. She is undoubtedly familiar with such situations and may be able to recommend something from the same manufacturer that can be adapted to the situation. Or she may have another solution. The dress does not have to be identical to fit into the wedding party. You need not feel embarrassed about this, and you should discuss the options right away. A wedding is a family affair. If your future sister-in-law is able to be in the bridal party, no one should "snicker" about it. If they do, pay absolutely no attention. It would be insensitive and inappropriate and reflects only on their bad manners.

As for the photographs, discuss it in advance with your photographer so her condition can be taken into account when positioning the wedding attendants. If she has the baby early, she may not be able to attend the wedding, or she may have to sit it out. No problem. As I have said before, the number of attendants does not have to be even.

### ✻✻ QUICK TIPS FOR THE MODERN BRIDE ✻✻
# *Attendant Etiquette*

- Think carefully about selecting attendants too far in advance of the wedding—relationships can change over a long engagement, and you cannot retract the invitation once it is accepted.

- Consider your relationship with each person in selecting your attendants—you do not need to ask someone just because you were in her wedding.

- Do not feel compelled to have the same number of bridesmaids as you do groomsmen or ushers or vice versa.

- Choose flower girls and ring bearers who are between four and six years old. The behavior of younger children is often too unpredictable.

- Be considerate about costs—try to let your attendants know in advance if the financial burden will be heavy.

- Select clothing that will be flattering to all attendants. Remember that your bridesmaids do not *have* to be dressed identically.

# CHAPTER 6
# *What to Wear*

## *The Bride's Attire*

*I am confused about what is most important in determining the best style for my wedding dress. I have heard the style depends on the formality of the wedding—time of day, place, etc. Is that the key consideration?*

Those are points to be considered, but they are not the only criteria today. The bride's sense of style is more important: what she thinks looks wonderful on her and what makes her feel most beautiful. In general, a large and very formal wedding calls for a more elaborate dress—lace, beading, train, etc. But in truth, some women prefer a much simpler, understated look for such a celebration, while others having a smaller event want "the whole nine yards." The traditional guidelines are there if you want to follow them, but nothing is written in stone. So go for your dream dress regardless of what anyone tells you. (For the traditional guidelines, see *What to Wear* on page 68.)

*I thought a wedding dress purchased at a full-service bridal shop would be custom made just for me. But I am told that it is custom fitted. What is the difference?*

When you shop for your dress, the bridal consultant brings you sample gowns to try on. If you are smaller than the sample size, she will pull it in with pins to give you an idea of how the dress will really look. If you are larger, you may be able to try the dress on with the zipper open, or hold it up against you to get an idea of how it will look on you. Once you have selected your dress, you will be measured exactly, and the dress will be ordered to your closest size.

When the dress comes in, it will need at least one alteration, perhaps two, to be an absolutely perfect fit. If the dress were custom made, it would be done on the premises, and you would be going for fittings in stages as the garment was being constructed.

*According to tradition, the groom-to-be is not supposed to see the bride's gown before the wedding day. But I would like my fiancé to come with me when I shop to offer his opinion about what he thinks suits me best. Would it be bad luck to include him?*

Such superstitions should have gone the way of the Model T. We are approaching the twenty-first century. By all means invite your fiancé to help you shop for the wedding-dress look you both love!

*Our wedding date is 18 months from now. I do not plan to shop for my dress until closer to that time. What should I do if I like a dress currently featured in a bridal magazine?*

Your wedding dress should be ordered at least six months in advance. For the time being, retain photographs of all the gowns you like in the magazines. If you clip out the pages, be sure to label the name of the magazine, date of issue, and page number. When you begin shopping, present the photographs to the store's bridal consultant to identify the styles that interest you. It is possible that some of your selections will still be available. If not, the consultant will be able to help you find newly designed gowns similar to the ones you have selected.

*We will have a large, formal wedding in October. Even though it is fall and some-what cool, I am always warm and prefer to wear a short-sleeved dress. My moth-er thinks long sleeves are mandatory at that time of year. Is she correct?*

There is no required length of sleeve for a wedding dress based on the sea-son. Sleeve length has to do with the design of the dress and the style that looks best on you. Your comfort is also important. You might appease your mother by wearing long gloves for the ceremony.

*I will be wearing the same wedding gown my mother wore some 30 years ago. Would it be in poor taste to have this mentioned when the groom and I are announced by the master of ceremonies?*

Calling attention to the fact that you are wearing your mother's dress is a lovely idea. The M.C. may say: "Mr. and Mrs. _____: The beautiful bride has the good fortune to wear her mother's heirloom wedding gown."

*My wedding is not for 18 months, but I want to take my time shopping for my wedding dress, so I would like to start now. I am getting a lot of criticism from my family and friends for starting so far ahead. They claim that if I find something now, I will either change my mind and/or the styles will change. I disagree and feel that if I am lucky enough to find my dream dress, I should order it. How much do styles really change in one year? Am I rushing or is it okay to start now?*

It is not only okay, it is wise to start now. Styles will not change that much and, as noted earlier, a wedding dress should be ordered at least four to six months before the wedding. The more time you have the better. Those offering their advice do not know much about the process of obtaining a wedding dress.

*My wedding is at 4:00 P.M., followed by an evening reception. We have seven attendants each. The bridesmaids are wearing ankle-length dresses; the men will be in black tie. I found two wedding gowns I adore, one with a cathedral train and the other with a short, sweep train. Which of the two is more appropriate for me to wear?*

With 14 attendants, the men in black tie, and an evening reception, your wedding is formal. The longer train is fine. Be sure someone at the bridal shop shows your honor attendant or your mother how to bustle the train for comfortable dancing at your reception.

*The wedding gown I like is in a very light pink with a matching veil. However, my sister told me that only people who marry for a second time wear pink wedding dresses. Is she right?*

No, she is not. Light pink and pale peach wedding gowns are selected by first-time brides who love those shades. In fact, those color tones are very becoming to every complexion, more so in some cases than white or ivory. If that is your preference, you need not be concerned that you will be identified as a second-time bride.

*I have just put a deposit on my dress, and I have a problem. The cost of the dress is $900. When I told my mother and maid-of-honor, they were appalled that the gown I chose only cost that amount. My mother expected me to spend at least $1,500. The gown I purchased is an ivory, all-lace, full-length gown with long sleeves and a cathedral train. It is very heavily beaded with sequins. I thought it was appropriate for an evening wedding. Before I made the decision to buy this gown, I tried on a zillion dresses including couture designs at $4,500. I feel that I have pretty good taste, and I simply liked this dress best. Now I am concerned that I might have made a terrible mistake. I have noticed that there are not too many*

*all-lace gowns pictured in bridal magazines. Is a plain silk or taffeta gown con-*
*sidered more classy and elegant than a gown of all-lace? I am afraid that I will*
*look cheap and tacky at my own wedding, where everything from the flowers to the*
*favors will be the best money can buy. Is this type of gown a good choice for a very*
*lavish affair?*

An all-lace dress embellished as you describe is suitably formal for an elegant
evening wedding. High cost does not necessarily equate with good taste, nor
does a modest price signify cheap and tacky. You shopped extensively, tried on
many possibilities, and did not go for price, but rather for what you felt was right
for you. There is no mistake in any of what you have done.

*I am very close to my fiancé's mother. She is paying for most of our wedding. In*
*addition, she has given me her wedding gown and insists that I wear it. It is beau-*
*tiful, but it is dated and not in my taste. How do I tell her this without hurting*
*her feelings?*

Take some time to explain to your future mother-in-law that, although you
appreciate her kindness, you would prefer to wear a gown of your own. Tell her
that you have always looked forward to shopping for a wedding gown designed
to reflect your own individual style. If you invite her to shop with you when you
look for the gown, she may find your decision easier to accept. You should definitely be prepared to pay for the gown yourself and tell her you plan to do that.

*My fiancé is a traditionalist. He has asked that I wear a gown with a high wed-*
*ding-ring-style neckline. I look better in a sweetheart neckline, which I would*
*prefer. He thinks that this neckline is too bare. Where does it fit into the defini-*
*tion of traditional versus untraditional in appropriate choice for a bridal dress*
*neckline?*

A sweetheart neckline is one of the more traditional necklines. By today's
standards, it is not bare at all. Your fiancé should feel comfortable about that
choice and should not insist that you select something that you do not feel is
attractive.

*When my daughter and I were shopping for her wedding dress, we found ourselves*
*in a small, reputable bridal shop where my daughter tried on many current styles.*
*She did not find what she was looking for, so she asked to see the shop's discon-*
*tinued styles. She fell in love with a gown from a well-known designer. My*
*daughter went back several times to try it on. The gown needed work—some*
*bodice lace had been removed and needed to be replaced. (I can only guess that the*
*lace was cut away and used for other purposes.) The pearls and sequins needed to*
*be resewn in some places, and the zipper was broken. But in all other respects, the*

*gown was in good condition. The dressmaker assured us that the gown would look like new when she finished refurbishing it. The cost of the gown "as is" was very inexpensive: Adding the extensive work to be done and the cleaning, the final price would be an additional $450, but still within our budget and far less than the original price. We did not have a picture of the original gown at the time; therefore, we had to rely on the seamstress's familiarity with the dress when it was new to restore it to its original beauty. Subsequently, we found a picture of the gown in a back issue of a bridal magazine. Now, we want to be sure the gown will look exactly the same, and we worry it might not be possible to achieve this. What advice would you give to anyone who may be thinking about purchasing a gown that needs more than the basic alterations?*

My advice to anyone thinking about purchasing a shopworn wedding dress with lace and beading missing and requiring *extensive* work is, "Don't do it!" Not if you expect it to precisely replicate the original. Some bridal designers use very special laces and beading for which they have exclusivity. Each dress is made to order with their unique detailing. It would be unlikely that a dressmaker could make an identical match. If price is limiting, I would recommend selecting a less expensive gown or having a dressmaker make a gown from the beginning.

*I am being married in the winter. I need to choose my gown now when magazines are featuring only spring and summer gowns. What do I do about that?*

Although the dresses are presented for spring and summer weddings, they are not limited to those seasons. For the most part, these wedding dresses are made of fabrics that transcend all seasons and will be just as appropriate in November as they are in June.

# Headpiece, Veil, and Accessories

*I have seen photos of the type of headpiece and veil that I like, but have not been able to find them in any bridal shops. I would like some direction as to what style headpiece and veil would be most flattering on me, and I would like to keep the price under $150. If my dress is simple, may the headpiece be more embellished?*

It is best to try on headpiece and veil possibilities *with* your dress before making a decision. If your dress is simple, the headpiece may be detailed with lace, flowers, pearls, beading, whatever you wish that complements the dress; $150 would be the minimum for something with those elements. Show the consultant at the shop where you purchased your wedding dress the photos of the headpieces that you like. She may have something similar or be able to get it for you. She may also have suggestions for other pieces that will look even better. It is really wise for a bride to select her headpiece and wedding dress at the same place. If she does not select them at the same time, the headpiece can be chosen when she has her first dress fitting.

***I like the idea of wearing a veil over my face when I come down the aisle. What is that called?***

The veil is known as a blusher. Some religious ceremonies require it, and some brides prefer to have one even when it is not required. It is quite dramatic when the bride's father lifts the veil just before presenting her to her groom. (Historic note: Originally, the bride's face was kept covered to keep evil spirits from identifying her, not as a symbol of virginity.)

***I am wearing a floor-length ball gown with a full skirt. Rather than have the train come from the dress, I want a cathedral-length train of tulle veiling to come from my headpiece. Is this appropriate?***

Indeed, it is very elegant. You can have veiling that comes from your headpiece in layers attached to each other with Velcro tape. Once you have made your grand entrance into the reception, you can easily detach the train for dancing. (To learn how to handle a long train on your dress, see "Other Quandaries" on page 112.)

***I live and work in an urban area, but will be marrying in the suburb where my parents live. My hairdresser is in the city, and I would like to ask him to do my hair on my wedding day. How do I handle this? Should I invite him for the day? How do I pay him for this excursion? Should I invite him and a guest to the wedding? Or should I find a local hairdresser?***

If you feel more secure having your usual hairdresser do your hair for your wedding, you should definitely discuss the possibility with him or her. If he or she is willing, ask about the fee. Ultimately, your arrangements depend on the relationship you two have. He or she might be happy to receive the fee plus transportation, do your job, and leave. Or your hairdresser might be delighted to do your hair, attend the wedding, and make that a gift to you. If he or she prefers that, and has a spouse or partner, that person should also be invited.

***My mother has a beautiful piece of handmade French lace veiling that she wore with a pillbox headpiece at her wedding. I would love to wear her veil, but the headpiece does not look good on me. Where can I go to have someone adapt the veil to a headpiece that suits me better?***

A bridal salon with a good reputation for service to their customers should be able to work with you to convert your mother's veiling to a new headpiece.

*Please give me some pointers on how to select the shoes for my wedding day. Happily, there is quite a variety to choose from these days. Can you provide a quick list of things to keep in mind?*

You are right. It is no longer just plain old satin or silk pumps. There are also moiré, faille, and brocade pumps as well as slingbacks and sandals. Some pumps have lace, beads, and bows similar to what is on your dress, or you can get the materials and have shoes custom designed to match. You may also purchase shoe clips to dress up a plain pump. Choose a style that flatters your leg and complements your gown: high heels or slingbacks for a short dress or sheath, mid-heel pumps or flats for a floor-length ballgown. Order shoes in advance of your first wedding gown fitting. Wear your shoes around the house *a lot* to break them in before the big day.

*My fiancé and I are planning a country-and-western–style wedding. My dress comes to just below my calf, and my fiancé thinks I should wear my leather cowboy boots in keeping with our theme. But I do not want to hide my legs. Is there a shoe that will satisfy both purposes?*

Yes, there are lace and satin booties (more shoe than boot) that will flatter your legs and tie into the theme. Coloriffics, Dyeables, Marionat, and Saugus, major resources for wedding shoes, can usually provide footwear to solve such a dilemma. (Saugus has sizes up to 14 wide.)

*My dress has long sleeves, and I want to wear short lace gloves. Is this the right choice? What do I do about the gloves during the exchange of rings?*

Your choice of gloves is perfect. When the ring is to be placed on your finger, the officiant will tell you to give your bouquet to your honor attendant. Remove your gloves and give them to her too. Later, she will return the gloves for you to put on just before she hands you your bouquet.

*I plan to wear long gloves. May I keep my gloves on during the receiving line?*

You may wear your gloves during the receiving line and throughout all the festivities except when you are eating.

*No one is going to see my legs under my full-length wedding dress. Is there any reason why I should buy special hosiery for the day?*

I can think of a couple. Everything you wear on that day should be special, and hosiery is no exception. Also, there will be times when you will lift your skirt: getting in and out of a vehicle, perhaps dancing and, certainly, when the groom removes your garter. There is a wonderful array of hosiery available from which to make your choice. Hosiery really is an important accessory, so much so that I recommend you take a swatch of your dress so you can match the hue when you purchase it. An ivory or candlelight dress needs hose with a beige or grayish tinge; a pink or peach cast looks best with a very light pastel in that shade. Comfort is important, and you will find thigh-highs as well as pantyhose in an array of textures and patterns, including rosettes and rhinestones.

*My mother believes that pearls—necklace and earrings—are the only appropriate jewelry to wear on a wedding day. I think they are lovely, but I have other jewelry in mind. Is it wrong for me to wear something else?*

Pearls are traditional, of course, as are lockets, diamond stud earrings, heirloom bracelets, or a special wedding-day gift from the groom. In general, conservative jewelry complements a classic bridal look; eye-catching pieces accent a more sophisticated or dramatic look. Today's older brides often favor the larger pieces that complement the chic look and make a fashion statement. It is not a matter of right or wrong; it is a matter of your style.

# Full-Figured Styles

*I am a large-sized bride, and I become so frustrated when every model wearing a bridal dress is a perfect 10. Also, most of the bridal shops have only small-sized samples. How can I determine what will look attractive on me?*

There are bridal manufacturers and bridal salons that provide a selection of wedding dresses and bridesmaids dresses in sizes 18 and up. Michele Piccione, designer for Alfred Angelo, has an extensive selection of large sizes to 44. She advises that the most important thing for full-sized brides to remember is that the proportion of your body determines styling to a great extent. She says that some size 18 and 20 brides look stunning in a body-hugging sheath because their proportions can carry it. Other figure-flattering tips: Choose sleeves that are elbow-length or to the wrist; select an open neckline that is soft and effective in drawing attention to your face, such as the court neckline and the V—neckline. The latter is slenderizing and built up on the shoulder so a bride can wear her choice of undergarment. High collars are a bit too much, but a straight sabrina is fine. An illusion yoke is a good way to have both a little sheerness and a high neckline. The elongated, basque waistline makes a full-sized bride look thinner because it lengthens the torso. A full ballgown skirt gives a regal appearance. The most slenderizing dress for the majority of body types is one with a dropped torso, very deep waistline, and full skirt; the skirt helps shape the waistline and covers the hips. (For a list of manufacturers that specialize in large sizes, see *Resources* under "Special Size Resources.")

*I am concerned that the two heavy-set bridesmaids in my wedding party will not look as good as the others who can wear just about any style. What can I do to assure that all look and feel equally attractive?*

The advice given previously applies to the selection of your bridesmaids' dresses as well. The trick is to select what works best for the heavier participants, because the others will look fine in whatever you choose. In the case of attendants, you also have the option of two-piece ensembles that are easily altered and becoming to a variety of shapes and sizes.

# Petite Bride

*I am only five feet tall and want to be sure my dress is perfectly proportioned. Do I need a special fit?*

Yes, a wedding gown for a bride under five feet four inches requires special attention. Priscilla of Boston recognized this 30 years ago and has an extensive line designed with the needs of petites in mind. Other designers have followed her lead. (See *Resources* under "Special Size Resources.")

# Wedding Dress Rental

*I do not want to invest a great deal of money in my wedding gown, but would like to be able to wear something traditional and very beautiful. Would it be tacky to rent my wedding dress?*

No, it is not tacky to rent a wedding dress, if that enables you to have the dress you want within your budget. But before you pursue that route, be sure you shop around to see the many beautifully designed, moderately priced wedding dresses now available from $300 to $800. Rentals range from a couple hundred dollars to over a thousand, depending on the design selection and the shop's location. Dresses *must* be cleaned each time they are worn, and the fragility of the fabrics makes this a much more costly process than for men's formal wear. That is one of the reasons there are not very many wedding dress rental sources in business. Another reason demand for rentals is limited is that most brides desire something made just for them, their own heirloom that can be preserved and kept for others in the family, or simply for their own pleasure. While rental shops usually make some alterations so that the dress looks good on each bride, they cannot change anything on the garment. If you have taken all of these things into consideration and find your dream dress in a rental shop that keeps its stock clean and fresh, can alter the dress to look picture perfect on you, and save you a lot of money, then rent the dress.

# Preserving Your Gown

*My sister wanted to wear our mother's wedding dress, which was carefully stored in a box 30 years ago. When we opened the box, the dress disintegrated. On my sister's headpiece we were able to use some of the lace and veiling from our mother's headpiece that was stored with the dress. Of course, she purchased her own dress. Although I have no plans to wed in the near future, I might like to wear her wedding dress when I do, and we also want to be sure it is a possibility for any daughters born into the family. How can we avoid another disappointing experience?*

The following tips on wedding gown preservation will assure that your sister's gown will be as good as new whenever it is unpacked. Have the dress cleaned immediately. The longer a stain is imbedded in the fabric, the more difficult it becomes to remove it. This is true of perspiration, makeup, and perfume, as well as any food or drink that is spilled on a dress. Do not try home-cleaning remedies and *never* rub a stain. Find a professional dry cleaner who can identify the stain in the material and apply the appropriate cleaning agent to handle it. Of course, if you know what was spilled, it will help.

Once the gown is cleaned, most dry cleaners wrap it in acid-free tissue paper and place it in an acid-free box. It is also possible to wrap the dry-cleaned gown in a freshly washed cotton sheet, then store it in a cedar chest. Whichever way you choose to store it, certain elements of the gown should be removed before it is stored. Padding will decompose and release a residue that stains. Metal hooks and buttons often corrode. They should be wrapped separately, then placed in the storage box. The same procedure should be followed for a headpiece and veil that will be kept safe surrounded by the acid-free tissue paper. For further reassurance that the gown will remain in perfect condition, it is recommended that it be removed once a year or every other year to be sure that an overlooked stain has not begun to yellow. If it has, a dry cleaner can remove it then. Some things *not* to do: Never keep a wedding gown in a plastic garment bag; plastic gives off gases that will cause yellowing. Do not store your gown on a hanger because it places too much stress on the fabric. Keep your gown storage box out of the basement and the attic because of extreme temperature changes. Any other room that is not extensively trafficked is fine.

# The Groom's Attire

*I am wearing a traditional white gown, chapel train, short sleeves, and mid-length veil for our church ceremony that begins at 5:30 P.M. on a Saturday. I have read plenty about formal and semiformal attire after 6:00 P.M. as well as what is appropriate for daytime formal and semiformal attire, but do not know where to draw the line for appropriateness in our case. The ceremony is during daylight, but the dinner and dancing reception goes well into night. Will a cutaway and ascot be out of place?*

Because the ceremony is before 6:00 P.M., the cutaway is certainly acceptable. However, today for late afternoon ceremonies followed by a full evening reception, the choice of a tuxedo is just as appropriate.

*We are having a daytime formal wedding. I want my fiancé to wear a cutaway, but he does not like it. Is there another choice for a traditional, elegant daytime wedding?*

A stroller jacket is an alternative to the cutaway. I think your fiancé will like that better. Go with him to a local formalwear specialist to see what is available, and you will have no problem finding something you both like.

*Our wedding is at 4:00 P.M. in December. My fiancé wants to wear white tie and tails. We both are aware that this is ultraformal and should not be worn prior to 6:00 P.M. We live in a small southern town where many of the guests follow the traditional guidelines. Would it be a serious breach of etiquette for him to wear his preference?*

Today, such guidelines are a good frame of reference, but not written in stone. The fact that a formal reception going into the evening follows shortly after the ceremony leads many couples to choose ultraformal attire at this time of day. If your groom wants to do this, while his attendants wear tuxedos (or even white tie as well), he should be able to without worrying about what other people think. After all, it is his wedding, not theirs.

*My father says that all the men in the wedding party must wear the same attire. My fiancé would like to wear something a little different from the rest. Can he do this in good taste?*

Certainly. Traditionally, the differentiating factor is the boutonniere. The groom's matches a flower in the bride's bouquet, while the other men might all have carnations. But if the groom wants to select formalwear that is different, but complementary to the degree of formality that is chosen for the attire of all the men, that is fine. Here, again, the men's formalwear specialist can help you find very handsome combinations. (Some other ways to distinguish the groom: different color accessories, a top hat, even a cape!)

*Our wedding is in the afternoon. My mother is firm in her belief that the groom and his ushers must wear morning suits to follow strictly proper etiquette. My fiancé is strongly opposed. He feels his wishes should take precedence over my mother's "rules," and he should be allowed to wear a classic tuxedo. Is wearing something other than a morning suit considered to be against all standards of etiquette for an afternoon wedding? Can my future husband wear what he wants and still make my mother feel that no standards are being violated?*

I repeat, traditional guidelines are just guidelines, they are not rules etched in stone. If your fiancé has his heart set on wearing a classic tuxedo in the afternoon, the world will not come to an end. I believe the line should be drawn at a morning wedding. There, the cutaway or stroller with striped pants is the best choice. I attended a 10:00 A.M. wedding where tuxedos were worn. It looked ridiculous. Only croupiers or waiters should be in tuxedos at that hour.

# Mothers' Dresses

*I was told by my relatives that the mother of the bride is supposed to wear pink and the mother of the groom should wear light blue. I have attended weddings where the mothers wore colors that reflected the color scheme of the wedding. Which is correct?*

The latter. Mothers select colors that coordinate with what you have chosen for your wedding party. But they should also be colors that look good on them. Rather than make an arbitrary decision, discuss it with the mothers so each will be able to wear something especially attractive for this occasion.

*My fiancé's mother already has a dress that she wants to wear to the wedding. I always thought that the bride's mother is supposed to make her selection first; then the groom's mother chooses something that coordinates in color and style. What can I do about this situation?*

Most important, do not worry about it. See what your future mother-in-law plans to wear. As long as it is in keeping with the formality of the wedding and the color is not in horrendous conflict with what you have in mind for your wedding colors, you and your mother will be able to work with that. It is not even terrible if she has chosen a color that is the same or similar to what your mother wants. In fact, it may turn out to look more coordinated than you think.

*My mother does not want to wear a "typical mother-of-the-bride dress." She wants something really chic that she will wear to other special occasions, too. I think that makes sense. My fiancé's mother is uncomfortable with that idea and prefers to stick with a more traditional choice. Should my mother feel obliged to find something more in keeping with that philosophy?*

Not at all. Each mother can follow her preference by selecting a style that is most becoming to her figure and one that reflects her personal sense of style.

# Fathers' Attire

*My fiancé's father has his own tuxedo, which he would like to wear for our wedding. The problem is that ours is a noon ceremony with the reception immediately following. All the other men will be in daytime formalwear, and I do not want him to look different. Should I insist he go with the rental?*

In this case, I believe you should. It is one thing to wear your own tuxedo when others will be in tuxedos. It does not have to match exactly, but it will be close enough. However, in your circumstances, he would really look like odd man out wearing his tuxedo.

*The men in our formal evening wedding party will be wearing white tie and tails. Both dads would prefer to wear tuxedos instead. Is that all right?*

As long as they *both* want to, it will be fine.

*My dad will not be actively participating in the wedding party, though he will be sitting up front. He would prefer not to have to dress formally. Does he have to?*

No, he does not. He may wear a dark business suit.

# Guests' Attire

*We are having an extremely elegant evening formal wedding and want everyone attending to dress accordingly. I know that "Black Tie" on the invitation indicates that men must wear tuxedos. I hesitate to do this because some of our family and friends may not be able to afford the rental, and I do not want them to regret because of this. Is there a way to communicate that to them?*

Yes, there is a solution to that quandary. You may print "Black Tie Invited" on your invitations. That way, guests are informed that yours will be a very formal affair; the women will dress to the nines, the men who have tuxedos will wear them, and those who do not will know a tuxedo rental is in order. If finances prevent some men from doing that, they will realize they must at least wear a dark business suit.

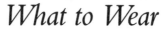

# What to Wear

The size of the wedding, the time of day, the location, and the formality of the bride's dress are what determine the style of the wedding. This chart is a guide to assist you with everyone's attire, but it is always subject to changes in fashion. For example, styles in menswear have become more versatile. Local formal wear specialists throughout the country can advise you on the newest choices for rental or purchase. Your preferences, guided by your bridal consultant's advice, will help you plan a beautiful wedding. In a second marriage, the bride should feel free to follow her wishes, and white is a valid choice.

| TYPE OF WEDDING | BRIDE | BRIDESMAIDS |
|---|---|---|
| FORMAL DAYTIME | White, ivory, or delicate pastel-tinted, floor-length wedding dress with a cathedral or a chapel (sweep) train. Long veil covering the train or extending to train length. Or ballroom dress with full skirt and optional sweep train. Bouquet or prayer book; shoes to match gown; long gloves with short sleeves, otherwise gloves are optional. | Floor-length, ballerina, tea-length, or short dresses; hat, wreath, or decorative hair comb; gloves to complement length of sleeves; shoes to match or blend with dresses; honor attendant's dress may match or contrast with other attendants' dresses. |
| FORMAL EVENING | Six o'clock is the hour that separates the formal evening wedding from the formal day wedding. Wedding dress is the same as for the daytime; fabrics and trimmings may be more elaborate. | Long or ballerina-length evening dresses; accessories same as daytime. Fabrics can be more elaborate. |
| SEMI-FORMAL DAYTIME | White or pastel floor-length or ballerina dress. Veil: elbow length or shorter. Same accessories as formal wedding. | Same as for formal wedding, although style and fabric should be simplified. |
| SEMI-FORMAL EVENING | Same as daytime. Fabrics or trim may be more elaborate. | Long, ballerina, tea-length, or short evening dresses; accessories same as daytime. Fabrics may be more elaborate. |
| INFORMAL DAYTIME AND EVENING | White or pastel floor-length, ballerina, or tea-length dress or suit. Short veil or bridal-type hat. Small bouquet, corsage, or prayer book. Gloves and complementary shoes. | Same length dress as bride wears; however, if bride wears floor-length style, it is permissible for attendants to wear a short dress. Accessories should be simple and suitable to the ensemble. |

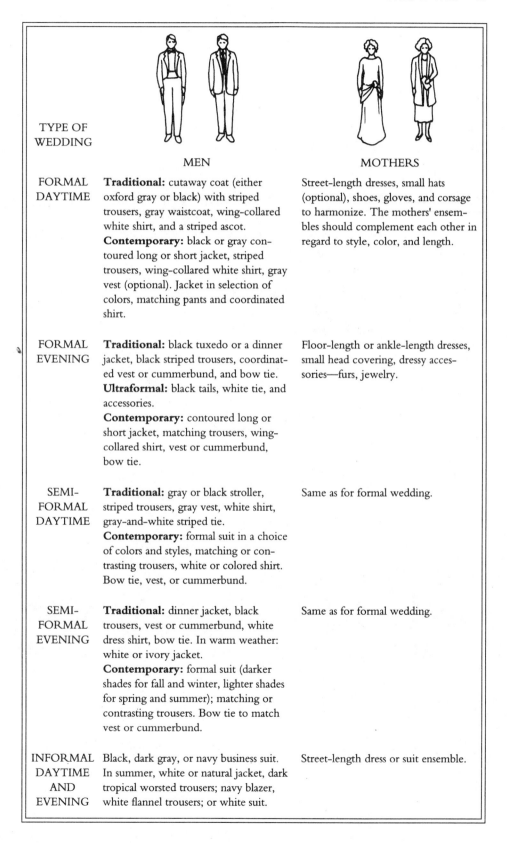

| TYPE OF WEDDING | MEN | MOTHERS |
|---|---|---|
| FORMAL DAYTIME | **Traditional:** cutaway coat (either oxford gray or black) with striped trousers, gray waistcoat, wing-collared white shirt, and a striped ascot. **Contemporary:** black or gray contoured long or short jacket, striped trousers, wing-collared white shirt, gray vest (optional). Jacket in selection of colors, matching pants and coordinated shirt. | Street-length dresses, small hats (optional), shoes, gloves, and corsage to harmonize. The mothers' ensembles should complement each other in regard to style, color, and length. |
| FORMAL EVENING | **Traditional:** black tuxedo or a dinner jacket, black striped trousers, coordinated vest or cummerbund, and bow tie. **Ultraformal:** black tails, white tie, and accessories. **Contemporary:** contoured long or short jacket, matching trousers, wing-collared shirt, vest or cummerbund, bow tie. | Floor-length or ankle-length dresses, small head covering, dressy accessories—furs, jewelry. |
| SEMI-FORMAL DAYTIME | **Traditional:** gray or black stroller, striped trousers, gray vest, white shirt, gray-and-white striped tie. **Contemporary:** formal suit in a choice of colors and styles, matching or contrasting trousers, white or colored shirt. Bow tie, vest, or cummerbund. | Same as for formal wedding. |
| SEMI-FORMAL EVENING | **Traditional:** dinner jacket, black trousers, vest or cummerbund, white dress shirt, bow tie. In warm weather: white or ivory jacket. **Contemporary:** formal suit (darker shades for fall and winter, lighter shades for spring and summer); matching or contrasting trousers. Bow tie to match vest or cummerbund. | Same as for formal wedding. |
| INFORMAL DAYTIME AND EVENING | Black, dark gray, or navy business suit. In summer, white or natural jacket, dark tropical worsted trousers; navy blazer, white flannel trousers; or white suit. | Street-length dress or suit ensemble. |

*I have seen so many women guests at weddings wearing black dresses, which I do not particularly care for. Is it acceptable for me to place an enclosure card in the invitations requesting that women not wear black to my wedding?*

Although you do not care for black at weddings, it is an elegant choice, especially at formal evening affairs. Guests should have the freedom to select whatever color they wish to wear. Therefore, it would not be appropriate for you to mention this with the invitation.

*I am planning a daytime formal wedding. To set the proper tone for the wedding, I would like to have guests dress up. I am not talking about black tie, just suits for men. The problem is, I have attended weddings similar to what I am having where men have come in sports jackets with no tie and even without jackets. What do you suggest I do to prevent this from happening to us?*

Tell your family and close friends that you expect men to dress in business suits and women to wear daytime dressy attire (silks, chic suits, etc.) and enlist their help in spreading the word.

# CHAPTER 7
# *Choosing*
# *Resources*

## *Choosing the Photographer and Videographer*

*I want to have both still photos and a video. My parents are concerned that there will be too much confusion with a photographer, a videographer, and all of their equipment. My parents also are worried about the intrusiveness of the process. I know what they mean because I have been to weddings where the photographer or the videographer and sometimes both get in the way of just about everything. How can we be sure that will not happen at our wedding?*

You take plenty of time to interview the photographers and videographers you are considering. If you have attended some weddings where these resources have been unobtrusive, they are the ones to call. If that has not been your experience, ask people you know who have recently married for their recommendations. If you have no such contacts, ask the photographer and videographer for names of their customers. The good ones are delighted to provide references. The way you and your fiancé interact with these two key recorders of your wedding is a good indication of how well they will deliver the kind of photos you want. You have to feel very relaxed with them in your planning meetings. You have to love the work they show you from other weddings. If it is possible, arrange to observe them doing a wedding in your area; that is a good way to be sure you are making the right decision. Be as certain as possible that the photographer and videographer you select are the ones who will be at your wedding. That should be clearly stated in your contractual agreement. Sometimes unforeseen circumstances such as illness or a family crisis might prevent the contracted person from being able to make it, so it is a good idea to ask how such a situation would be handled. The point is that you must feel confident that the photographer and videographer understand what *you* want and will do all they can to deliver. Here, as in your search for all resources, the best recommendations come from satisfied customers.

*I know that it is customary for the bride's parents to pay for the wedding photography. Does that mean they also have to pay for photographs that the groom's family wants? What about the ones for the grandparents?*

The bride's family and/or the bride and groom usually pay for one large album for the couple. Smaller ones with the same choices or perhaps fewer selections may be given by the couple to their parents and grandparents or purchased by those people for themselves. These are general guidelines. The final decision depends on each family's preference and budget.

*Our photographer wants to take the posed shots of my groom and me before the wedding ceremony in order to avoid taking time from the reception later. The caterer is also encouraging me to do this because she says I will be constantly interrupted and taken away for photographs when I should be enjoying the celebration with my guests. Is there a way to avoid having my groom see me before the wedding and still not have to worry about when those photographs will be taken?*

You should not feel pressured to be photographed with your groom before the wedding if this makes you uncomfortable. It is a good way to save time for brides who are not superstitious and who do not have their heart set on the groom seeing them in full bridal regalia for the first time walking down the aisle. I believe your reluctance to do the pre-wedding session is representative of the majority of brides. Do not hesitate to tell your photographer and the caterer that this is not what you want. Always remember, you are the customer and it is their job to accommodate you, not vice versa. Arrange with the photographer to do all the posed shots with your parents, attendants, and any other family members before the wedding. Then, you will need to do only the ones with the groom, his attendants, and the full wedding party following the ceremony. A good photographer should be able to do that in 30 to 45 minutes, subsequent to the receiving line while guests are being served beverages and hors d'oeuvres and are mingling. There should be no need to take you away during the balance of the reception because that is when the photographer takes the candid shots that catch the spirit of the celebration as it is taking place.

*My fiancé and I will have a photographer at the wedding and reception, but we do not want our wedding videotaped. My future brother-in-law always brings his video camera everywhere. His wife will be in the wedding party. We do not mind his photographing her with a regular camera, but we do not want anyone using a video camera. How can we get my future brother-in-law and anyone else who always has a video camera ready for action to save it for someone else's wedding?*

Feeling as strongly as you do about this, you and your fiancé should tell his brother-in-law and any other guests who are known to bring video cameras to such events to leave them at home. Undoubtedly, they will be somewhat surprised by your request, but whatever they think, they should respect your wishes. If some guests do attend your wedding with video cameras in tow, the ushers can inform them that only still photography is permitted. Flashes on still cameras are often considered intrusive and may be prohibited in the sanctuary. If you feel that way or the officiant has such a policy, he or she will tell guests to refrain from taking flash photos during the ceremony.

# Choosing Ceremony Musicians

*We do not belong to the church where we will be married. A friend of ours is a wonderful organist, and we would like him to play at our wedding. Can we just tell the officiant of our preference during our meetings to plan the ceremony?*

When you reserve a church for your wedding, the use of the church organist is usually part of that arrangement, even though the fee for using the church usually does not include the fee for the organist. Rather than "tell" the officiant what you want, you should ask about the policy. It is likely that you will need to discuss your preference with the music director, who is often the organist. If there is no objection to bringing in another musician, you still may have to pay some fee to the resident organist.

*We would like to have two or three instrumentalists play at our wedding ceremony. How do we go about finding that talent?*

Your first resource is the music director at the church or synagogue where you are planning to be married. Often the director will have a list of qualified people. If not, other contacts include the local symphony orchestra, the music department of local colleges and universities, and the musicians' union in the area. Be sure you have an opportunity to hear any vocalist or musicians you are considering before you make a commitment. Your wedding music should be presented by trained performers, not by just anyone who dabbles in this field.

*We do not know much about wedding ceremony music, but we want ours to be especially beautiful. We would like a list of possibilities and a way to hear the options before we make a choice. How can we manage to do this?*

The type of wedding you plan—traditional, religious, formal, or informal—is the determining factor in the music you select. Ask the church's or synagogue's music director for suggestions to consider for the prelude, processional, meditational, and recessional selections. This is the time to find out if there are any restrictions on secular music. Hard as it might be to believe, the very familiar "Here Comes the Bride," which is the "Bridal Chorus" from Wagner's *Lohengrin,* and the equally popular "Wedding March" by Mendelssohn are secular, nonsacred pieces that are not permitted in some religious wedding rituals. The music director should be able to either play the selections from his or her list for you or have any other musicians he recommends do the same. If that is not possible, you can hear recordings of the pieces at a local music library or music store. There are also recordings of suggested wedding music on tape. (See *Resources* under "Music.")

# Choosing the Reception Musicians

*We plan to have a small sit-down luncheon reception with no dancing. What is the appropriate musical accompaniment for such a reception?*

Consider a harpist, violinist, cellist, or guitarist. Of course, piano music is always lovely and may be combined with one or two of the other instruments.

*My fiancé is very fussy about the band we hire because we have been to quite a few weddings where the music was not that great. Often it is too loud, and the band's repertoire is not sufficiently varied. How can we be certain to get a band that delivers what we expect?*

Start your search early and be sure you hear *and* see the bands you are considering. Listening to an audio tape is not sufficient because you do not know how many musicians are playing or what kind of electronic enhancement is being used to give you a good impression. The best way to determine if you like a band is to see it actually playing at a wedding. Some facilities will allow you to unobtrusively stand in the back or just outside the door to witness the group in action. If that is not possible, view a videotape of the band performing. When you make your choice, be sure the contract indicates the following points: the musicians and vocalists you heard will be the ones actually playing at your wedding; the attire you expect them to be wearing; the number and duration of breaks and provisions for music during those interludes; the need for any special sound system and cost, if applicable; extra charges not included in the fee (travel, set up time, continuous music, overtime); payment schedule; and cancellation policy.

*We want live music, but have a limited budget. Are there some guidelines that will help us determine how many musicians we need for our reception?*

A large guest list leads to a large space to accommodate all of the people, and that dictates the size of the band you will need. In general, a five-piece group is sufficient for 150 guests. Add another one or two pieces for 200 and a full ensemble of ten to twelve pieces for 300 or more guests.

*My fiancé and I want to have a disc jockey for two reasons: First, we believe there is much more choice of selections because he brings something from every era, and we do not have to worry about whether he knows this or that; second, it is a considerable savings over a band. My parents have never been to a wedding with a DJ, and they think it would be tacky to have one at our wedding. Can you help me convince them otherwise?*

Disc jockeys are becoming increasingly popular for precisely the reasons you have stated, and it makes a lot of sense. A good DJ can be counted on to get people dancing and keep the party moving, and that is what you want at your reception. Your parents may think that the DJ has to be funky with long hair and casual attire. Some are, but you do not have to select that type. When you are interviewing resources, tell them the type of demeanor you expect and arrange to see them perform at a wedding to be sure they are capable of living up to your expectations. Often a two-person team is the best choice for seeing to it that everything runs smoothly and there are no lapses. One person acts as the music mixer (plays the discs), and the other is the announcer. The same amount of planning for selections and order of activities is necessary with a DJ as with a bandleader.

*Our caterer recommended only one band, and it is never available for us to make contact. How can we find other possibilities to interview and see perform?*

You often will find local bands advertised in the regional pages of *Modern Bride.* They are also listed in your *Yellow Pages* and in bridal supplements of your area newspapers and in regional bridal publications. Check with friends and relatives who have recently attended weddings to see if they have any recommendations. Think about weddings you and/or your fiancé have attended where there was good music. If any come to mind, contact the couple.

*Neither my fiancé nor I know much about what music to play or the timing of events during the reception. We would like to rely on the bandleader for that expertise. Is it reasonable to expect him to give us the right mix and to act as master of ceremonies during the evening?*

If you follow all the previous advice about finding a band that has the style you want, you should feel confident that the bandleader will be able to deliver great sound, to vary musical selections for guests of all ages, and to keep traditions, as well as the tempo, in synch.

*Ours is an intercultural marriage, and we want to have ethnic music representative of both our backgrounds at the reception. Can we assume that most big bands know how to accommodate our needs?*

If you learn nothing else from reading this book, you must remember that you can *assume nothing.* You must check into everything before you make a commitment to any of your resources. Explain your ethnic music requirements to the musicians you are considering, and be sure you hear them play representative pieces so that you know they can provide music to the satisfaction of both your families and to the enjoyment of your guests.

# Choosing the Florist

*We know that flowers are a very important decorative element in the wedding picture. Unfortunately, we cannot have all that we would like in the church and at the reception. How can we find a florist who will help us stretch what we can afford to maximum creative advantage?*

At the risk of being tediously repetitious, I say once again, start early, interview a few florists, ask lots of questions, and rely on word of mouth from people you know who have faced the same limitations and found a great resource. A good florist will start with *your* budget and not try to talk you into spending any more. Working with that budget, he or she will find ways to economize with flair. Here are some things that will help to keep the costs in control: familiarity with the locations of your ceremony and reception to give the florist a head start on knowing what tricks can be employed to provide more for less; using in-season flowers; selecting loose arrangements vs. those that require labor intensive design; renting shrubs and trees to fill large spaces; utilizing some of the decorations already in place at the site. All of these will contribute to cost containment.

*I think it is confusing to follow the traditional guidelines that indicate the groom is supposed to pay for the bridal bouquet, mothers' corsages, men's boutonnieres, and rehearsal dinner flowers. How do we separate these costs and is it really necessary to do so?*

No, it is not really necessary. Usually, all the floral selections for the wedding are made by the bride and her family or whoever else is hosting the wedding. In the interests of economy and artistic coordination, that is the most practical way to handle it. The expenses will be itemized in the contract and on the bill, so if floral costs are being split in any way, those who agreed to the purchase can either each give their own payment or one person can pay the total cost and then be reimbursed by the others.

*A number of women close to me and my fiancé will not have an active role in the wedding, but we would like to acknowledge them somehow. Of course, our mothers and grandmothers will have corsages. Will it diminish their status or hurt other relatives' feelings to give a corsage to the nanny who raised me, my god-mother, my fiancé's very dear aunt, etc.?*

The flowers you give to those special people should be different from what you give to your mothers and grandmothers. A little corsage of carnations, perhaps a single long-stemmed rose, or a Victorian tussie-mussie arrangement (a very small bouquet of fragrant flowers in a little hand held silver holder) are thoughtful gestures of appreciation for the important influence these women had in your lives. The gesture should not detract in any way from your mothers and grandmothers, and other relatives have no reason to feel hurt by your recognition of anyone who has earned a special spot in your lives.

*We would like to have silk flower arrangements for the wedding attendants and for my own bouquet, then be able to keep them as mementos of the wedding. Is there any reason not to do this?*

None whatsoever, if that is your preference.

*I have always thought that a full-service florist does everything. Is there a difference between such a person and a floral designer?*

A full-service florist does just about everything: bouquets, arrangements, corsages, and spatial decorations. A floral designer does that, but in addition he or she creates a total environment in the most nondescript space. If yours is a theme wedding or if you want some type of fantasy excitement that involves special lighting and other effects, a floral designer is the person to do it. The best way to find this resource is through word of mouth or by contacting corporate party planners or those who organize charity events and often use such artists.

*I would like to save my wedding bouquet so it can be dried and kept as a memento. What do I do about tossing the bouquet?*

You may have your bouquet designed with a "break-away" section to toss and keep the rest to be dried. Or you may have another smaller arrangement made just for tossing.

# Transportation

*I have heard some disturbing stories from brides who hired a limousine service that arrived late and some who had drivers who did not know how to get where they were going. We are looking forward to the luxury and convenience of having this special treat, and I do not want to have to worry about such an unnerving experience. What can I do to insure it will not happen to us?*

The National Limousine Association is a professional organization representing 900 member companies nationwide. By contacting one of its members, you are likely to get the most reliable service. (For referrals, see *Resources* under "Transportation.") Do not rely on a phone conversation—meet personally with the owner or manager of the company. Look at the cars they have available. Ask to see a list of the customers they service. If they have a significant list of businesses, it is an indication of their reliability. Phone some of their previous brides, as well. Verify insurance protection and the qualifications of the drivers. Be sure the company is licensed by the appropriate licensing authorities (state and municipal). This is essential if the vehicles will cross state or county lines transporting you.

*We have to economize in some areas to do more of what we want in others. Is it really necessary to have limousines for the wedding party?*

It is not a requirement, but many consider it an important element on this once-in-a-lifetime day. Rather than eliminate the limousine altogether, plan to have one for you and your father to go to the ceremony and then for you and your new husband to enjoy in those first moments of marriage as you go to your reception. Other members of the wedding party can be transported with private cars, but if you can manage to include one limousine in your budget, you will be very glad you did.

*My mother thinks that she should ride to the ceremony in the limousine with me and my father. What is the usual protocol?*

Mothers usually ride in a limousine with the honor attendant and bridesmaids or they go with another member of the family, whichever is personally preferable. If the bride wants her mother and father with her, that is fine. Also, when the bride's father is deceased or if her parents are divorced and her father is not actively involved in the wedding, she will probably want her mother to be with her in the limousine.

*Some friends told us that they were not able to have champagne in the limousine on their way from the wedding to the reception. We think that is so romantic and were looking forward to toasting each other. What could have been the reason they were prevented from doing this?*

The prohibition from serving champagne in the limousine is undoubtedly due to local liquor laws that restrict the consumption of alcoholic beverages in a moving vehicle. Check on your local liquor laws to see if they will affect you. If such laws exist, there are no exceptions to them.

*I have seen advertised a luxury bus with living-room-style appointments, a refrigerator, TV, etc., that accommodates an entire wedding party. My fiancé and I think this is a great idea and want to hire one. We would then meet my parents at the church. But my parents are appalled at this breach of the traditional mode of transporting the bride, and they also think it is too expensive. Is the bus as inappropriate as they think it is?*

It is fairly new, and it is certainly a departure from tradition, but it is a viable option. While it is expensive, if you plan to hire limousines for everyone in the wedding party anyway, the bus will cost the same or perhaps less. When the wedding party consists of many out-of-town friends who have traveled a distance to be with you, this is a great way to maintain the camaraderie. Even if your attendants are all local residents, it is a fun way to begin your wedding celebration. There is nothing wrong with renting the bus, if it is what you both want.

# Dealing with Legal Issues

*I have heard so many horror stories about bridal shops overcharging, not delivering on time, and even going out of business before the bride-to-be gets the dress for which she already has paid a 50 percent deposit. How can I prevent this from happening to me?*

Thankfully, such experiences are more the exception than the rule. However, if it happens to anyone, it is a disaster for that person. To rest easy, contact the Better Business Bureau in the trading area where the shop is located to see if there are any outstanding complaints against it. For further peace of mind, you might also want to contact the state attorney general's office to learn if it has anything on file.

*I am concerned about the liquor liability law as it affects guests driving home from the wedding after they have been drinking. Is the reception facility and/or the host liable if an accident occurs with one of the wedding guests behind the wheel?*

The contract you sign with the reception facility relieves them of any responsibility. The host(s) whose signature is on that contract bears the liability if there is an accident resulting from drinking at the wedding reception. You are wise to be concerned about this and should make every effort to be sure that guests do not drink to excess and that any who do have either someone who did not drink available to drive or a place to sleep it off.

*The contracts that I am getting from the caterer, photographer, florist, and band all have an advance payment schedule with full payment due shortly before the wedding. All have a refund policy if they are able to rebook their services. If something totally out of our control necessitates a postponement at the very last minute, will that money be applied to a future date?*

I believe most wedding professionals will be glad to do that, but it has to be when they have an opening, not when you think they should accommodate you. It is something to question, and if it is not in your contract, ask that it be added. I strongly recommend that engaged couples and/or their parents have an attorney review the contractual agreements before signing them.

## ೯ఁ❀ะాఁ♥ QUICK TIPS FOR THE MODERN BRIDE ೯ఁ❀ะాఁ♥
# *Hints on Choosing Resources*

- Be sure that you and your fiancé have agreed on the wedding style and budget before you make any decisions.

- Ask for recommendations from couples who were happy with the services provided at their wedding.

- Check with the Better Business Bureau to see if any complaints have been registered against the companies you are considering.

- Ensure that all your wishes are in writing and agreed to by both parties before you sign anything.

- Spend enough time talking with bands, caterers, photographers, florists, etc., to be sure that you share the same vision of your wedding.

- A DJ is certainly an acceptable modern option if you cannot find a band to meet your wishes and budget.

- If you choose to have your wedding videotaped, be sure that the videographer will be unobtrusive and will not disturb the ceremony or your guests.

- Use a checklist or timetable to organize your planning—there are lots of details to keep in mind!

- Consider hiring a wedding consultant to coordinate everything, which will very likely save you time, aggravation, and money.

# CHAPTER 8
# Guest Accommodations

## Arrangements for Out-of-Towners

*I live in New York, but will be getting married in Florida. In trying to help with arrangements, I have spoken with several hotel managers and have gotten special rates for groups. Reservations have to be confirmed a month before the wedding, and a minimum number of guests must be guaranteed in order to get the discounted rate. I am also hoping to help with car rentals and transfers from the airport. Communicating this to all of our guests through word of mouth is impossible. How can I do it appropriately on an invitation? Should I order separate inserts that say, "Please check here if you need assistance with hotel accommodations and transportation. Discounts are available"? Should I include hotel brochures with the invitations? Also, because one quarter of the guests invited will be from out of town, may I send the invitations considerably in advance of the preferred two months before the wedding day?*

You are smart to want to provide information about hotel and other accommodations as early as possible to those who will have to travel to attend your wedding. That way they can mark their calendar, avail themselves of lower air fares and hotel discounts, and even plan extra days to vacation in Florida, if they wish. Rather than put all of the material into the wedding invitation, write a letter to them now. Tell them how much you hope they will be able to make the trip for the wedding, and let them know the arrangements you are trying to make to keep their cost down. Choose one hotel that is convenient to everything and make your deal for discount rates with that facility. Enclose all the information for your guests to determine what will best suit their needs. Ask them to let you know about preferences for airport transfers and car rental. Provide hotel reservation cards with rates indicated and advise them to return the cards directly to the hotel at least one month before the wedding. You may photocopy the letter you send. Then, six to eight weeks before the wedding, mail the invitations in the usual manner. The arrangements you have made for airport transfer and car rental can be noted on an insert with the invitations. Upon arriving at the hotel, guests should have an envelope waiting for them containing maps and any other details about the wedding events.

*I am planning to hold my wedding at a state park resort lodge about an hour and one-half away. It is close enough for most guests to drive there and back the same day. However, the lodge is nice enough that ideally I would like to see everyone stay the night and enjoy the facilities as well as the late night wedding reception. I definitely want the wedding party and close family to stay overnight. Am I responsible for their accommodations? How do I inform them of what I have in mind, and how do I tell the guests about this option?*

Encouraging your guests to stay at the state park resort following the reception revelry, which undoubtedly includes drinking, is a great idea for safety reasons as well as for the fun of enjoying the facilities. The guests and your family should expect to pay for their own accommodations. However, you are obliged to assume the cost of the rooms assigned to the members of your wedding party. Arrange for discounted rates with the resort, then write out-of-towners with the information as noted in my previous response. Call your local family and friends or mail them a copy of your letter to let them know what is available, if they would like to stay overnight. Then leave it to them to call and make their own reservations.

*Our wedding ceremony takes place at 1:30 P.M., and the reception is scheduled to begin at 5:30. There are quite a few guests from out of town. We are not able to invite them to either parents' home. Because my fiancé and I are paying for the majority of our wedding, cost must be minimal. Is it our responsibility to provide something for our guests to do during the time lapse and, if it is, what suggestions do you have?*

Yes, something should be provided for out-of-towners during that interlude. Some suggestions are: a hospitality suite at the hotel where they are staying stocked with snacks, coffee, tea, and soft drinks; if that cost is prohibitive, enlist help from local relatives and friends who could invite the guests to their home(s) or take them sightseeing. A Chicago bride who had more leverage in her budget, hired a sightseeing bus and driver to keep her guests busy in between the festivities.

*Some family and friends from out of town will be arriving a couple of days before our wedding. Are there any guidelines about who should be responsible for entertaining them?*

If there are parties being held in honor of the bride and groom, those who have traveled to be at the wedding should be included on the guest list. Immediate family of the bride and groom and close friends who live where the wedding is taking place should make every effort to assist the parents of the couple or the couple themselves with plans to provide meals and organize activities for the out-of-towners.

*I am very close to an aunt and uncle who are coming from out of town for my wedding. My father also has an aunt and uncle who will be coming from out of town. Ordinarily, when they visit, they all stay with my parents. We do not want to hurt any feelings, but I am worried about overcrowding, congestion, and general craziness in our house on my wedding day. My godmother has offered to accommodate one couple, and the other couple has a friend in town who will be coming to the wedding and is willing to have them stay with her. Would it be all right to make other arrangements for them this once?*

Explain to your relatives your concerns not just about the organization and smooth flow of dressing for your wedding, but also for their own comfort and timing to get ready for the celebration. Tell them you have arranged to have them stay where they will be welcome and have more flexibility.

# Parking and Other Amenities

*The hotel where we are having our reception charges for parking. The banquet manager has given us the option of adding those charges to our expenses or letting the guests pay for their own parking. What is the best way to handle this?*

The hosts should take care of the parking fees. Whether guests park their cars themselves or there is valet parking, ideally they should not have to pay anything to attend your wedding. That applies to coat check as well. If these costs destroy your budget, you may leave either or both for the guests to handle.

*Our wedding will take place in my hometown in New Jersey. My fiancé and his family come from Long Island. There will be many people coming from there, including quite a few elderly relatives and friends. We are thinking of renting a bus to transport them from a central location near their homes to the wedding and back. Is this a good idea?*

It is more than good, it is excellent. People do not have to worry about directions or getting lost. That is a thoughtful way to accommodate guests who have to drive a couple of hours each way and who would enjoy the reception so much more if they did not have to worry about the long drive home.

*Quite a few of the couples who are coming from out of town are bringing their children for the weekend. We want to have the couples at the rehearsal dinner the evening before the wedding, but we do not want youngsters at it or at the wedding. They will be staying at a hotel that has a pool and an arcade with games. There are also movies in the neighborhood. How can we tell these parents that their children will not be included in the wedding events?*

First, determine whether you want to provide a sitter or two at your expense or if you expect the parents to pay for that. If it is the former, secure the dates with the sitter(s). Then, write or phone the parents to tell them what arrangements you have made so there are no surprises and they can prepare their children. If you cannot handle that expense, still write or call to inform the parents that no children will be attending the festivities, therefore you are providing them with the names of sitters whom they can contact directly to take care of their children during the events. Provide them with the sitter rates so they can determine whether they want to do that or to arrange to leave their children at home.

*I would like to have a token of welcome at the hotel for our guests when they arrive. What do you suggest?*

A basket of fruit, cheese and crackers, a bottle of wine, an arrangement of flowers sent to each guest's room with a note of thanks for coming to share your celebration—any one of these is extremely thoughtful. But so is anything you put together yourself, such as a tin of home-baked cookies, your own assortment of fruit, or even a long-stemmed rose or a few carnations in an inexpensive bud vase. It does not have to be elaborate or expensive to be thoughtful.

# ꙮ QUICK TIPS FOR THE MODERN BRIDE ꙮ
## *Ways to Accommodate Your Guests*

- Arrange for group discounts at hotels well in advance.

- Inform any out-of-town guests in advance of available accommodations, transportation, etc. However, they are responsible for making their own reservations.

- Check to be sure that parking is available at the reception, and pay for it in advance if there is a charge. Ideally, your guests should not have to pay for anything at your reception.

- Include precise directions to the reception site with your invitations.

- Consider hiring a sitter to look after any young children who will be at the reception.

- Do not assume that people who have not responded to the invitation are not coming. Have someone call to get an accurate count for the caterer.

- If there is a significant lapse of time between the ceremony and the reception, provide someplace for out-of-town guests to go. A hospitality suite is a good idea.

# CHAPTER 9
# The Ceremony

## Finding an Officiant

*Believe it or not, I am marrying the boy next door! Our parents are great friends. We want to have a garden ceremony in our backyard and the reception in his. Problem: We are Catholic and want a Nuptial Mass. We have heard that priests will not perform that ceremony outside of a church. Is that true?*

Yes, it is. And there are other orthodox and conservative faiths that will not allow a marriage ceremony to be performed outside their sanctuary. Check with your officiant before making plans for a ceremony outdoors or at any other location other than your church or synagogue.

*My parents are members of a congregation but do not attend services very often. I never do. However, my fiancé and I would like to have a church wedding. Since he has no particular religious involvement anywhere, we would like to be married at the church my parents occasionally attend. Do you think there will be any problem with that?*

Not if you make an appointment to see the pastor before you start making other wedding plans. You may be asked to start attending services regularly in order to make your wedding arrangements there. Meeting with the pastor to learn what marriage preparation is required and to set a date that works into the church calendar, as well as into your own schedule, makes the preparations run much more smoothly.

*We live in a Catholic diocese that requires a year's advance notice to confirm a wedding date at our church. That seems excessive. What if we are unable to plan that far ahead?*

It is not too much lead time to expect when you realize that engagements average 15 months. The reason for doing this is twofold: 1. Without this requirement, couples would make their reception arrangements at least that far in advance, then come to the pastor shortly before the event and insist that they must be married on that date which, for a variety of reasons, might not be available. 2. Marriage preparation sessions are required during the engagement, and often waiting to contact the priest about the wedding date did not allow the couples enough time to take part in the program. The order of priorities was reversed, and the need for a full year's advance notice is the result. If there are very good reasons why that time frame does not work for a couple, I am sure an exception is possible. But it has to be a very important consideration, not a capricious whim.

*Ours will be an interfaith marriage, and we would like to have a rabbi and a priest officiate. How do we manage that?*

You will need plenty of time to locate a rabbi and a priest willing to co-officiate at your wedding. It is unlikely that this can be accomplished if you want to be married in a synagogue, but if one of you is a practicing Catholic, it might be possible to have a rabbi in attendance at a church service. There are not very many rabbis who will officiate or co-officiate at an interfaith marriage. The Catholic partner's priest might know of one. If not, there is a reference resource in New Jersey with a list of rabbis willing to perform such marriages. (See Resources under Interfaith Marriage.) Also check the classified section of bridal publications, city magazines, and newspaper bridal supplements for rabbis and other clergy available to perform interfaith ceremonies. Such weddings are often performed at the reception location rather than in a house of worship. (See "Choosing the Location" on page 103.) To find a priest to co-officiate, consult with the pastor of the Catholic partner or with the Diocesan Family Life Office.

*We want to have a civil ceremony. Who can perform this, and how can we find that person?*

Judges, city officials, some notary publics and, of course, justices of the peace are licensed to perform marriages. To locate these resources, check with the local marriage license bureau, as well as with the municipal and district courts.

*We have no idea what to pay our celebrant. Are there guidelines?*

First, ask the officiant or the secretary in the church or synagogue office about their policy. Some have a fee, others may prefer a donation. Those performing an interfaith marriage often charge more and may have travel expenses. Second, please remember how important the celebrant is in the wedding ritual. Many spend considerable preparatory time with you. Your payment should reflect that. Civil officiants have set fees they will provide when you make your arrangements.

***We do not follow any formal religion, but do believe in God and would like to be married in a church. What is the best way to accomplish this?***

Look for a nondenominational minister to help you with the arrangements. You will find contacts in the *Yellow Pages* under "Churches." (For other options, see *Resources* under "The Ceremony.")

# *Personalizing Your Service*

***We would like to write our own wedding vows. How do we do this?***

There are three steps to follow: 1. Meet with your officiant to learn what parts of the traditional service are mandatory and how much latitude you have to create original material. Even if you will be married in a civil service, you should consult with the officiant about your desire to write your vows. 2. Think about what you want to say. Together with your fiancé, compile a list of what you want to state publicly about your relationship, your hopes and dreams for the future. Some suggestions: the meaning of commitment, keeping individuality and equality in your marriage, your definition of love, the importance of trust and your feelings on fidelity. Another possibility: excerpt from a favorite song or poem that means something to the two of you. (See *Resources* under "Personalizing Your Service.") Individually write down your thoughts and feelings, then share what you have written with each other. Choose the most pertinent ideas to include in your ceremony. 3. Decide what form your vows will take. The content of your vows should be approved by your officiant. Plan time to practice with each other so you will be relaxed and everyone can hear you.

***We would like everyone to be able to follow the sequence of the ceremony. Some friends handed out programs at their wedding. Is this common?***

It is a growing trend to print a program that identifies all the participants, provides the order of the service, lists musical selections, and even carries a special message from the couple to their guests. The vows you have personalized could also be included. Be sure ushers hand a program to all guests when they are seated. (For information on multilingual ceremonies, see "Different Cultures" on page 159.)

# Wedding Rings

***I'm confused about what to do with my engagement ring when we exchange our wedding bands. How is this handled?***

Most brides wear their engagement ring on their right hand during the wedding ceremony, then switch it afterwards. Another option is to have your honor attendant wear it until later.

***My nephew is our ring bearer. I am concerned about his being responsible for two expensive wedding bands. Is this too much to expect of a five year old?***

Usually, the rings sewn onto the pillow carried by the ring bearer are inexpensive ones from a novelty store. The real rings remain with the best man. In a double ring ceremony, the bride's honor attendant may wear the groom's ring, but it is more common for the best man to have them both in his pocket.

***I am wearing long over-the-elbow gloves that will be very difficult to remove when I receive my wedding ring. Must I remove them or can I have the ring slipped over the glove?***

If your ring is sized to your finger as it should be, it would not fit over the glove. Instead, slit the two side seams on the ring finger of your left glove to permit the ring to slip on easily. Do not worry; it will not ruin the glove or be noticed and the seams can be resewn at a later date.

***I am not certain of how to wear my wedding ring with my engagement ring. What is the correct order?***

Your engagement ring goes in front of your wedding band. To clarify, the wedding ring is worn closest to your heart and the engagement ring closest to your fingertip.

# Seating

***We are being married in my hometown and my fiancé comes from elsewhere. There will be considerably more people from my side of the family than from his. Is it all right to eliminate the traditional bride's side/groom's-side seating arrangements in the church?***

If the number of guests is greater on one side than the other, by all means instruct the ushers to fill in the rows evenly on both sides without concern for the family connection. The only exception is immediate family—the bride's family should occupy the first few rows on the left, the groom's the same on the right.

*We do not have a center aisle in our church. How do we handle seating the parents and follow the bride's-side/groom's-side formula in this case?*

The bride's parents would occupy the left end of the front pew and the groom's parents the right end. Rather than leave an empty expanse between them, it would be nice to seat grandparents and/or other close relatives from both sides up there before the mother of the groom and mother of the bride are escorted to their aisle seats.

*My parents are divorced, and my mother does not want to be seated anywhere near my father's wife, who will be attending the wedding with him. He is escorting me down the aisle. How should I arrange their seating at the service?*

Your father's wife should be seated along with other guests three or four pews behind your mother. Have an usher give her the aisle seat and leave a space there for your father to join her after leaving you.

*My fiancé's parents are divorced and both remarried. How should they be seated at the wedding?*

Your fiancé's stepmother should be escorted in by an usher, with his father walking behind, to their seat in the same manner as the other guests. If your fiancé's father and stepmother are on good terms with his mother and her husband, they could be seated in the first row with them. Otherwise, they should sit a row or two behind or as far back as is comfortable for both couples. His stepfather should walk in alone to take his assigned seat up front. Just before your mother is escorted up the aisle, your fiancé's mother should be ushered in to take her seat next to her husband in the front pew on the groom's side.

# Escorting the Bride

*I love both my father and my stepfather. If I have to choose one to give me away, the other would be deeply hurt. How can I include them both?*

Just before the wedding processional have your stepfather, rather than an usher, escort your mother to the first pew, left side, where they both take their seats. He should be dressed as your father and all the men in the wedding party. Let your father escort you in the traditional manner. If you want your stepfather to have more participation, ask your officiant to help you select a prayer or scriptural passage for your stepfather to read. It is a nice way to have him share in the ritual. An alternative is to have your father and stepfather both escort you if they are amenable enough to do this. Another way to handle the problem of "too many fathers" is for the bride to walk in alone, with her groom, or halfway down the aisle alone to be met by the groom. (For more about handling parental divorce situations, see "Dealing with Divorced Parents" on page 153.)

*My father died when I was a child. Would it be okay to have my grandfather give me away? If so, what should he reply when asked, "Who gives this woman . . . ?"*

You may certainly invite your grandfather to escort you. When the question is asked, he answers, "Her family." It is also possible to arrange in advance with your officiant to omit that question if you prefer.

*I come from a single parent home. My mother and I are very close. Is it appropriate for my mother to walk me down the aisle or should I ask my uncle?*

Your mother would be an excellent choice. Nowhere is it written in stone that a man must be at your side for that important time.

*My father passed away, and I want my middle brother to walk me down the aisle. We have been quite close, while I really have very little contact with the older one. My mother says the oldest brother should escort me. Is that an inflexible rule?*

No, it is not. If you feel much closer to your middle brother, he should be the one to escort you. Age is not the determining factor. What counts is the relationship you have with your middle brother.

*The number of friends my fiancé has invited to be his attendants precludes including my three older brothers in the wedding party. I am the youngest and the only girl. I want my brothers to have an important role, so I am thinking about having each take turns walking a few steps down the aisle with me to reach my father, who will be last and the one who gives me away. What do you think of this?*

I think your idea sounds more like a musical stage production than a wedding procession. My advice is to have your father walk with you and invite your brothers to each read a scriptural passage and/or a poem during the ceremony.

*My fiancé and I have attended Jewish weddings where it is the custom of the parents of the groom and the parents of the bride to escort them down the aisle. Although ours will be a Christian ceremony, we would like to incorporate this custom. Is there any reason not to do it?*

This symbol of the love and support that both parents have given to their daughter and son would be appropriate at any wedding ceremony. Discuss it with your officiant and if he or she has no objection, inform your parents of your desire to have them participate in this manner. Most would be very happy to oblige. (Be sure, however, that your dad will not feel cheated. Some fathers look forward to that special walk. And many mothers are not comfortable tampering with that tradition.)

# Order of Processional and Recessional

### *We have not attended many weddings and do not know how to position the attendants. How is this handled?*

In general, ushers and bridesmaids enter according to their height, shorter ones going first. Whether they walk in single file or in pairs reflects the procedure usually followed in the place where you are marrying. Your own preference should also be considered when determining the order at the rehearsal. The bride's honor attendant is last to enter before the bride and stands at the left. The best man and groom enter from a side door just before the processional begins (except for Jewish weddings where they are in the processional). Where ushers and bridesmaids stand (or sit) during the service depends on the customs followed in your particular wedding ritual. The officiant will provide all of that direction at the rehearsal. The order of the recessional is just the reverse of the processional. (For Christian and Jewish ceremonies, see the chart on page 96.)

### *I am not sure when the official processional begins. Is it when the mothers enter or after that?*

The last two people to be seated before the wedding processional begins are the groom's mother, followed by the bride's mother. Then, two ushers roll down the white aisle runner (if there is one), and the official wedding processional begins. Usually, the organist and/or musicians indicate this with appropriate wedding march music. After all the attendants have taken their places, the wedding march music changes to something more dramatic to accompany the bride's entrance.

### *My fiancé has a best man and two ushers. I have a maid of honor and four bridesmaids. How do I handle the processional and recessional?*

The two ushers may lead the processional single file followed by the bridesmaids, also single file. In the recessional, two bridesmaids may double up directly after the maid of honor and best man; then the ushers escort the other two

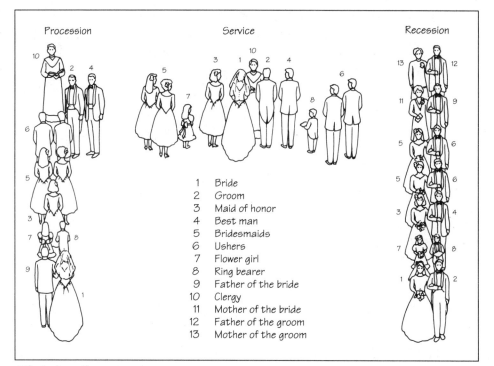

1    Bride
2    Groom
3    Maid of honor
4    Best man
5    Bridesmaids
6    Ushers
7    Flower girl
8    Ring bearer
9    Father of the bride
10   Clergy
11   Mother of the bride
12   Father of the groom
13   Mother of the groom

**Christian Ceremony**

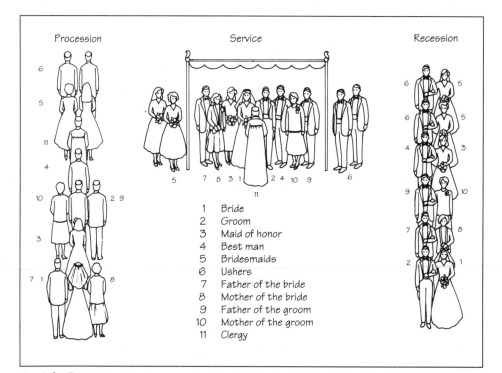

1    Bride
2    Groom
3    Maid of honor
4    Best man
5    Bridesmaids
6    Ushers
7    Father of the bride
8    Mother of the bride
9    Father of the groom
10   Mother of the groom
11   Clergy

**Jewish Ceremony**

bridesmaids. It is also possible for one usher to escort two bridesmaids, one on each arm, in the recessional. When there are more ushers than bridesmaids, the single file processional is best as well. In the recessional, ushers either double up or one bridesmaid can walk between two ushers.

***I know that the honor attendant enters behind the bridesmaids and just before the bride. But I have two. How do I determine which one is just before me and where each stands at the altar?***

The height rule works here, too. Other options: flip a coin, pull the numbers from a hat, or alphabetically by last name. Or have them walk side-by-side. They will both be next to you during the service, so which one is closest does not matter. Just decide at the rehearsal, either by closing your eyes and pointing or flipping the coin.

***I would like the exiting of guests to be as orderly as the recessional. How can this be accomplished?***

Following the recessional, two of the ushers who first reach the door of the sanctuary should return immediately to the front of the church to stand at the end of each pew, directing the guests to leave one row at a time. That should make the exiting run smoothly. If there is no receiving line at the front door, it will move along swiftly. If there is a receiving line as guests exit, it will keep them from getting out of sequence and encourage them to wait patiently for their turn to greet you.

# *Interfaith Accommodations*

***My fiancé and I come from different religious traditions. Although neither of us feels strongly about our religion, both of our families practice their faiths. They have accepted our decision to marry in a civil ceremony at the hotel where we are also holding the reception. We would like to incorporate some of the traditions that are associated with each faith, but are not versed in what those are. What is the best way to accomplish this?***

First tell your parents what you want to do and ask for their suggestions. Go to the library and read about the wedding rituals practiced in each of your faiths. If you have difficulty finding the information, phone the clergy at the house of worship your parents attend to ask for suggestions or sources to consult. For example, if one of you is Jewish, you could marry under a canopy representing the traditional *chuppah,* symbolic of the tent home in which newlyweds dwelt in ancient times. Our *Modern Bride* book *Wedding Celebrations* describes wedding rituals specific to 15 different religions, as well as 40 different ethnic and cultural traditions. (See *Resources* under "Interfaith Marriage.")

*Because my fiancé and I are from different religious backgrounds (he is Greek Orthodox and I am Protestant), we will be having two wedding ceremonies on the same day! This is the only way we can satisfy both families. Our first wedding service will be held in my family church at 2:30 P.M. The second service will take place at the Greek church at 4:00. We want one invitation to indicate both services. It is very important to us that our family and guests be present at both ceremonies. How do we word the invitations?*

My suggestion for the wording is:

Mr. and Mrs. _____

request the honour of your presence

at the marriage of their daughter _____

to

_____

Saturday, the sixth of November

at 2:30 o'clock

Protestant church

address

and at 4 o'clock

Greek church

address.

During the first service the Protestant minister, a family member, or friend could explain to the guests how much it means to have them all witness the second ceremony as well. Some guests might phone after receiving the invitation to question the two times and churches, which will provide an opportunity to clarify your plans. I also advise you and your families to personally tell as many relatives and friends as possible about your plans in advance to help overcome any confusion resulting from this departure from ordinary circumstances.

*My father is Jewish and my mother is Catholic. My fiancé is Catholic, and we are planning a Catholic wedding ceremony without the Mass. My father would like us to smash a glass at the end of the service as is customary in a Jewish ceremony. How can I incorporate this tradition, and what does it mean?*

The smashing of the glass is a universal Jewish symbol of marriage. At the conclusion of the ceremony, the groom crushes a very inexpensive glass under his right foot. To avoid accidents from flying splinters, the glass is placed in a paper bag before the ceremony, ready for the officiant to place under the groom's foot. (To make it more attractive, a large white napkin is often wrapped around the bag, and some wedding accessories resources have designed pretty coverings to slip the glass and paper bag into, as well.) Some explain the meaning of the gesture is a reminder that even in happy moments, we must be aware of the fragility of life. Over the centuries, however, this act has become a symbol of the destruction of the Temple and of mourning for Jerusalem. Today, it is an act of celebration and continuity, as well as a reminder of those other more serious considerations. It would be lovely if your priest agrees to include it at the end of the service, just before your groom kisses you.

# Candlelight and Candle-Lighting

*We would like to have a candlelight ceremony. Are any special arrangements necessary?*

Check with someone at the site where you plan to hold the ceremony to be sure there are no fire regulations that prohibit the use of candles. In a church or synagogue it would be the sexton; at other locations, it is the banquet or special events manager. Along with doing the floral arrangements, the florist is usually responsible for positioning the candle holders and placing the candles in them. Tell your photographer that there will be candlelight, so he or she has the necessary equipment and lighting to capture the mood in clearly focused, sharply reproduced pictures.

*We are being married early in the afternoon, but would still like to have a candlelight ceremony. Does it have to be dusk or evening to do this?*

To benefit from the drama that comes from an abundance of candlelit pedestals and candelabra, the ceremony should be held at dusk or in the evening. Candlelight creates a special effect, and that purpose is totally lost if bright daylight is pouring into the sanctuary. On the other hand, if you are being married in a place that has little or no access to daylight, the time of day will not matter at all.

*I have two nephews, ages 11 and 13, who have no role in the wedding party. I would like them to be the candlelighters. May they do it, or is an adult required?*

Unless the facility has a policy limiting this responsibility to an adult, it provides a good opportunity for your nephews to take an active part in the ceremony. At the rehearsal, they will be instructed about the time frame for the candle-lighting.

*I did not plan on assigning the candle-lighting to anyone in our wedding party. Is this necessary, or is there another way to handle it?*

Although often two ushers are the most likely choice for this assignment, there are alternatives to having it done by members of the wedding party. Acolytes may do it, the florist can take care of it, or you might consider it an honor you want give to a dear friend or relative who is not otherwise involved. (This is a good time to note that acolytes and altar boys should be given a cash token of appreciation.)

### *I like the idea of having a unity candle at my ceremony. What is the procedure for doing this?*

During the service, there is one candle burning on the bride's side of the altar and another one on the groom's side. A taller, unlit candle stands in the middle. After the bride and groom are pronounced husband and wife, they each take their respective candle, meet at the unlit candle, light it, and blow out the two other candles in a symbolic gesture of the unification of two families and two hearts. Parents and other members of the bride's and groom's families might come up to the altar to join the couple at this time.

### 𝒮𝒾𝓈𝓈𝓈 QUICK TIPS FOR THE MODERN BRIDE 𝒮𝒾𝓈𝓈𝓈

# Planning the Ceremony of Your Dreams

- Meet with your officiant well in advance to plan the ceremony.

- Discuss any special considerations such as an interfaith wedding—be sure to find an officiant who will work with you to conduct the type of service you both want.

- Insist that photographers and videographers be inconspicuous during the service.

- Think about seating options and special circumstances ahead of time, and let the ushers know of your plans.

- Remind ushers to escort guests as they arrive, and not to be distracted by seeing old friends.

- The bride can choose who, if anyone, should escort her down the aisle. In Jewish weddings, both parents traditionally do the honors. This is becoming more common in Christian weddings as well. The bride may also walk down unescorted, or even with the groom if she chooses.

- If you have people you wish to honor who are not in the wedding party, consider having them do special readings. Discuss other options with your officiant.

- Check to see if your location allows throwing rice (or anything else). Many prohibit this custom.

# CHAPTER 10
# The Reception

## Choosing the Location

*I have read that one should start looking for a reception site at least 12 months before the wedding. However, many of my friends tell me that some reception facilities have a two-year waiting list. How far ahead should I plan?*

With so many weddings taking place on weekends, the most popular reception locations are often reserved far in advance. For weddings in spring, summer, and fall, two years is not too soon to begin. There is more availability and flexibility for weekends during January, February, and March. Week nights throughout the year can be reserved with less lead time and often at discounted rates.

*I have always dreamed of a garden reception, but my fiancé is worried about the logistics and is especially concerned about the weather. How do you recommend we deal with this?*

Look for a reception location that can accommodate an outdoor reception, if weather permits, and can also provide an indoor alternative if it does not. Hotels and catering establishments often have such facilities. Also contact the local parks department, historical society, or party planners to locate places with suitable outdoor sites. If you choose an outdoor site, you should arrange to rent an all-weather tent and a dance floor. This is important even if the weather is perfect. All of this is expensive, and the uncertainty might be unnerving. An alternative is to plan an indoor reception filled with rented trees and shrubbery, and lovely floral arrangements that simulate the outdoors. In your search for the right reception facility, you might even find one that has an atrium where receptions can be held.

**We would like to hold our reception at someplace other than a hotel or catering establishment. What suggestions do you have?**

A desire for imaginative settings has led many couples to look for more untraditional wedding sites. These include yachts, mansions, museums, historical buildings, lofts, and botanical gardens. Resources for such places are wedding consultants, party planners, or your local Chamber of Commerce, parks commission, or historical society. Also look for *Places*, a publication that provides a nationwide directory of location possibilities. (See *Resources* under "Reception Locations.") You will have to hire a caterer to provide the reception fare. Availability of kitchen facilities is an important consideration when making your plans both for convenience of preparation and as it affects cost. Significant equipment rental—tables, chairs, dinnerware, flatware, glasses, linens—is usually required. Often the caterer and/or florist can provide these, but you pay for it, either built into their fees or itemized as extras. Be sure you inquire about that and plug the costs into your wedding budget as you do your research. The contact person who has managed weddings at these sites before will undoubtedly have catering and rental resources to suggest to you. Their familiarity with the facility is often an asset. If you like what they propose, and get good word-of-mouth references on their work, you would be wise to choose them.

**Most wedding receptions take place in a catering establishment or a hotel. I had always thought that is where mine would be. My fiancé is not sure that is what he wants. What can I tell him to convince him that it is the best choice for us?**

These are the most popular choices because they have all the services needed on site and generally have a variety of packages from which to choose. They are usually centrally located as well. A hotel is especially convenient if you have a lot of out-of-town guests, who then will not have to drive in a strange city after the reception. While you can arrange to reserve blocks of rooms for your guests at a discounted rate elsewhere, you might be able to get an even better rate on your wedding reception if you do everything in the same hotel. In addition, a hotel often provides a complimentary honeymoon suite for the newlyweds. However, some couples do not want their reception to be one of many taking place at the same time in the same establishment. Perhaps your fiancé is thinking of that, though he has not put it in those words. The overlap is more noticeable in some places than in others, and it is something to be aware of when you are looking for the location that most pleases you both. Some other things to do before making your decision: Try to visit the facility while another wedding is going on to unobtrusively observe how the staff runs the affair; sample the food; inspect the kitchen and the rest rooms.

# *Choosing the Caterer*

*Knowing that the reception food and drink is the most costly aspect of our wedding, we are worried about being disappointed* after *paying for everything. What can we do to minimize the likelihood of that happening?*

Allow plenty of time to shop around. Talk to the banquet managers of several establishments, and be sure you have a good personal rapport with anyone you might later be entrusting with your reception plans. Request a sample meal to ensure that the food and style of presentation pleases you. Discuss menus and *ask questions.* It may be a mistake to think that you can save money by serving only champagne and hors d'oeuvres if, for very little more per person, you can have a seated luncheon, dinner, or hot buffet, and much happier guests. Can the caterer accommodate any dietary restrictions? If you know couples who have had their reception in the places you are considering and they were very pleased, you are ahead of the game. If not, ask for previous customers you can contact for references. Get a written contract with detailed cost breakdowns including exactly what will be served, components of the place settings, number of servers, cost of bartenders, taxes, gratuities, and an inflation cap for dates of more than a year in the future. Discuss deposit and payment schedules. Before signing a contract, carefully check the contractual obligations (with a lawyer, if possible), the cancellation policy, and the liquor liability. In the light of recent legal cases, you must know who will be responsible for the safety of a guest who has had too much to drink at the wedding.

*While making my reception plans, I was shocked to hear from my banquet manager that I have to pay for dinners for the five band members, the photographer, and the videographer. That is a considerable amount of money in addition to what I am already paying for their services. The banquet manager also said they must be seated with guests because the room cannot accommodate more than the 10 tables planned for my 100 guests. Must I incur such expense and crowd these strangers into my seating arrangements?*

The band members, photographer, and videographer will be spending a substantial number of hours working at your wedding. To do their best, they should be provided with something to eat and drink during a logical break in their services. They do not require the same meal served to guests, nor should they be seated with the guests. I consulted some highly respected professional wedding caterers and consultants throughout the country about this problem. They offer the following guidelines: When contracting for your wedding menu, arrange the type of refreshment that will be served to the musicians, etc. It could be a family-style platter or even a sandwich plate. It could also be a minimal selection from the entrée on your menu without any of the other courses. Beverages should be served then and may also be at the band area, but no musician or any other person employed for the wedding should walk around among guests with a drink in hand. A reasonable charge for the food and drink (nothing close to what you pay for each guest) should be written into the contract as well as the provision that the caterer will have a separate and inconspicuous place for the musicians and photographers to sit and eat away from the main guest area. If any banquet manager insists otherwise, take your business elsewhere.

*I am not sure who to tip at the reception. Should a lump sum be given to the caterer or should something be given to each bartender and butler?*

It is not necessary to tip the caterer if that person is the owner of the business. Usually, gratuities are included in your contract. If not, the gratuities should be added to your payment to the caterer to be distributed among the help that the caterer has provided. The amount of the gratuity varies between 15 percent and 20 percent, depending on prevailing local custom. If you contracted for your own help without assistance from the caterer, add the tip to what you agreed to pay each person. If you have contracted with a hotel or facility that assigns a banquet manager or maitre d'hotel to work closely with you, and the service is extraordinary, you might want to give that person an additional 2 percent tip. Often, the bartenders provided by the hotel or caterer are extra, but usually that is indicated in the contract. Their gratuities should be included in the contract as well. Check and be sure it is. Under no circumstances should there be a receptacle for bartender tips at your wedding.

*For our only daughter's wedding, we are planning a lovely reception for 175 people. The groom's parents and the couple are sharing the expense with us. Neither of our families are drinkers, and we do not wish to spend a great deal on an open bar. The caterer tells us that others have had a cash bar in similar circumstances. Is it proper to indicate "Cash bar available" on the reception card?*

Absolutely not, nor is it appropriate to have such an option at your wedding reception. A "No Host" bar, as this arrangement is called, is truly an oxymoron. When a formal wedding invitation is extended, it is the responsibility of the hosts to provide food and beverage. (Would you invite guests to your home for dinner and charge for their drinks?)

The trend toward offering a cash bar at a wedding is the result of reception facilities finding a way to make their profit on alcohol when those hosting the wedding cannot afford to commit to that expense. While such an arrangement is appropriate at fund raisers, class reunions, and other such events, it is not at a wedding. Rather than do such a thing to keep within budget, I recommend the following alternatives: cocktails *limited* to one hour and/or champagne for toasting during dinner; just champagne punch or wine during the entire reception; a "soft bar" which consists of wine, beer, and soda.

Generally, people are drinking less alcohol today. Therefore, it might be more economical to arrange with the caterer to pay for the alcohol by the drink consumed rather than by a flat per-person rate. Ask about the option of running a bar tab. (You must feel confident that it will be an honest accounting with no padding.) Finally, there is no reason for a couple or their families to feel compelled to serve alcohol at the wedding reception. This is a celebration of the commitment the bride and groom make to their lifetime partnership. It is not necessary to serve liquor to have a wonderful party. Sparkling grape juice, non-alcoholic punch festively presented, mixed drinks without the alcohol, sodas, and mineral water are all that is needed for those who do not wish to serve alcohol for economic, religious, or other personal reasons.

# Menu Options

***I would like to have a formal reception and a nice menu, but finances are a problem. How can I provide something substantial within my budget?***

In general, let me assure you it is possible to have a lovely reception without incurring debt. Find a caterer who either has some packages that work in your budget or who is willing to break out of the mold and provide a menu of fewer courses. For example, have raw vegetables, dips, assorted cheese and crackers, and one or two other hot and/or cold hors d'oeuvres rather than an elaborate cocktail menu. Follow this with an appetizer, entrée, and sherbet instead of a multicourse extravaganza. Limiting the alcohol service helps considerably to economize on the reception costs. Remember, do not feel pressured to do what someone else has done; do what works for you.

***At our wedding reception I only want cake and punch, maybe champagne. My fiancé insists that people expect a full meal. Is that true?***

The type of food served at a reception depends on the time of day. A morning wedding presumes that some breakfast, brunch, or lunch be served. Late afternoon usually means a cocktail reception with hors d'oeuvres, often followed by a full dinner. However, if you plan a 2 P.M. ceremony with reception immediately following, cake accompanied by champagne and/or punch would be all right, but your guests might be happier if you also serve tea sandwiches, nuts, and mints. (Geographic locations and regional customs often affect the choice of food that guests expect and hosts should consider serving.)

***I am having a large evening wedding reception. I wish to offer my guests a choice between either filet mignon–and–lobster, or double filet as an entrée. I would like***

*to enclose a card with the wedding invitation requesting that the guests check their choice of entrée and return it with the response card. Is this acceptable?*

If the caterer needs the information in advance, there is no reason not to handle it in this manner.

# Receiving Line

*I have been to weddings where fathers are in the receiving line and those where they are not. What determines their participation, and what is the order in either case?*

It is a matter of personal preference. Often dads do not have the patience to stand in the line and prefer to mingle with their guests during that time, which is perfectly all right. The order is as follows: bride's mother, bride's father, groom's mother, groom's father, bride, groom, honor attendant, and bridesmaids. (The best man and ushers always mingle.) When the fathers are not participating in the receiving line, it is the bride's mother, groom's mother, the couple, etc. Sometimes, in order to speed up the time spent going through the receiving line, the bridesmaids are omitted. Child attendants are not expected to be in it.

*My fiancé's parents are divorced and both have remarried. Ours will be a fairly small reception. What is the best way to incorporate them all into the receiving line?*

Only your fiancé's mother should join your mother in the receiving line. Your father and stepparents greet and mingle with guests informally.

*For a variety of reasons, it would not be pleasant having our parents in the receiving line. What alternatives are there?*

You and your groom may be the only ones to greet your guests formally, or you may omit the receiving line altogether in favor of stopping by every table to see and speak with everyone during the reception.

# Seating Options

*My fiancé's mother says we are supposed to seat parents of the bride and groom at the bridal table. I do not want to do that. What can I tell her?*

Inform her that there are a number of equally correct seating arrangements. It is the bride's prerogative to choose the seating plan she wants. The choices are:

bride and groom with their attendants only; the couple's parents, the officiant and spouse, also, if the wedding party is small; a separate parents' table that includes the officiant and spouse; or two parents' tables so that the bride's parents and the groom's parents can each host their own table with close relatives and friends. The bride and groom may even choose to be seated alone at a centrally placed table. Their wedding party may be seated at tables around them, enabling the attendants to sit with their own husbands, fiancés, or significant others who are not in the wedding party.

*My fiancé and I are wondering whether formal name tags would be proper at our reception. We both have been to weddings where we knew hardly anyone at the reception. What do you think of this idea?*

Name tags at a wedding would be tacky, but place cards at the reception tables assigned to guests are a good alternative. They will help the guests to learn and remember the names of those around them and encourage conversation.

*I know that guests should be assigned to tables with others they know or whom they will enjoy meeting. Ordinarily their names are written on cards with the table assignment, and guests pick them up at the door to the reception. If we do not want to go that route, is there another way to indicate table assignments?*

You can have a master list, with names in alphabetical order and the table number assignment next to the names, posted prominently just outside the door to the reception area. But the other method is much more elegant.

*We have a flower girl and ring bearer in our wedding party. Should they be seated at the bridal table or elsewhere?*

If there are other children in attendance, it would be much more entertaining for the youngsters to sit with them. It is also wise to hire a sitter or two to look after the children, maybe even to bring some games or coloring books to keep the children occupied when they become restless. If there are no other children, they should sit with their parents; if their parents are in the wedding party, assign the children to a table with relatives who are not.

*We will be having an elaborate cocktail reception using both butler service and buffet. It will be at 9:00 P.M. Since no sit-down meal is planned, is a seating arrangement necessary?*

A formal seating plan is not required, but you should have plenty of tables and chairs for guests to sit down and eat comfortably, especially for your older guests.

# Schedule of Events

*I do not want to be concerned about what should take place and when during the reception. Who is in charge of that?*

It could be any one of the following: the banquet manager, the bandleader or disc jockey, or your wedding consultant, if you are working with one. He or she will have a list of what is usually done and discuss it with you well in advance to determine if you want to follow it or prefer to change it in any way.

*We have been to about a dozen weddings, and no two receptions seem to have the same traditions. Are there some wedding traditions that must always be included?*

Much depends on the couple's taste and their backgrounds. Every reception is different because no two couples are alike. There are really only two things that should be included at every wedding reception: something to toast the couple and a wedding cake. Everything else is adaptable. The events that most often take place and the order in which they occur are: guests sign the guest book as they enter the reception; the couple's parents and the wedding party are announced after all guests are seated; toasts are proposed by the best man and groom, fathers of the bride and groom, and other members of the wedding party, if they wish to do so; the bride and groom have their first dance as husband and wife, then the bride with her father, groom with bride's mother, then groom with his mother and bride with his father, then the wedding party, and finally the guests join in. Any of these can be omitted, if circumstances call for it. For example, if the parents are divorced, perhaps just the wedding party is introduced, or it is limited to only the formal entrance of the bride and groom. If a best man or groom is very uncomfortable proposing a toast, it is not mandatory; someone else can do it. I have received letters from distraught brides-to-be because their fiancé cannot dance and does not want to do the requisite first dance. No problem—just have the bandleader invite everyone to dance, so guests are not waiting for something that is not going to happen. The important cake cutting comes about an hour before the end of the reception. After cake is served, the bouquet is thrown to the single women and the garter is removed to throw to the single men, unless the couple prefers to skip that.

*My mother tells me that it is the bride and groom's responsibility to hand out favors at the end of the reception, and my fiancé says it should be the maid of honor and the best man. Who is right?*

Usually, there are two ways to handle the distribution of guest favors: 1. Have one favor at each guest's place at the table to take along whenever the guest leaves. 2. Put all the favors on one table near where the bride and groom will be toward the end of the reception. Then, as guests bid goodbye to the couple, they can thank them for coming by giving them the favor or telling them to take one as they leave. In most cases, the maid of honor and best man have nothing to do with that. An exception might be based on ethnic tradition, where the patron (best man) provides the favors.

# Wedding Cake

***We are having a 9:00 A.M. wedding followed by a breakfast. Is it too early to serve wedding cake?***

By all means serve wedding cake as the finale of your morning reception. Choose one with a lighter filling such as lemon or fruit. Use a royal frosting (egg- white based) rather than a buttercream. The cake should be beautifully decorated with sugar or real flowers. Serve it with sherbet or berries on the side.

***I do not want the usual white wedding cake. Instead, I am planning to have a chocolate cake and chocolate icing with peach and white decorations. My future mother-in-law is appalled by this breach of tradition. Is what I want so outrageous?***

On the contrary, today it is possible to have just about any kind of cake and filling flavor a bride wants—carrot, chocolate, piña colada, white chocolate, pra-line, mocha, and banana, to mention a few. Another popular variation is alter-nating flavors for different cake tiers. Although the traditional white icing is still the choice of most brides (and chocolate frosting does come in white), cakes that reflect individual taste both in filling and design are the focal point of many wedding receptions. Couples who love skiing have ordered theirs in the shape of a ski slope; sailors have had a replica of their boat. Often a couple's ethnic heritage is reflected in their choice of cake: rum filled for Italo-Americans; a cake made with honey, sesame seeds, and quince for Greek couples; those with a French background might have the traditional *croquembouche,* a decorative, cone-shaped tower of cream puffs glazed with caramel syrup. The selection is limited only by your imagination and the talent of the pastry chef.

***My fiancé would like to have a groom's cake. I am not familiar with this. What does he mean, and what do we do with it?***

Groom's cake is an old Southern tradition that has become popular through-out the country. Originally, it was meant for single women guests, who would place a slice under their pillows and dream of their future husbands. That cake was a fruitcake, but today the groom's cake, like the wedding/bride's cake, can be any flavor, color, or shape. In the South, it is German chocolate. For fun it might be designed to reflect the groom's hobby, occupation, or background (a football, the 18th hole, a cowboy boot, etc.). Sometimes it is served at the rehearsal dinner, more often at the wedding where it is frequently boxed as guest favors.

# Smoking and Allergies

*Both my fiancé and I smoke. Several members of the wedding party, family, and guests also smoke. I know a lot of other people do not smoke and might find it unpleasant if we do. What is the prevailing etiquette concerning smoking at a wedding reception?*

The answer to your question depends on the policy at the place where you hold the reception. Ask if the bridal table can be placed where smoking is permitted and still be the focal point of the room. If not, smokers will have to go to an area that allows smoking. Another important consideration is your guests' comfort. Many people find smoking offensive, especially when eating. Bearing that in mind, it would be thoughtful for the smokers, even you and your groom, to leave the room to smoke a cigarette.

*My mother is severely allergic to cigarette smoke. I would like to have no smoking at our reception, but I am unsure how to convey this to our guests without offending some. What do you suggest I do?*

Designate a specific place outside the dining area where smoking is permitted. Do not provide ashtrays, and arrange for the master of ceremonies to make an announcement informing guests where they must go to smoke.

*I have an acute allergy to perfume of any kind. I realize there is no way I can prevent guests from wearing a fragrance. If I get close to any of them, I will be miserable. What can I do to minimize the problem?*

Omit the receiving line to avoid the hand shaking, hugging, and kissing associated with it. Visit your guests at their tables, and chat without getting too close to them. When necessary, explain that your allergy prevents you from being as physically affectionate as you would like.

# Other Quandaries

*The number of dinners served at our reception will be limited to those who responded affirmatively, and the seating will be assigned accordingly. Budgetary and space limitations prevent us from being able to accommodate those who did not respond and any "walk-in" strangers accompanying single guests. What can we do to prevent this?*

Enclose with your wedding invitations a response card that indicates the date by which you must hear from guests. Either phone those who do not respond yourself or appoint someone to do it for you. Explain there will be assigned seating, and you must know now who is attending. Unless you indicate "and Guest" on the invitation sent to a single person, no one should bring one. When speaking to someone who indicates he or she plans to do that, you may explain that space is limited and, regrettably, an extra guest cannot be accommodated.

*I find the clinking of the glasses indicating that the bride and groom should kiss very annoying. Is there something else you can suggest to replace this custom at our reception?*

Yes, invite your guests to sing a song with the word "love" in it. At the beginning of the reception, the master of ceremonies announces that each table of guests should get together and think of a song that includes the word "love." Once they have done that, they stand together and sing the ditty until they reach "love," when the bride and groom kiss. They can do it as many times as they wish, and guests have great fun thinking about what songs to sing to keep the couple kissing.

*I would like to give away the centerpiece on each table in a unique way. I have been to weddings where guests pass around a dollar until the music stops, and the person who has the dollar gets the centerpiece. Or it goes to the person with a penny taped under his or her chair, or to the guest at that table whose birthday is closest to the date of the wedding. What other suggestion do you have?*

These are good ways to make the selection but, because you are celebrating your wedding, you might give the centerpiece to the couple at the table who has been married the longest. If it is a table of singles, it could be those dating longest.

*My wedding dress has a long train. Is there anything I can do with it when I am dancing besides holding it over my arm?*

Your train should be pulled up into a bustle for the reception. There should be hooks sewn into the dress for this purpose. At one of your fittings, be sure someone at the bridal shop shows your honor attendant or your mother how to do the bustle. (Today, you may also choose a gown that has a train attached with hooks and eyes or Velcro tape for easy removal at the reception. This is especially important with a tulle train because it is impossible to bustle that fabric.)

***We expect people to bring wedding gifts to our reception. When should we open them?***

Those gifts should be transported still wrapped to wherever the other gifts are kept, and opened at a future time. However, I discourage the practice of bringing gifts to the wedding reception because of the risk of loss, misplacement, even theft. Gifts should be delivered to the home of the bride's parents, the couple's residence if they are living together, or the home of the groom's parents if the guest knows them best. When a gift is not sent ahead, it should be delivered to the couple's home after the wedding. Although in some ethnic traditions bringing gifts is expected, it would be wise to think about following these suggestions as we move toward the twenty-first century.

***My sister feels that having the dollar dance and auctioning the garter at our reception would be extremely tacky and seems to be another way of asking for money. I never thought of it that way. I have always enjoyed the two traditions, but now I am having second thoughts about them. What is your opinion?***

If these two events are expected and acceptable customs at weddings in your families and among your friends, there is no reason to omit them from your plans. On the other hand, if they are not familiar, they would be inappropriate.

***The throwing of rice or anything else is not permitted at my reception facility. How can I tastefully inform people that to do this would cost me $150 in fines?***

Here are a few steps you can take: When speaking with relatives and friends invited to the wedding, tell them about the prohibition policy; enlist the help of your parents, siblings, and wedding-party members to pass along the information. Finally, if the ushers see anyone with bags of rice, confetti, or rose petals, they should quickly inform the guest that there is a prohibition and fine that is strictly enforced, and request that they please not violate it.

***My father is deceased and my uncle is giving me away. For the first dance, have you any suggestions other than "Daddy's Little Girl"?***

Some alternatives include "Thank Heaven for Little Girls" from *Gigi*, "Sunrise, Sunset" from *Fiddler on the Roof*, "The Times of Your Life" by Paul Anka, or "September" from *The Fantasticks*.

***Rather than follow the usual events at our reception, we would like to have some form of entertainment. What would be fun for our guests?***

Consider hiring mimes, celebrity look-alikes, or a professional dance team to perform.

*We cannot afford expensive floral arrangements at our reception, but want the tables to look pretty. Any ideas?*

Small, pretty flowering plants can be grouped together as centerpieces, then taken home as favors by the women at each table. Simple floral combinations in a vase that do not require extensive time to arrange are economical and attractive. Fill inexpensive little vases with miniature violets and cluster them together. These can also be the guest favors. Vegetables lend themselves to creative centerpieces at minimal cost. Carve out the center of an apple and fill it with a votive or other candles. You can do the same with pineapples (squash and pumpkin in the fall). A cornucopia on each table filled with fruit and greens is lovely, and guests can take the fruit home with them. Hurricane lamps surrounded by greens mixed with some dried flowers are another possibility. At Christmas, groupings of miniature poinsettias are pretty and inexpensive. (See "Holiday and Theme Weddings" on page 126.)

## ✧❧ QUICK TIPS FOR THE MODERN BRIDE ❧✧
# *Making the Reception Worry Free*

- Consider what influence the time of year your wedding takes place will have on your choice of a reception site and food.

- Try to visit the site during another wedding so that you can (unobtrusively!) observe.

- Make sure that your band or DJ has ample space and reasonable amplification.

- Do not require your guests to pay for their own drinks—if you choose not to have an open bar, serve just wine, champagne, and soft drinks.

- Do not allow the bartenders to put out tip jars or baskets. Whoever is paying for the reception should handle all gratuities.

- If you are having a master of ceremonies, be sure that he or she is clear on what his or her role is, and what you want to have—and not have—announced. Discuss that in advance.

- Have the musicians play a variety of music so that everyone can enjoy dancing at the reception.

- Be sure that your photo session does not last too long—you do not want your guests to notice a conspicuous absence.

- Assign someone to transport gifts from the reception to your residence. Ask that person to ensure that cards are not separated from the gifts!

- There is no one correct seating arrangement. Discuss your preferences with the manager of the reception site, whose job it is to accommodate you.

- Food need not be extravagant. Serve what is appropriate for the time of day.

- You do not have to settle for a traditional wedding cake. Pastry chefs welcome an opportunity to create something special and out-of-the-ordinary just for you two!

# CHAPTER 11
# *Specialty Weddings*

## *Destination Weddings*

*Our dream is to be married at our honeymoon location, and we are excited about our decision to do this. When our friends learned about it, we got a lot of static for not sharing this day with family and friends. After we return, we want to have a reception. Is this improper because it obligates guests to give gifts when they did not attend the wedding?*

There is nothing improper about your post-wedding reception, because guests have no obligation to give you a gift. For a variety of reasons, more and more couples are planning to marry at their honeymoon destination. Most resorts will make all the romantic arrangements for you. Some couples advise immediate family and close friends far enough ahead so they can plan to be there for the ceremony and celebration, then take their own vacation. A follow-up reception for those who cannot attend the wedding is a perfect way to share your joy. Show photos, or even better a video, and it will be as if your guests had been there!

*My fiancé and I are planning our wedding for a year from now. We vacationed several times in Key West, Florida, and fell in love with everything the island has to offer. We are considering planning a simple romantic wedding there and flying our immediate family members to Key West to join the celebration. My problem: I do not know how to get started finding a church, priest, hotel/restaurant, etc. How do I begin to arrange for this event?*

Contact the special events coordinators at the major hotels in Key West for information on the types of packages they offer. Discuss your plans with your priest, and ask him to recommend a celebrant to contact for the marriage ceremony and to provide you with a letter of approval. If that is a problem, the wedding coordinator at the hotel you select will probably be able to give you the name of a priest to call upon. If you would rather use a site other than a hotel, try to get some referrals of party planners or wedding consultants in the area to interview and possibly to hire so they can coordinate everything for you in Key West. Before making any written commitment, go on an exploratory trip to Key West to meet and interview possible resources to determine, in person, who makes you feel most comfortable about delivering the services you want. Also, check on requirements for obtaining a marriage license in the state of Florida. (For help arranging a wedding anywhere in the world, see *Resources* under "Destination Weddings.")

*We are planning to be married in Hawaii. Our close relatives and friends have expressed interest in being there for the wedding. We have asked a few others to join us, but have also assured them we understand that they might not be able to make such a trip. Should we send invitations to them and a larger list of people we would like to have at our wedding, but who could not possibly travel that distance?*

Your oral invitation already extended to relatives and friends should be followed up with a letter giving them the details: day, date, time, place, hotel accommodations, etc. Rather than send formal invitations to the extended list, mail those people a formal wedding announcement the day of your wedding or shortly thereafter.

*My fiancé and I are very fond of the water, and we are considering a simple wedding with our immediate families on a cruise ship. How do I begin to arrange this event?*

Contrary to common belief, ship captains are not certified to perform marriages. But many cruise lines do make arrangements for a couple to be married on board ship. For example, Hawaiian American Cruise Lines, sailing out of Honolulu, arranges for the ceremony to take place while the ship is in port prior to sailing; then the reception goes on as the ship leaves. Other lines offer similar services. Remember that your officiant must be licensed to perform in whatever town or city you hold your ceremony. A minister from New York cannot legally marry you in the U.S. Virgin Islands. The best way to make your arrangements for an on-board wedding is by contacting your local travel agent or the cruise lines in which you are interested. CLIA (Cruise Lines International Association) certified travel agents are especially knowledgeable about cruise ships. (See *Resources* under "Your Honeymoon.")

*Our wedding will be held in the Caribbean. We plan to have a reception a week later when we return home. May I wear my wedding dress to the reception, and how many of the reception traditions should we follow?*

By all means, wear your wedding dress. I suggest you wear a wrist corsage rather than carry a bouquet. You will want to choose a special song for your first dance as husband and wife in the presence of your family and friends. Toasts are certainly in order, as is cutting the first slices of wedding cake to give each other. There will be no bouquet to throw, so omitting the garter toss also makes sense.

# Remarriage

*This will be my second marriage and my fiancé's first. We plan to have a traditional church wedding with a best man and a maid of honor. I would also like to have my two daughters, ages six and seven, in the wedding. My parents are attending the wedding, but not giving me away. What is the best way to proceed down the aisle, or should the wedding party gather all at once in front of the pastor?*

You may walk in by yourself. Have your mother and father seated in the first pew, left side, just before the wedding ceremony begins. The best man and groom enter with the pastor and wait for you at the altar. As the processional is played, have your maid of honor and your two daughters precede you down the aisle. The girls can either stand with you during the ceremony or sit with your parents, whichever you all prefer. The order of the recessional is: you and your husband first, followed by the girls, the maid of honor and the best man, perhaps the minister (that depends on your church's protocol), then your parents and your husband's parents.

*I am 36 years old, marrying for the second time. My fiancé has never been married. We are hosting the wedding, which takes place at 6 P.M. followed by a formal reception. I want to wear a floor-length, somewhat elaborate gown in pink (I realize white would be improper). The dress has no veil or train. Yet, I am still receiving negative comments from members of my family who feel this type of wedding is inappropriate under the circumstances. My fiancé and his family are very supportive, and he feels that those who have voiced their objections are mean spirited. I do not want to commit a serious breach of etiquette. What do you think?*

The type of wedding dress you want is perfect for the wedding you are planning. Today, even white or ivory may be worn by a bride marrying again. Furthermore, white was symbolic of joy long before it was ever associated with virginity! Your fiancé is right. Anyone who makes a rude comment is mean spirited. To be blunt, do not let them rain on your parade. You have every right to have a special wedding celebration and to be a splendid-looking bride.

*My maid of honor wants to give me a shower. This is my second wedding (my first was very private), and I am concerned about the propriety of her doing that. Is it all right?*

A shower for you under such circumstances is fine. If your first wedding had been a big affair and there were showers for you then, it would not be as appropriate. Your maid of honor might like to plan a more sophisticated theme such as travel (luggage, small leather goods, American Express gift certificates), wine and gourmet products, or fitness—guests dress in work-out or sports clothes and bring sports or fitness-related gifts. (For other ideas, see "Showers" on page 133.)

*My fiancé and I are hosting our wedding, so the invitations will come from the two of us. I have retained my ex-husband's name. Is that a problem and, if not, what is the correct wording?*

No problem. The wording is:

*Mary Smith Jones*
*and*
*Thomas Allan Brown*
*etc.*

*At age 22 I was married in a beautiful wedding hosted by my parents. Unfortunately, the marriage was dissolved. Now, years later, I am engaged to a wonderful man. He has never been married, and he would like a traditional wedding. We will host our own wedding, which will be simple compared to my first. I have many new friends who will be attending the celebration, but I would also like my family present to share our happiness. Sadly, my parents do not think it is proper for me to invite other family members and close friends who attended the first wedding. I thought about indicating on the invitation, "Your presence is the greatest gift of all," to appease my parents, but I doubt it will change their minds. May I invite the people I have known all my life, or do I have to send them a wedding announcement after the fact?*

It is acceptable and desirable to invite those friends and family to your remarriage, even though they attended the previous wedding. This is the 1990s, and there is no longer a stigma attached to marrying again. Your thoughtful notation concerning gifts is not necessary. Guests need not feel obligated to give a gift to be present, but if they wish to do so, it is their prerogative. I hope your parents will realize how fortunate you all are to have this second chance. It is a time for joy and celebration, without any recriminations or embarrassment.

*My fiancé would like to have his 13-year-old son as his best man. Is that all right?*

It is fine for the boy to be at his side for the wedding, but he cannot sign the marriage certificate as the official witness unless he is 18. However, any adult present may do that.

*I have a 6-year-old daughter, and my fiancé has an 11-year-old daughter. Mine will be our flower girl and his will be a junior bridesmaid. They are not as thrilled about our plans as we had hoped. Is there something we can do to encourage them to share our happiness?*

In the case of second weddings, children from a previous marriage often feel excluded from the event as a whole. To overcome this, the Reverend Roger Coleman, chaplain of urban ministry for the Community Christian Church in Kansas City, Missouri, has designed a "Family Medallion" for circumstances just like yours. The medallion—three circles merged together, symbolizing the new family—would be a good gift to give the girls to make them feel more secure about your marriage and their role in your lives. He has also created a special ceremony called "Celebrating the New Family" that includes a reading on the importance of children followed by a prayer for the child. (See *Resources* under "Remarriage.")

# Military Weddings

*I am in the military, and I would like to honor my commitment to the service by having a military wedding. My fiancée is in favor of this, but we have no idea how to go about planning a military wedding. Do you have some guidelines?*

Military weddings are formal, usually held in a chapel at a military site or in a house of worship. Military personnel wear full dress uniform. There is nothing different about the religious service. What differentiates the military wedding is the arch of swords (navy) or sabers (army) under which the bride and groom pass following the ceremony. This occurs just outside the church or chapel. As the couple exits, they walk under the arch created by four to six saber/sword bearers. Ceremony and reception decorations often include the American flag and standard of the military unit in addition to traditional floral arrangements. The couple always cuts the wedding cake with the sword or saber. For enlisted personnel and noncommissioned officers, the invitation wording is:

*John Wilson Smith*
*United States Army*

For senior officers above captain in the army and lieutenant senior grade in the navy it is:

*Major Thomas Lee Jones*
*United States Army*

For junior officers the title appears on the second line:

*James Arthur Richardson*
*First Lieutenant*
*United States Air Force.*

(For complete details, see *Resources* under "Military Weddings.")

*My son is an ensign in the navy, as is his bride. They are having a military wedding at 1:00 P.M. It is formal with the bride wearing a traditional white satin gown. Two ushers are civilians and two are naval officers. What is the correct formal attire for the civilian ushers?*

They should dress in daytime formalwear, either a cutaway coat (in oxford gray or black) or a stroller jacket with striped trousers, a gray waistcoat, and a wing-collared white shirt. A striped ascot is worn with the cutaway. The ascot or a striped four-in-hand tie may be worn with the stroller jacket. Shoes and socks should be black.

# Long-Distance Weddings

*My fiancé and I live in New Hampshire now, but we both come from Arkansas. My parents as well as his have relocated to different areas. However, most of the family and friends that we want at our wedding still live in Arkansas, so we would like to have the wedding there. What must I do to plan this efficiently?*

Start as far in advance a possible. Make lists of what needs to be done, following the *Modern Bride* planning checklist available in every issue of the magazine. Identify what family members or close friends in your hometown might be willing to help you follow up on details on site. Even better, consider hiring a wedding consultant there to take care of everything. Arrange to use your vacations and/or holidays to go to Arkansas to interview the services you are considering before you make any commitment, and then return at least once more to be sure everything is going the way you want it. Include those travel expenses as well as long-distance phone calls, photocopying, and fax charges in your wedding budget. If your attendants will be coming from different parts of the country, you need to select their attire early to allow for mailing dresses to them. Provide complete transportation information to those who must travel to the wedding. Many air, rail, and bus carriers have discounted rates for groups traveling together. Secure a block of hotel rooms at discounted rates for the out-of-towners. If any of this becomes too burdensome, you might consider marrying in an easily accessible central location that is most convenient for you, your fiancé, closest family, and friends, then follow up with subsequent small receptions on a visit to the places where other family and friends reside.

*I have relocated to Delaware with my fiancé, who is from New Jersey. My family is in Massachusetts, where we plan to be married. His family seemed happy about that, but we have learned that many of them will not be able to make the trip because of the expense and travel time. I would be willing to change the location to New Jersey, but then the situation would be reversed. Either way, one of us is going to be disappointed on what is supposed to be the happiest day of our lives. Do you have any suggestions?*

Since you both agreed to have the wedding in Massachusetts, try to arrange with family and friends there to provide overnight accommodations for his closest family. That would help defray some of their expenses. For those who cannot come under any circumstances, you could plan an informal party in New Jersey after returning from your honeymoon. Or you could turn that around, if his family is better able to make provisions for yours. Talk over all the options and come up with a reasonable compromise that, while it might not bring all the family you want together, allows some from each place to be with you.

# Garden or At-Home Weddings

*Ever since I was a little girl, I have envisioned being married at our family home. Ideally, I want to have it in the garden, weather permitting. My parents are concerned about the logistics of doing this successfully. What preparations are necessary?*

There is nothing quite as special as a wedding and reception in the friendly surroundings of your own home and garden. But you must have alternate plans in place for inclement weather. Renting an all-weather tent solves this problem. Whether your outdoor wedding is at home or in a public park, your town may require a permit for erecting a tent. Check ahead. A tent should be reserved at least five months in advance. Refer to the *Yellow Pages* under "Party Tents and Equipment" for rental firms in your area. Some brides we know have even held their at-home wedding in the dead of winter, renting heaters to keep everyone comfortable. In summer, outdoor fans or air conditioners should definitely be budgeted. Be sure electrical outlets are sufficient to handle those power requirements as well as what will be needed for musical instruments, lighting, and cooking equipment. Tables, seating, tableware, and a dance floor are additional rentals, as are portable toilets. (The latter depends on how many bathrooms are in the house and how many guests attend.) Often a larger, well-known caterer who has worked with many party specialists can offer a package price that includes everything you will need. In general, hiring one person, either a caterer or wedding consultant, to take care of all aspects of planning will provide some savings and, more importantly, peace of mind for you and your parents. Finally, you must have adequate parking available, and hiring a parking attendant or two is strongly recommended. (You do not want to replicate the Steve Martin experience in *Father of the Bride!*)

# Marrying Abroad

*I met my Prince Charming while on vacation in Italy. We want to have a wedding there in the presence of his family, then another one in the United States for my family. Are there any legal issues we must consider, such as both of us living in Italy for a certain amount of time?*

Marrying in a foreign country is a complicated process and requires advance inquiry with the country's consulate office in the United States, but you will ultimately have to reach the provincial authorities for full details. Every country has its own legalities, which must be met in order for the marriage to be valid. Often it requires a period of residence. The Italian Consulate at 690 Park Avenue in New York City, (212) 737-9100, can give you some information. To return to the United States with a foreign spouse, and for any plans your spouse might have to become a U.S. citizen, you need to contact the United States Immigration and Naturalization Service. (For others considering a foreign wedding, the U.S. Department of State, Bureau of Consular Affairs, has guidelines and resource information. See *Resources* under "Marrying Abroad.")

# Double Weddings

*My sister and I are planning a double wedding. Do we have to wear identical dresses? Do our attendants? How can our father escort us both down the aisle?*

You need not wear identical wedding gowns, but they should reflect the same degree of formality. The selection should be what is most flattering to each of you. If one of you looks best in an off-the-shoulder neckline and the other prefers a sweetheart neckline, that is fine. The choices should be complementary, not clones. However, the men's formalwear should be the same to give a sense of unity to the whole wedding party. Bridesmaids may wear different colors, as long as they do not clash. Here, too, the degree of formality should be similar. Your father escorts the first bride down the aisle (usually the elder sister, but you may prefer to flip a coin), then returns for his other daughter. An alternative is to have a brother or your mom walk with the second bride.

### *My parents do not think it is possible to have a double wedding unless there are two aisles in the church. Is that true?*

With two aisles, the two processionals and recessionals can take place simultaneously, but the procedure can be adapted to work with only a center aisle. Both sets of ushers, paired by height, lead the wedding procession. Bridesmaids and honor attendant of the first bride follow, then comes the bride with her father; next, the second bride's attendants followed by the bride with her father or other escort. Once at the head of the aisle, the first bride's attendants stand at the left facing the altar and the other bride's attendants take places on the right. The two couples stand next to each other in the center in front of the officiant. Their father stands behind the bride on the left side until responding to the officiant's query, "Who gives...," then moves to the other daughter to do the same before taking his seat. The recessional is lead by the two couples. In the interests of fairness, the second bride to enter in the processional becomes the first to leave in the recessional.

### *A double wedding will save our parents considerable money, but my sister and I are concerned about the logistics of the receiving line, the bridal table seating assignments, the first dance, the wedding cake(s), and the time it takes to do the photography. We fear it will be very complicated. Is there a way to keep it relatively simple?*

The receiving line can be pared down as follows: your mother, each groom's mother, the bridal couples, and the honor attendants. Fathers and bridesmaids mingle with the guests in the interests of keeping the line moving. If the wedding parties are small, you may have a joint bridal table, but if they are not, separate ones are in order. Each couple chooses their own first song, taking turns on the dance floor alone. You might be happy with one cake extravaganza that both couples cut together, or each of you might want your own to be cut at the same time. Discuss the photo schedule in advance with your photographer. Separate photos of the wedding parties should be taken, but other shots can combine you and your groom, your sister with her groom, and your parents. Arranging considerable formal poses before the ceremony will help reduce the time away from guests later on.

### *My best friend and I are marrying brothers, and we would like to have a double wedding. When sisters do this, one invitation from their parents is all that is needed. May we issue one invitation from my parents and hers or do we need one from each?*

You may do it on one invitation, but it will have to be a large size to accommodate all of the names as follows:

*Mr. and Mrs. Donald Louis Anderson*

*and*

*Mr. and Mrs. Roger James Barrett*
*request the honour of your presence*
*at the marriage of their daughters*
*Laura Elizabeth Anderson*

*to*

*Peter Francis Smith*

*and*

*Melanie Ann Barrett*

*to*

*Ralph Thomas Smith*

*etc.*

If each set of parents wishes to send its own invitation, that is fine and probably preferable. (Guests need send a gift only to the couple they know.)

# Holiday and Theme Weddings

*I love the thought of a Christmas wedding and have chosen December 19 for ours. My mother says that our relatives and friends will not come because of parties and other commitments at Christmas time. She is also concerned that the weather might be a problem. We live in the Northeast and would have quite a few guests traveling to the wedding, which could be difficult in snow. My fiancé says those who care about us will be there. Am I being inconsiderate to expect guests to come at a time when driving and even flying might be dangerous?*

A Christmas wedding can be absolutely spectacular, and if that is what you both want you should be able to have it. Your fiancé has a point. Caring family and friends will make every effort to be present unless all transportation is disrupted because of inclement conditions. Weather is always an unknown at that time of year, so you must face the possibility that a bad storm could prevent traveling. However, some caterers and reception sites offer blizzard insurance, which you might want to investigate. If not, they will usually reschedule your event at the earliest date available that works for you. Ideally, most of your out-of-town guests and, certainly, immediate family and attendants will arrive a day or two in advance of the wedding date, when you should plan lots of activities to entertain them. As for working around the holiday parties and other commitments guests usually have at that time of year, write to everyone who must travel to be there far enough ahead to let them know your plans and how much you hope they can be with you. That should give them plenty of time to make arrangements to avoid conflicts. Inform local friends and family ahead as well so that when they receive their invitation six weeks before the wedding, they will say yes.

***We are planning a Christmas wedding because most of our attendants live out of state and will be coming home for the holiday. Do you have suggestions for the ceremony and reception to emphasize the Christmas theme?***

Red and white poinsettias are ideal for a Christmas wedding, as are Christmas trees aglow with white lights. Brides marrying at this time of year are often fortunate to find Christmas arrangements already in place where the ceremony is being held. Christmas music is also a wonderful way to bring the holiday spirit into the celebration. One bride I know walked down the aisle to "Angels We Have Heard On High." Christmas trees, wreaths, etc., may also be at the reception location already, requiring only festive table arrangements to complete the holiday wedding decorations.

***We are being married on the Fourth of July, and we want to carry that theme through the wedding colors and entertainment. Fireworks seem perfect for such a celebration. Do you think that is appropriate?***

You have chosen a wonderful holiday to work with for your color and decorating theme. Fireworks are a great way to celebrate your union as long as you have an outdoor location that can safely accommodate them and qualified professionals doing the display.

***I would like to have a "snowball wedding" with all the attendants and mothers wearing white. Is this most appropriate during the day or in the evening, and what flowers complement this theme best?***

You may have such a wedding at any time of the day, but it is particularly impressive for a late afternoon or evening formal celebration with men dressed in tuxedos or white tie and tails. Attendants could carry red roses while your flowers are all white. But keeping everything white with touches of green and gold in the floral decorations is wonderful as well. There are many creative ways to enhance all-white wedding attire, and your florist is the best resource for suggestions on what will look great at your ceremony and reception locations.

***Halloween has always been my favorite holiday. This year it falls on a Saturday, and my fiancé agrees it would be such fun to have our wedding then. Of course, we want the theme to be evident in the attire and decorations. His mother is hyperventilating at the idea. How can we assure her that it is appropriate and will be tasteful?***

Tell her to envision it as a masked ball in the best European tradition. It can be very elegant when done with this in mind. Think of bridesmaids dressed in elegant black cocktail or evening gowns carrying a profusion of fall mums reflecting the holiday colors. Orange tablecloths covered with white or ivory sheer organdy or lace are decorated with centerpieces such as glowing hurricane lamps or scooped-out pumpkins or squash with candles inserted, surrounded by colorful fall foliage arrangements. Once again, a talented florist is your best resource to develop holiday and other themes imaginatively and tastefully so that your parents will feel comfortable and guests will appreciate the efforts made to have a reception that is exceptionally memorable.

*My fiancé and I met through the miracle of computers. We would like to carry that theme through our wedding and reception. What ideas do you have for doing this?*

Send computer generated invitations—either computer calligraphy on "traditional" invitations or sent via modem, network, disks, whatever is necessary to reach your list. Create wedding ceremony programs done as computer printouts. Have computer-programmed robots at the reception to serve drinks. Rather than assign guests to table numbers, identify the tables by computer terminology names. Hire a DJ who provides high tech laser disc music.

*My fiancé and I are history buffs, and we would like our wedding to reflect some period from the past. What lends itself to accomplishing this?*

Starting far back and working forward: Medieval, Elizabethan, Colonial, Victorian, Western, Roaring Twenties, Art Deco, The Sixties. Once you have determined your theme, the local historical society may be able to provide you with resources. In addition, there are several books devoted to helping couples carry a theme through every aspect of their wedding. (See *Resources* under "Holiday and Theme Weddings.")

# Reaffirmation

*We have been very happily married for almost ten years, and we would like to acknowledge that with a formal reaffirmation service and gala reception to celebrate our tenth anniversary. Is this appropriate?*

There are several reasons to plan a formal reaffirmation celebration. Couples who grow closer with each passing year, as you have, want to reaffirm their choice and commitment on a special anniversary. But it can be done at any time. For a couple whose original wedding was orchestrated by parents in keeping with their taste and ideas, a renewal celebration provides the opportunity for the couple to have it the way *they* wanted it. Just as soon as they are able to afford it, they may plan the event. The same is true for couples who did not have the time or money available for a festive celebration the first time around. (I even heard from one bride who said the only thing about her wedding she would not change is the groom and her dress. Everything else was a horror story, including an intoxicated officiant. Her reaffirmation celebration will rectify that!) If you have children, you have the added joy of including them in the planning and the ceremony. How proud they will be to see their parents publicly renew their vows. How exciting to participate in this important rite. You will also be more relaxed for this event and, perhaps, savor it more than you did before.

*We were married by a justice of the peace and now plan a religious ceremony because a civil marriage is not considered valid in our faith. The wedding will be followed by a formal reception. My parents are sharing the cost with us. May I wear a bridal gown? How should the invitations be worded? What roles do you suggest for my children, who are 4, 3, and 15 months?*

You definitely may wear a bridal gown. Suggested wording for your invitations is:

*The honour of your presence*
*is requested at the religious affirmation*
*of the marriage of*
*etc.*

Your 3- and 4-year-old children may be flower girl and/or ring bearer. The 15 month old is too young to be in the wedding party. Have a babysitter mind the little one and take care of the others when they get restless. She could even take them home to play or nap if they become very restless.

*We are planning a formal renewal after 11 wonderful years of marriage. Do we need new rings?*

It is not necessary to purchase new wedding bands unless you wish to. If so, your renewal is a great excuse!

*My husband and I were married in the county courthouse two years ago with no family or friends present. We said then that someday we would have a real wedding. That will take place on our anniversary next year. As hosts, how do we word the invitation? Also, I really do not expect guests to give us gifts, but if they want to do so, I would like them to know what we need. Is it in poor taste to register our preferences for a reaffirmation?*

Suggested wording for your invitation is:

*Please come to help celebrate our joy*
*at the reaffirmation of our wedding vows*
*etc.*

Registering your gift preferences is a good idea. Since none of the people you are inviting were at your civil marriage, they are likely to want to give you something on this occasion and will appreciate the fact that you are registered at a conveniently located store.

**Our children are hosting a reaffirmation celebration for us on our 25th anniversary. How should the invitations be worded, and what can we do to discourage guests from giving us gifts?**

The options for wording are:

*Robert and Marie Johnson*
*request the pleasure of your company*
*at the reaffirmation celebration of their parents*
*Mr. and Mrs. Aubrey Johnson*
*in honor of their twenty-fifth anniversary*
*etc.*

or

*The Johnson Family*
*requests the pleasure of your company*
*to celebrate the reaffirmation of the wedding vows of*
*Melinda and Aubrey Johnson.*

Your children may include a line on the invitation as follows: "No gifts please" or "Only the present of your presence is required." Some friends will want to give you a gift in spite of this. Accept it graciously and write prompt thank-you notes.

**Because we had a very small wedding, we were not able to have attendants. Would it be all right to invite those who would have been in the wedding then to do so at our reaffirmation?**

Certainly, you may do that. However, be especially practical about what you expect the women to wear. Sophisticated, wear-again choices that become *them* in color and style should be a primary factor. (For those who did have a wedding party and would like to invite their attendants to serve in those roles again, this is also a key consideration.) The men will have no problem; they simply rent the latest formal attire!

# ✿ QUICK TIPS FOR THE MODERN BRIDE ✿
## *Hints on Specialty Weddings*

- If you are planning a holiday or out-of-town wedding, let guests know several months to a year in advance so that they can make arrangements.

- Be sure that your musicians can play the appropriate music for your theme wedding, if you have one.

- Check into legal requirements if you are marrying out of state or out of the country.

- A remarriage can be as formal or informal as you like. There is no reason not to wear white or register for gifts, if that is what you want.

- Specialty weddings require more planning and attention to details—if you do enough advance work, it will be well worth it!

- A reaffirmation celebration is a wonderful way to have the kind of wedding you may not have been able to arrange when you were married.

# CHAPTER 12
# Related Parties

## Showers

*My mother and I disagree on who should give a shower. She wants to have one for me, and I am uncomfortable with that. Who should host a shower, and who should be invited?*

Members of the immediate family—mother or sister—should not host a shower. Close friends, aunts, or cousins would be fine. There may be extenuating circumstances that change those guidelines. For example, if the couple is giving their own wedding, the bride's or the groom's mother might want to give a shower. The "rules" concerning who gives a shower have relaxed considerably in recent years, and that trend will probably continue. Determining the guest list is easier to control. It should be close friends and family, those who welcome the opportunity to give you a variety of gifts. The best showers are intimate rather than elaborate parties.

*Along with two other bridesmaids, I want to plan a shower for the bride who tells us she wants to have* **fun***! I have never done anything like this, so I do not know where to begin. What can we do to ensure a good time for everyone?*

A bridal shower may range from a brunch to a lunchtime celebration, a dinner party, or simply dessert and coffee. It may focus on particular items such as kitchen, bed and bath, or lingerie and other personal gifts. Or it could be a miscellaneous shower. Opening the gifts takes most of the time. You can make that more fun if, prior to the shower, a short story is written about the bride and groom. Key descriptive words are deleted from the story. Then, as the bride opens each gift, her words of exclamation are substituted for the blanks, in order. The bride or her maid of honor then reads the story aloud. Another way to entertain your guest of honor and learn something as well is to bring in talent, for example, a makeup artist, a flower arranging expert, or a cake decorator. Some hosts indicate a "wishing well" where, in addition to a theme gift for the home, guests bring an inexpensive household item for the "well." Others fill a piñata full of little gifts for the bride and have fun trying to break it open.

*I am my friend's maid of honor. There are no other attendants, so I must underwrite the shower alone. My budget is **very** limited. What can I do that is not costly?*

Weekend brunches are convenient and less costly than buffets or sit-down dinners. You can make your own omelettes, salads, molds, and/or casseroles to serve. An afternoon tea shower is lovely, and requires only some small sandwiches, cookies, or cake with beverages. For an evening shower held after dinner, you need only serve dessert and coffee or tea.

*We are planning to hold a shower for a bride-to-be who has a fully furnished residence. She does not need any of the usual shower items. We would like to suggest to the guests that they give her gift certificates to a variety of different resources that we know she will appreciate. May we do this on the invitation?*

Yes, where the type of shower is ordinarily mentioned on the invitation, you may elaborate that it is "A gift certificate shower to any of the following places: restaurant, lingerie boutique, hardware store, music store, lighting fixture store, health and fitness or beauty salon."

*As maid of honor, I plan to organize the shower for my friend. Her mother insists that I must invite every woman who is on the wedding guest list. We are looking at more than 100 women! I feel this is absurd. I also know that the bride-to-be would rather have a coed party. What should I do?*

You should *not* invite every female on the wedding guest list. I repeat, shower guests should be close family and friends of the bride, and that includes the groom's immediate family. Those invited should also be among the wedding guests, unless it is an office shower for the bride. Given your friend's preference, plan a "Jack and Jill" shower where you invite partners of the friends of the bride-to-be along with friends and their partners who are close to the groom-to-be. In addition to the enjoyment of opening the gifts, you might have some entertainment such as a classic movie comedy on video or instruction on the latest dance steps to keep the event lively. You might even plan it as a bowling evening. Whether yours is a fashionable cocktail party, an informal barbecue, or an everybody-bring-one-dish affair, its purpose is to be relaxing and fun for the couple and their friends.

*I am concerned about those who have to buy shower gifts and a wedding gift for me. The expense can be draining, especially when there are a lot of weddings around the same time, as is the case among my friends. This is particularly true for wedding attendants. Is there a limit to the number of showers that should be given?*

There is no limit to the showers given in honor of the bride-to-be, but there is a limit to how many gifts one should have to give. Therefore, it is considerate not to ask the same people to more than one shower, except for immediate family and members of the wedding party, who should be told that they are not expected to bring a gift to each event. Knowing that, if they still choose to do so, it is their prerogative.

*Most of my guests are from out of town and not familiar with this area. My maid of honor wants to hold the shower at my house because everyone knows how to get to it. Is this all right?*

The location of your shower is fine because it is convenient for your guests to find. The important difference is that it is being hosted by someone who is not a member of your immediate family. Of course, with shower "rules" so much more relaxed, if you have sisters in the wedding party who want to arrange a shower, it is fine.

*I want to have a shower for my best friend. She and her fiancé really need money more than anything else. May I indicate this on the shower invitations? I have also heard that it is all right to invite out-of-towners even though there is no possibility they could come, but it permits them to send a check to be opened at the shower. Does this sound right?*

No and no! I am sure your intentions are well meaning, but to do what you are considering is crass. If you do not think your friend will appreciate a theme-centered or miscellaneous shower, you need not arrange one for her. Instead, save your money for the wedding gift and give your own check then. You might privately encourage others you know to do likewise, but never mention money in an invitation. Also, do not invite out-of-towners you know cannot come to a shower unless they are members of the wedding party, who need not feel obligated to send a gift.

*My favorite aunt has offered to host a bridal shower for me. But to my embarrassment, she intends to insert a list of all the gifts I need with the shower invitation. I feel uncomfortable about such directness, but I have not had the heart to tell her so. Would it be tacky to include a gift list with the invitation?*

Yes, it would be tacky. There is another way to guide guests toward the purchase of items you want if you have registered with a department and/or gift specialty store. (See "The Bridal Gift Registry" on page 143.) Then, she may indicate on the invitation the name(s) of the place(s) at which you are registered. For example, she writes in: "For your convenience, you might like to know that Jane is registered at _____." It is not impolite to do this because a shower is solely for the purpose of "showering" the couple with items they need for their home or gifts they will enjoy in their leisure. But it must never be done on a wedding invitation because the wedding is the celebration of a rite of passage. While it is customary for guests to give the couple a wedding gift, no one should feel that they would be unwelcome if circumstances prevented them from giving a gift, nor should those who receive an invitation and are unable to attend the wedding feel obligated to send a gift.

# Bridal Luncheon

*So much has changed in terms of types of pre-wedding parties being held today, I wonder how many brides-to-be are still hosting a bridal luncheon. I want to show appreciation to my attendants, but a luncheon sounds so stuffy. What else can I do?*

Although such a formal fete is not as prevalent as it once was, there are still plenty of brides-to-be and/or their mothers who entertain the attendants in this fashion. Others prefer a more informal gathering such as a breakfast, brunch, dinner out, or just a casual get-together. It is often held at the bride's home a few days before the wedding or earlier when all of the attendants live locally. Otherwise, it is scheduled quite close to the wedding, so as many out-of-town attendants as possible can be there. The bride may present her gifts to the attendants then or at the rehearsal dinner.

*My future daughter-in-law and her mother cannot afford to have any type of party for the bridal attendants. I would like to offer to host the party for them even though we are also doing the rehearsal dinner. Would it be appropriate to make that gesture?*

Not only appropriate, but very thoughtful and sure to be appreciated. In fact, anyone who wants to help with entertaining for the couple and their guests should not hesitate to offer that option. With tight budgets, engaged couples really welcome such gestures of hospitality from caring family and friends.

# *Bachelor Bash*

*I always thought the best man and/or ushers were responsible for the bachelor party. I have read that the groom sometimes gives it. What is the story?*

Ninety-nine percent of the time, the men in the wedding arrange the bachelor bash. After all, it is theoretically the "last hurrah" for the groom with all of his pals. In some circumstances—none of the male attendants live where the wedding is held or they cannot afford to host a party—the groom may decide to handle the event. The bachelor party certainly is not a prerequisite to a successful wedding. (In fact, it has been known to cause more dissension between the bride and groom than good will!) Read on.

*I am really upset about the plans for my fiancé's bachelor party. The horror stories I have heard (female "entertainment," dreadful hangovers, etc.) make me extremely nervous, and I do not see why guys feel they have to do this. When I think about all the time and money going into making our wedding truly beautiful, I get angry when my fiancé talks about how much he is looking forward to this evening that I consider pure debauchery. What is he going to look and feel like at the wedding two days later? If most brides-to-be feel as I do, why do the grooms-to-be keep doing this?*

They do it because it represents their farewell to bachelorhood, theoretically, their last opportunity for a night out on the town with the boys. Actually, most brides worry a lot more than necessary about these events because the revelries are usually more benign than threatening. It is true, however, that the classic bachelor party does result in painful hangovers, which is a good reason to schedule it *considerably* in advance of the wedding day. A week is ideal.

*My bride-to-be is not comfortable about the traditional bachelor party, and I am not convinced that it is what I want either. I do want to have something. Are there alternatives I can consider?*

There certainly are: 1. A "Jack and Jill" celebration, mentioned earlier, that includes men and women. 2. A black-tie only dinner in an elegant restaurant where toasts are offered or the groom is roasted. It might include a video of the groom's life before and after meeting his fiancée. 3. A bachelor weekend centered around a sporting event—perfect for male bonding. 4. Arrange separate bachelor and bachelorette dinners on the same night with plans to meet with everyone afterward. Being out with her friends while you are enjoying an evening with yours, and having an appointed time to meet later, may make your fiancée feel more comfortable about a male-only bash. Bear in mind that those participating in any of these activities are dividing the cost of everything among themselves. The expectations for what is feasible must reflect that reality.

# Rehearsal Festivities

*My fiancé's mother is planning the rehearsal dinner either at her home or at a restaurant. Should members of the wedding party be allowed to bring their spouses or fiancés if they are not attendants? Is the guest list left up to the groom's parents to determine?*

If space and/or finances are limited, only the members of the wedding party need be invited to the dinner following the rehearsal in appreciation for their participation. *But* the real purpose of the rehearsal dinner, usually held the night before your wedding, is to provide an opportunity to visit and relax with those closest to the bride and groom. The bride and groom and her parents work with the groom's parents to compile the guest list. Ideally, guests include attendants with their spouse, fiancé, or live-in partner; immediate family of the bride and groom (that is, siblings and their partners as well as parents, and often grandparents), officant and spouse, and the out-of-town guests. The event may run the gamut from a sit-down dinner, to an informal buffet, to a backyard barbecue. It gives people who know and love the couple the chance to tell them so in an informal manner. Toasts (serious, funny, short and sweet) and other tributes (poems about the bride and groom, a video of their childhoods leading up to how they met and courted) are given during the course of the evening. This is also the occasion when most bridal couples present their gifts to their attendants.

*At the rehearsal dinner for our son's wedding, I have planned on having a head table for six: bride and groom, best man and matron of honor with their spouses. Is there any arrangement required for seating the balance of the wedding party? Also, is my husband expected to make a toast or speech?*

Formal seating is not required, but often people feel more comfortable if you at least have a table assignment for them. Talk it over with the bride and groom to determine which of the following options they think is preferable: Allow the guests to select their own table and put together who will join them during the cocktail hour, or determine compatible groupings in advance and assign the guests to tables with numbers or names. Your husband need not make a speech, but should welcome the guests when all are seated and propose a toast to the couple during the evening.

*I do not believe we need to send invitations to the rehearsal dinner because everyone in the wedding party knows about it. My mother thinks we should have invitations. Who is right?*

Mailing invitations is a thoughtful reminder to your attendants and to the members of your family who will be attending the dinner, but are not in the wedding party. It is absolutely essential to send invitations to the out-of-town guests who will also be included. Mail them shortly after the wedding invitations are sent.

*My future in-laws are hosting the rehearsal dinner at a very nice restaurant. They have been extremely cooperative about inviting everyone my parents and my fiancé and I want. Now, several of the single attendants have asked to bring an escort. How should we handle that?*

As with invitations to the wedding, there is a limit. This is a private, not a public, celebration. Again, I say, if space and/or finances are limited, you should tell those attendants that, though you would like to accommodate their request, your in-laws are hosting the dinner and cannot be expected to add any more to the guest list.

*I am the best man at my brother's wedding. From what I understand, I am to make a toast at the rehearsal dinner. What type of sentiments should I include, and do you have any tips on stage fright?*

The evening will be full of convivial fun, so do not worry about stage fright. Think about a humorous story involving your brother that guests would enjoy, then commend him on his choice of bride, and toast the couple's happiness. Keep it brief and you will find that less is more.

*My fiancé's parents are deceased. Neither my parents nor my fiancé and I can afford to host a rehearsal party. Would it be terrible not to have one?*

Remember, it does not have to be formal or elaborate to say thanks and to provide some food and beverage. If your parents cannot invite the attendants back to their home for a few hours, maybe some other relatives on his side or yours or even a very dear family friend could host this get-together for you. It could be their wedding present.

*Of course, my fiancé will be at the rehearsal dinner, but I am not sure he should be at the rehearsal itself. I have heard that if the rehearsal takes place the night before the wedding, as it will, a stand-in should take his role. Then, I heard it is okay for the groom to come to the rehearsal; he is just not supposed to see the bride the day of the wedding. Is it bad luck for the groom to take part in the rehearsal or to see his bride before the ceremony on the wedding day?*

I have never heard of a stand-in for the groom, but at some rehearsals, though the bride is there, someone else stands in for her. These admonitions and practices are superstitions that hark back to the days when people believed that evil spirits would hex the couple's chances for happiness, so every precaution was taken to keep the evil forces from identifying the bride. Few adults today adhere to such folklore. Now, a bride is more likely not to want her groom to see her in her wedding gown for romantic reasons and to preserve the anticipation of both partners, not because of impending doom. Your fiancé should participate in the rehearsal. What could be more unlucky than an unprepared groom?

# Pre- and Post-Wedding Receptions

*We will be married in Ireland where my fiancé lives. My immediate family will be there, but no one else can come. Subsequently, we will live in Ireland; therefore, I will not be back in the United States for quite some time. My fiancé will be here for a few weeks before the wedding, and we would like to have a reception then for my extended family and my friends to share our happiness. Would this be considered precipitous or presumptuous on our part?*

Neither. It is a fine way to have those who cannot be with you wish you well. Plan it along the lines of the rehearsal dinner, so that there will be toasts, tributes, and some fun history about the two of you to record in your wedding journal or scrapbook. Be sure to have a photographer present, either a professional or an amateur who you know takes good pictures. If you are lucky enough to have siblings, seek their assistance in putting the event together.

*My fiancé and I are being married in Illinois. We live in Rhode Island as do most of his family. Many of his uncles, etc., are elderly and will not be able to make the trip, and a considerable number of our friends will not be able to afford the trip. We do not want to leave these people out of our celebration, so we would like to have a second reception in Rhode Island after our honeymoon. If this is appropriate, should we include a separate reception card in the invitation to those people, or should we make it a separate party invitation mailed after our return?*

What you plan makes a lot of sense. Include only the wedding reception cards with the wedding invitations that will be mailed to everyone. (Some may surprise you and find a way to get there.) When you return from your honeymoon, send the invitations to your subsequent reception three to four weeks in advance of the date.

*After our elopement, we are going to host a reception. What is the best way to issue invitations?*

Send wedding announcements worded:

*Mary Ann Smith*

*and*

*John Paul Jones*

*announce their marriage*

*day, date*

*place.*

Enclose the reception invitation with the announcements. To make it less formal you might say:

*Please join us to celebrate*

*day, date*

*time*

*place.*

*Although we are having my daughter's wedding here in her hometown, many of the friends she wants to attend reside across the country where she currently lives. Knowing they cannot come, she wants another reception there later and would like to wear her wedding dress and repeat some of the traditional reception customs as well. I do not want this to become a road show, but I would like her to be able to celebrate with her dear friends. Should I go along with this plan?*

Yes, as you can see from my responses to the many other couples who find themselves in similar circumstances. The prohibitive distance makes sharing one or more post-wedding receptions the only logical solution.

# QUICK TIPS FOR THE MODERN BRIDE
## *Party Etiquette*

- Anyone who wants to can give you a shower. Traditionally, family members were not supposed to, but attitudes on this are relaxing considerably.

- Except for family and attendants, the same guests should not be invited to multiple showers.

- If the bride does not need household items, arrange a shower based on another theme—but never ask guests to bring money.

- Bachelor parties should be held well enough in advance of the wedding so that the aftereffects have worn off!

- There is no reason that showers and bachelor parties today cannot include both the bride and the groom and their friends of both sexes.

- The rehearsal dinner need not be a formal occasion. The wedding party and both families at least should be invited, but it is nice to include their spouses and any out-of-town guests, if finances and space permit.

- Couples who marry far away from one family may have a "post-wedding" reception for friends who could not travel to attend the wedding. This can be formal or informal.

# CHAPTER 13
# All About Gifts

## The Bridal Gift Registry

*I think the gift registry is a wonderful idea. My fiancé and I attended one of the* **Modern Bride** *department store shows and learned a great deal about how to make informed choices when selecting the items we need for our home. We returned on another day to spend some time with the consultant, who gave us much-needed guidance to keep us from wasting money or making major mistakes because of our inexperience in setting up a household. We have registered for all our tableware, linens, housewares, small electrics, home electronics, even lamps and decorative accessories. We also have lots of inexpensive items on our list. I am concerned that the people attending my showers and the wedding will not know about the registry. How can we tactfully tell them where we are registered?*

In the course of conversation with family and friends, talk about visiting the registry and the fun you had selecting the products you would like for your new home. Your parents and siblings can spread the word about the convenience of using the registry. They can explain that only a phone call is necessary to learn what you want in a variety of price ranges. When a guest makes a selection either in person or by telephone, the gift will be sent directly to you, which is preferable to bringing gifts to the wedding. (See *The Reception.*) Using the registry is not just a way for the engaged couple to get gifts they need and will use and to prevent duplications and the time wasted returning them, but it is also a great advantage for guests who do not have time to go shopping and especially for out-of-towners. (Some stores have an 800 number for customers calling the registry.) It is also possible to indicate where the couple is registered on shower invitations (see "Showers" on page 133.)

*This is a second marriage for both of us. We have more than enough household furnishings between the two of us, but frankly, I would like to start over, making the choices together. Am I crazy to think of doing this?*

Not in my view—new partner, new life! I have often recommended that couples in your circumstances have a gigantic tag sale to make room for the updated products and exciting designs you and your fiancé can enjoy selecting for the home you will be sharing. You may feel a little uncomfortable going into the registry at this stage of your life, but most of your family and friends will want to give you a wedding gift, so it makes sense to direct them to the place where they can be sure what they buy is what you want.

*My fiancé lives in Chicago, and I live in Los Angeles. His relatives and friends live in Minnesota and mine in California. I will relocate to Chicago at least six months prior to the wedding, but the ceremony will take place in Los Angeles. I would like to register in a department store in Minnesota and one in California, but worry about whether they will both carry my patterns and about how to avoid duplications. My most important concern is how I let guests know I want the gifts sent to our home in Chicago.*

When you register, you will fill in the address where gifts should be sent. (If there is a wait because of back order, notification of purchase will be sent to you and the gift delivered just as soon as it arrives.) To avoid duplications, do not register the same items at more than one store (unless it is part of a chain that has computerized its registry so that each gift purchased is recorded throughout the system). In Minnesota you might select appliances and linens and leave the tableware choices for a California store.

## Displaying Gifts

*I have heard that brides should display their wedding gifts. In our family, the majority of gifts are presented at an engagement party and/or shower. Wedding gifts are usually money brought to the reception. Am I supposed to display my engagement and shower gifts and, if so, where?*

You are not expected to display your gifts. This is a custom established a long time ago among brides from socially prominent families. When life was a lot more leisurely and family friends made afternoon social calls, the bride's gifts would often be displayed on the dining room table in her parents' home during the month before the wedding, which is when the majority of gifts arrived. Of course, someone was always at home then, and the probability of theft was not a concern. Today, some brides who are having a large wedding and come from families with a tradition of doing this still arrange an attractive display, but along with special insurance binders. Some even hire security protection.

*We are going to display our wedding gifts. Do we set out every piece of china, etc., and what about checks?*

One place setting of your dinnerware, flatware, and crystal is sufficient. You may or may not display the gift cards relating to the presents near them. Checks are noted with an envelope or card simply indicating "Check" and the name of the giver. Never mention the amount.

# Cash and Other Alternatives

*My fiancé and I have lived together for a number of years and have everything we need for our home. We do need help in paying for our reception and would like to indicate that to the people invited to the wedding. May we enclose a note to that effect in the invitation?*

One more time—*never* mention a preference for money with a wedding invitation! You may *tell* close family and friends of this preference and hope that they will mention it to others. But I caution you not to plan your reception based on what you hope to "collect" as gifts. You should budget what you are able to afford before gifts are received. Cash gifts may be money put *back* in the bank, but should not be counted on to pay wedding costs.

*We are being married in my hometown in the United States and moving to my fiancé's home in Italy immediately after the wedding. Taking or sending gifts over there would be an expense we cannot afford. How can we inform guests about this problem?*

Word of mouth is a good way to convey the fact that transporting gifts to Italy would be difficult. Through conversation and letters, people invited to your wedding should be told that you will be living in Italy. Then they may ask about how to handle gifts or simply plan to write a check or put money in an envelope because it is easiest for them and you.

*We are fortunate to have our home fully furnished, and we would like our guests to make a donation to our favorite charity in lieu of wedding gifts. May we indicate that on an enclosure with the invitations?*

My response to this is the same as that for noting a preference for cash—not with the invitation. You may certainly mention it to your family and friends. Also, if someone asks where you are registered, you or your family may reply that you have not registered because you prefer a donation be made to charity and then give them the name of your preferred recipient.

*My fiancé and I own our home. We do not need any household items and do not want the hassle of returning wedding gifts. To prevent this, we want to have a money tree at the reception, but we do not know how to word it on the invitation so that it does not sound like guests have to give us money. What is the best way to handle this?*

The money tree is a custom that some cultures engage in, but if it is unfamiliar to your guests, it is not something you should have at your reception and, of course, it should not be mentioned on an invitation. Those invited to your wedding should know you well enough to be aware that you have a home and are settled in. Based on that, they might realize that a card with money or a check would be appreciated and present that without prompting. There might also be some very special items for your home that you and your fiancé would not purchase for yourselves but that would be worth selecting at the gift registry in your favorite store. That way, those who are not comfortable giving money would give you items you can enjoy, and there is no risk of duplicating products you already have. Or you might want to register at some other resources in your community, such as a home supply or hardware store, gourmet shop, music store, liquor and wine shop, museum shop, beauty and fitness spa, or even a honeymoon registry set up with your travel agent.

*My husband and I disagree on how much money we should give to the bridal couple. Are there any guidelines?*

The amount of money you give or spend on a gift for the couple should be determined by your relationship with them and what you can afford. There is no formula for something so personal. Some couples would like to believe that guests will spend at least as much as the per-person cost to invite them to the reception. That is a crass and totally erroneous assumption with no basis in fact.

# Gifts for Attendants

*I have an honor attendant and bridesmaids in my wedding, plus cake servers and guest book attendants. When should I buy gifts, and who should receive them?*

Purchase gifts for your attendants whenever you find items that are appropriate. The honor attendant usually receives something of a little more value than the gifts for the bridesmaids. Give the cake servers and guest book attendants a token memento and a corsage to wear at the wedding.

*I have 11 attendants in my wedding, and I would like to give them each something special, but not too expensive. Do you have some suggestions?*

I recommend that you visit the gift registry in a department or specialty store because, in addition to the tableware products you expect to find there, the same manufacturers are designing a wonderful array of reasonably priced gift items for every member of the wedding party. Some examples are: perfume bottles, atomizers, purse vials and vanity items, desk accessories, bud vases, letter openers, small porcelain art objects, art deco pins, and silverplated, glass, and leather picture frames. You will find lots more possibilities in the display cases especially devoted to this purpose.

*I want to do something very special for my attendants. I plan to purchase gift bags and fill them with accessories such as the pantyhose and jewelry they will wear for the wedding and some breath mints. I would also like to give them something personal, and I am thinking of cologne because they can wear it for the wedding and enjoy it on occasions afterward. Do you think this is a good idea, or do you have another suggestion?*

Giving your bridesmaids bags filled with accessories for the wedding day is a creative and practical idea. They will surely appreciate the thoughtfulness and time you put into assembling those gifts. For the more personal memento, consider crystal, silverplated, or porcelain atomizers filled with cologne. Or simply present each with an atomizer that she can fill with her own favorite fragrance.

*We plan to give monogrammed picture frames to our attendants as their gift. Later, we will send them their photo in the wedding to put in the frame. If attendants' gifts are normally given at the rehearsal dinner, how can we explain that the frame is intended for that wedding photo?*

You may present your attendants with the frames at the dinner and enclose a note informing them that you also plan to give each one a special photo of them from the wedding. One bride drew silly pictures of the wedding party in color and placed one in each frame to indicate her intention. (She reports some liked her sketch better than the photograph!)

*My fiancé has absolutely no idea what to give his best man and ushers. What can I recommend?*

Possibilities for the men include: cuff links, tie clasp, or tac; desk accessories, special pen, or pen/pencil set; radio/headset, calculator; items that can be engraved such as picture frames, beer mugs, shot cups, money clips, card cases, and whiskey flasks; crystal or silverplated shaving accessories. Something not so lasting, but fun, might be tickets to a sports event.

*We have a four-year-old flower girl and a six-year-old ring bearer. What kind of gift would they enjoy?*

Some things that both a boy and girl would like are: a picture frame to hold their photo from the wedding, a cartoon character watch, a computer game or a video classic for children. Girls would love the *Modern Bride* bridal dress-up accessories or bridal clothes for dolls available at toy stores. They would also enjoy a bracelet, ring, or locket.

# Gifts for Each Other and Parents

*While I can generally find the right gift for my fiancé, selecting a wedding gift for him poses a problem. He has a watch, he wears no other jewelry, and I recently gave him a money clip in appreciation for his support through my bar exams. Can you give me some help?*

One of these should do the trick: a sterling silver key chain with the wedding date engraved or a sterling silver or crystal picture frame with your wedding photograph in it and the date engraved. Other not-so-traditional gifts are season tickets to his favorite sporting event or to the theater or concerts, if he prefers that; some special wines; a gift certificate to a spa; or a membership to a club in which he has expressed interest.

*My mother insists that I must give a piece of jewelry to my bride-to-be as a wedding gift, but she does not wear any jewelry. I want her present to be something that she will enjoy. What options do I have?*

True, most brides expect a special piece of jewelry from their groom to wear at the wedding and forever after. But there are exceptions to every rule, and your bride might appreciate some of the untraditional ideas listed for the groom above, as well as some very special decorative object for your new home, or even a pet, if that would make her happy.

*Our parents have been wonderful in helping to plan and pay for our wedding. We want to show our appreciation with something special for my parents and his. What is appropriate, and does it have to be the same for both?*

The gifts do not have to be identical for both sets of parents. A picture frame to hold a wedding photograph of you two with the date engraved will always be cherished, but there are many more items that can be engraved and will be appreciated: a clock, vase, bowl, pitcher, or wine cooler. Statuary and porcelain art objects are also perfect mementos.

# *Thank-You Notes*

*My fiancé and I have discussed how we will handle writing thank-you notes for our wedding gifts. We agreed we will share the responsibility. However, after reading a handful of wedding etiquette books, I have found it is solely the bride's responsibility. I like tradition, but find this custom ridiculous. The gifts we receive will be enjoyed by both of us. Is there some hidden, logical reason why only the bride should write the notes?*

There is nothing hidden, and the logic goes back to when men did not do a lot of things that only women were supposed to do and vice versa. Happily, that is no longer the case, and your fiancé can certainly help with gift acknowledgments. A good split is to have him handle those from his family and friends, you take yours, and divide equitably those you both know.

*We have been married for three months, and my mother-in-law is very upset with me because I have not acknowledged my wedding gifts. I am waiting for a wedding photo to be printed to go with my thank-you notes. Is that all right?*

No, your mother-in-law has good reason to feel embarrassed. A bride-to-be should write thank-you notes as gifts are received. If time and pressures intrude on keeping current during the week or two preceding the wedding, it may be postponed for a while. But within two months of return from your honeymoon, all gifts should be acknowledged. Later, quite independent of the thank-you note, you may mail a copy of your wedding photo to the family and friends who would welcome it. The others, aggravated by having had to wait so long to hear from you, probably would not appreciate the photo. You will save money on the photo order and avoid unpleasant thoughts about your lack of appreciation by sending those notes pronto.

*I was one of many people not invited to a wedding, but who felt close enough to the couple to send them a gift. It is almost two years since their marriage and none but the invited guests received a thank-you note. Are we wrong to have expected an acknowledgment?*

Not at all. Thank-you notes should always be written upon receipt of a gift. The couple might have been embarrassed because they did not invite you to the wedding, but that is no excuse for such a breach of common courtesy.

*I am contemplating different "thank-you" messages. I have attended weddings where there were small scrolls at each table saying, "Thank you for sharing our day, etc." Is this an appropriate substitute for a thank-you note sent after the wedding?*

Absolutely not. There is no substitute for a handwritten thank-you note. Guests are entitled to know that you received their gift and appreciate what they chose. That is why each gift must be personally acknowledged with mention of the item and how it will be used. To have the scrolls at each table in addition to writing a note is fine, but not in place of it.

*My new husband and I will go directly from our honeymoon to a temporary residence while he goes through a two-month job training program. Our wedding gifts will remain unopened at home until we return. Since I do not know what anyone gave us, may I wait until I get back to write thank-you notes?*

No, it would be more appropriate to mail printed acknowledgment cards worded: "Mary Jane and Richard Alison wish to acknowledge receipt of your gift. A personal note will follow." Then, make opening your gifts and acknowledging them a priority when you get home. At very large weddings where hundreds of gifts are received such an acknowledgment is sent to allow the bride and groom the extended time needed to write all of their thank-you notes.

### ❦❦❦ QUICK TIPS FOR THE MODERN BRIDE ❦❦❦
# *Handling Gifts*

- Using a department store registry is not tacky—it provides guests who wish to consult it with a list of your preferences. Indicating the name of the store where you are registered on a shower invitation is also not tacky. Putting that information on a wedding invitation *is* tacky.

- Be considerate—include items of varying costs on your registry list.

- Wedding gifts can be displayed in the home to which they are sent, but do not have to be. If that is your family tradition, by all means do it. If it is not, skip it.

- The bride and groom traditionally give gifts to their attendants. These can be presented at the rehearsal dinner or any other pre-wedding gathering.

- Wedding gifts should be acknowledged with a thank-you note as they arrive—even if that is before the wedding. All gifts should be acknowledged within two months after you return from your honeymoon.

- Guests traditionally send a gift before the wedding, but may do so within one year after the event.

- Cash gifts should be acknowledged immediately, so the giver is sure that the money was not lost.

- Thank-you notes must contain a personal message—a preprinted "thank you for the gift" is not sufficient.

- The acknowledgment need not be from the bride only—in today's world, the groom can share the note writing!

# CHAPTER 14
# *Special Situations*

## *Dealing with Divorced Parents*

*My fiancé's parents are divorced due to an extended affair his father had. He is still dating this woman, but they are not engaged or living together. We have met her only a few times. His father and mother are on good terms, but his mother feels a lot of resentment toward the other woman. In order to keep our wedding a happy event, may we invite his father alone?*

Your fiancé should speak with his father about how uncomfortable it would be for him and his mother to have the woman at the wedding. You can hope that his father has no expectation that she would be invited. However, if he does, knowing in advance of his son's feelings, he might readily agree to omit her from the guest list. Because they are not engaged or "officially" committed, and you and your fiancé hardly know her, there is no reason for her to be there.

*I am divorced from my daughter's father and have raised her with little help from him. We are not on good terms now. My daughter wants her father to walk her down the aisle. He has a daughter from his present marriage, and my daughter also wants her half sister to be the flower girl. This disturbs me because they will be in the photographs and the video, all calling up unhappy memories for me. I do not feel my daughter is showing any concern for my feelings. I know this is her wedding, but I want to enjoy it, too. What can I do to make her realize how difficult this is for me?*

Talk with your daughter about the feelings you have regarding the participation of her father and half sister. But keep in mind (as you mentioned yourself) that this is her day. Although you may not agree with her decisions, if she feels close enough to her father to want him to give her away, he should be able to do that. If she is not that close to his daughter, she might be willing to forgo the flower girl. Unless you tell her what is bothering you, she cannot be expected to know you find this hurtful. While you cannot ask your daughter to leave her father and his family out of her wedding album, you can arrange with her to have those photos omitted from the album you get for yourself. Whatever the outcome, any unpleasantness between you and your ex-husband should be put aside for the few hours you will be at her wedding.

*I am the groom's mother, divorced from his father who has remarried. I would like to know who is responsible for the rehearsal dinner and, if I am not paying for it, do I still have the right to say where it is held, who will be invited, etc.?*

Even though you are divorced, you and your ex-husband should try to make arrangements for the rehearsal dinner together. The financial circumstances and the status of your relationship will determine how feasible that is. But in the interests of the couple's happiness, you should do all that is possible to be cordial and cooperative with the groom's father and stepmother while planning and attending the dinner. Sharing the expenses should make it easier to effect mutual decisions concerning the details of site and guest list. If either you or your ex-husband is more financially able to handle the expense than the other, the costs could be divided with that in mind. But if you are both hosting it, decisions about the type of affair, location, and guest list should be mutually agreed upon, bearing in mind that the people with the most to say about it all should be the couple for whom it is being given.

*Nearly six years ago, my fiancé's parents were divorced, and his father has remarried. I get along very well with his father's wife and intend to invite her to our wedding. Recently, my fiancé's mother has told me she does not want this woman at the wedding. She expects her ex-husband to come alone and sit with her during the ceremony and reception. While I do not want her to be uncomfortable or hurt on what should be a happy day, I feel she is being unrealistic. How can we explain this to her?*

It is unreasonable and totally inappropriate for your fiancé's mother to expect her ex-husband to attend the wedding without his wife, if she wishes to be there. Moreover, whether his father's wife is there or not, his mother cannot expect her former husband to be her escort at the wedding and reception. Your fiancé must make that clear to his mother.

*My father has remarried. Neither I nor anyone in my family has met his wife. He divorced my mother to marry her, and we are bitter about that. I do not want her at our wedding. I would like to address the invitation only to my father. Everyone else will have escorts and I do not want my father to feel left out, but I am very close to my family and want them to be comfortable first. I have heard that the acrimony caused by divorce should be put on hold for this one special day, but it goes a lot deeper than a simple divorce. Is this really the right day to "unite" the family?*

If you want your father at your wedding, his wife should also be invited. Perhaps she will realize it would be more comfortable for everyone if she encourages your father to attend without her. If not and she does come, have your dad and her seated by the ushers for the ceremony in the same manner as the other guests, in a pew considerably away from the front left side. At the reception, assign them to a table with other guests who are not familiar with the circumstances. This is not an attempt to "unite" the family, just a compromise that will allow your father to be at your wedding celebration. On the other hand, if the woman's presence causes you distress, there is the possibility—although not a happy alternative—of not including your father at all.

*Help! I am at my wits' end!! My parents divorced when I was eight, and they are not on good terms at all. My brother and I still have a relationship with my dad even though he has done some things in the past that were hurtful and selfish. Of course, my mother's side of the family constantly reminds us of all the unkind things he has done, and this causes a lot of tension in my wedding planning. I want my father to escort me down the aisle. My mom wants my brother to escort me and my father to have no part in the wedding except to pay for the caterer. I think this is nasty, spiteful, and inconsiderate of my feelings. Now my mom is really angry at me for asking my father to walk with me, and I am angry at her for reminding me of things I just want to leave in the past. I am so fed up with being caught in the middle that I am considering calling the wedding off in favor of eloping. To have the wedding my fiancé and I are planning, I need my parents' financial assistance, but we cannot handle the tension. What should I do?*

*Tell* your mother that the problems between her ex and herself are *theirs*, not yours. He is your father and you are entitled to have him escort you down the aisle, if that is what *you* want. End of discussion! Your mother may have good reason to be resentful, but it is inconsiderate of her to try to exert such control over *your* wedding because she hates your father. It would be wise to talk with your clergyperson about the possibility of interceding with your mother to make her understand the need to put your feelings first for the wedding day. If that does not work, rather than elope, consider a small, private celebration now, and a grander reaffirmation celebration in the future when you can do it yourselves. Or, have a much longer engagement and save to do the big wedding on your own. There is also the possibility of a wedding at your honeymoon destination (see *Specialty Weddings*).

*My parents divorced and remarried. I like my stepfather very much, but am not fond of my stepmother. My fiancé and I do not want her in any of the wedding pictures, but we do want my father in the photos. I know he will try to include her. How can we avoid this?*

Meet with the photographer in advance to discuss who should be photographed and the groupings you prefer. Appoint a friend or relative to help identify those people for the photographer. You cannot eliminate your stepmother totally, but you can tell the photographer to limit the takes with her and to be sure he snaps your father with you and others exclusive of his wife. A good photographer is used to handling these situations, so you can rest assured. Furthermore, when you make the selections for your photo album, you have the option of omitting those with your dad's wife from the final choices.

*My mother recently remarried, but my father has not. However, they are cordial. When the bandleader introduces my parents, should my mother enter with her husband or my father?*

Your mother should enter with her husband and be introduced as the bride's mother and stepfather, Mr. and Mrs. _____. Your dad enters solo or with another daughter or other female relative.

*My parents divorced and both are remarried. In the 12 years since they split up, my mother and father have not had one nice word to say about each other and have not seen or spoken to each other except through lawyers. We are having a Jewish ceremony in which it is customary for both parents to give the bride away. I love my four parents very much and want all of them to give me away and to be an integral part of my wedding. Any suggestions?*

Speak to your rabbi about your concerns for getting the parents together in the ceremony. Hope that he will be able to convince your mother and father to arrange a truce for the wedding day enabling their full participation in the celebration.

## Parents Who Object to the Wedding

*My fiancé and I plan to be married in less than a year. We want a large, formal wedding. However, our families do not like each other and are against our marriage. How can we get both families together on this?*

Unfortunately, there is no magic formula I can give you to make your families overcome their objections to your marriage. I can only tell you that under these circumstances, you cannot expect financial help from either set of parents, so you would be wise to scale down your wedding plans to something the two of you can handle without their assistance. More important is the prospect for success of a marriage where the two families cannot get along. I urge you and your fiancé to seek premarital counseling from your clergy or a professional family counselor before making any confirmed wedding plans.

*My mother does not approve of my fiancé. Although she says she wants me to have a wedding and will not cause a scene, she has also said that she is not sure she can hide her feelings during all the pre-wedding activities. Her disapproval of my fiancé is expressed in verbal criticism and frequent crying. I dread shopping for my wedding dress, compiling the guest list, attending my shower, or doing anything else associated with the wedding with my mother. My parents are paying for a large part of the wedding, and my father, while not overjoyed, does not share my mother's intense dislike for my fiancé. How do I deal with this?*

You need to learn why your mother objects to your fiancé. She obviously has your welfare at heart or she would not try to go along with any wedding planning. She may have some very valid reasons for her concern about the suitability of your choice of partner. It is in your best interest to discuss those issues before the wedding takes place. Meeting with your clergyperson or a marriage and family counselor to help you resolve the problems before entering marriage is worth whatever time and money it takes to avoid future family estrangement and unhappiness.

*My mother and I have been at odds ever since I began dating the man who is now my fiancé. She denies having anything against him, but we know that is not true. We plan to be married in two years. We do not want my mother to have any part in the wedding. Money is not a problem—his parents will pay for the wedding. I want my father to give me away, but I do not think he will if my mother is not invited to the wedding. Should I ask my future father-in-law or another good friend to escort me? What should I do?*

With two years to go until the wedding, you have time to try to establish some constructive communication with your mother. This is much too soon to write her out of the most important day of your life, or to ask your father to attend without her. As with the other cases of parental estrangement discussed here, family counseling is recommended.

*I am Roman Catholic and my fiancé is Greek Orthodox, but neither of us is religious. We would be satisfied with a civil ceremony, but have agreed to respect our Christian traditions by having a ceremony performed by a Methodist minister at the reception location. My parents have accepted this decision, but my fiancé's mother adamantly objects and has told us that she will not attend our wedding if it is not in a Greek Orthodox church. She is making the experience miserable for both families, causing a lot of heartbreak and resentment. She says we do not respect her, but we believe she is being selfish and inconsiderate. What can we do to make her understand that what we plan is a reasonable compromise?*

Because of your fiancé's mother's strong religious ties to the Greek Orthodox church, it is not possible for her to consider a marriage valid in any other context. If neither of you has such a tie, but both still want a Christian ceremony, and provided a Greek Orthodox priest agrees to marry you, why not do so in the Greek Orthodox tradition? You must understand that your fiancé's mother is not being selfish or hurtful; she is being honest. If you both decide to go ahead with your plans, you will have to carry on without his mother's blessing or participation. That is a reality you need to face, not just for the wedding, but also for how this might affect the relationship you both have with his mother throughout your marriage. It is a sad situation, but not unusual in families with strict orthodox backgrounds. You need to feel very confident about your commitment to each other to be able to withstand the emotional strain that such a conflict could have on your future family life.

*My fiancé is in state prison, but when he gets out we are to be married. My parents say if I marry him they will disown me. What should I do about this?*

If your fiancé is serving time for a felony, pay attention to your parents! If the sentence is for a misdemeanor, you will have to choose between him and your parents.

# The Pregnant Bride

*My fiancé and I want to have a traditional wedding even though I will be six months pregnant. My parents are happy that we are marrying, but they do not think we should have any type of formal celebration. They think it should be very private. Are they right?*

Your desire to share your commitment to each other and celebrate your love in a formal marriage ceremony witnessed by family and friends need not be rejected because of your pregnancy. Speak with your clergy about his or her willingness to perform the service under these circumstances. If that presents no problem, a formal celebration can be tastefully planned. When you shop for a wedding dress, tell the consultant about your pregnancy so she can help you select a dress that will be attractive and accommodate the changes in your figure. It can be a wedding gown in white or ivory. Keeping your dress as well as everything else simple and low-key is the secret to making yourselves, your parents, and your guests comfortable.

# Teen Marriage

*I am 17 and my fiancé is 20. Our wedding is in two years. Because my parents married young and were subsequently divorced, they feel that I should wait until I am 21. Unless I agree, they will not pay for anything. My fiancé's parents are very happy about the engagement and are willing to help with expenses. How can I bring my parents around to share their outlook?*

I discourage you from trying to do that because your parents have your welfare in mind and have good reason to want you to wait. Seventeen is too young to even *think* about getting married. Before you start making wedding plans, consider the awesome responsibility that marriage requires from both partners. Now is the time to concentrate on pursuing an education and/or specific job training to determine what you are capable of achieving as adults before you undertake marriage and the possibility of other family commitments. Statistically, teen marriages have a significantly higher risk of divorce because the couple is not emotionally or realistically prepared to deal with the work it takes to be successfully married. I encourage you both to pursue and complete a postsecondary education and/or to secure a good job before planning a wedding. If your love is solid, it will survive the postponement and grow stronger as you mature, thereby increasing your chances for a happy, long-lasting marriage.

# Different Cultures

*My fiancé and I come from extremely different backgrounds. Although my parents like him, they have nothing in common with his family. The very formal wedding we are planning will be a totally unfamiliar experience for his family and their guests, many of whom do not speak English. I am worried about the reception. How can I try to make it pleasant for everyone?*

If you are planning to invite people unfamiliar with formality to an ultraformal wedding, you should tell them in advance what it will be like and what they are expected to wear. If they seem uncomfortable about it or express hesitation about attending, it might be more considerate not to include them now, but to invite them to an informal gathering after you return from your honeymoon. Discuss this option with your fiancé and have him talk with his parents about it. Then, you would plan the wedding to include only his immediate family and do all that is possible to help them shop, dress, and be prepared for the formal festivities. If they agree to your scheduling the subsequent event for the rest of their family and friends, they can personally let the others know and thereby avoid hurt feelings. In the long run, everyone is likely to feel more comfortable. From your letter it seems that such disparate backgrounds would make it impossible to please everybody at one reception.

*My fiancé and I are planning a formal wedding with 200 guests. My parents have forbidden alcohol because of my family's strong religious beliefs. My fiancé's family will be very disappointed if we do not at least serve champagne. We would be happy to pay for it. But that will not sway my parents. We are thinking of arranging for the caterer to serve it anyway and perhaps telling my parents after the ceremony on the way to the reception. What is your opinion?*

I discourage you from doing that. Most likely your parents will be disappointed and hurt that you deceived them, and this will ultimately put a damper on your wedding day. Instead, ask the caterer about serving sparkling grape or apple juice and/or a festive, nonalcoholic punch that everyone can enjoy while toasting to your happiness. Your fiancé's family may not realize that there is no alcohol in it, but if they do, it is a compromise they should be willing to make because of your parents' religious convictions and the fact that they are the hosts.

*My parents are being very generous in their wedding arrangements: an elegant reception location, a Rolls-Royce to transport me and my groom, and an expensive wedding dress. The problem: Our family is Pentecostal, which means there can be no alcohol served or dancing at our wedding. I have no difficulty with the former, but I do feel there will be a terrible void at the reception without music. I proposed we have some soft jazz music, not for dancing, just for ambiance. My father refused. I am concerned about the enjoyment of the members of my wedding party as well as other guests in their twenties. All I can picture is a dull reception with guests eating their dinner, talking with each other and complaining about a boring time, and leaving disappointed. That is the last thing I want to happen. I feel that I am so close to having the best day in my life, but still have so far to go, and I do not know how to make it complete. I have always attended wedding receptions that are not as restrictive. They were exciting and lively. Is there anything I can do to alleviate my anxiety about my own reception?*

Explain to your parents that you respect their beliefs and appreciate their generosity, but that you are concerned about your friends not enjoying themselves. Request that your father allow soft classical or semi-classical background music on tape or performed by a string ensemble. No one would dance, but it would be a pleasant sound in keeping with the celebration. While the reception will not be as lively as the other receptions, it will be lovely and your friends will enjoy themselves with excellent food and good conversation. You might also suggest hiring a vocalist, some mimes, or a magician to provide some entertainment that your father will not find objectionable.

*My fiancé has 14 nieces and nephews ranging from 10 months to 13 years of age. My parents and I did not plan to invite children to the wedding. When we told my fiancé's parents, they were insulted and angered because children always attend weddings in their family. Our history is just the opposite. I do not want to begin our marriage with hard feelings, but I also do not want the per-plate expense for children who hardly eat, nor do I want to have them running all over and disrupting the celebration. I am also concerned that his family will not mingle, dance, or have fun if they are feeding babies and holding one another's children. What is the best way to handle this?*

Your fiancé's nieces and nephews are members of his immediate family and should be invited to the wedding if this is a custom that means a lot to his parents and siblings. Speak with your future brothers- and sisters-in-law about the possibility of their getting together to share the cost of a babysitter for the infants, who would be much better off left at one of their homes where they can nap and crawl about and cry without disrupting any of the wedding festivities. The same is true for toddlers under the age of five, who would enjoy being able to play with each other away from this adult event. If the parents want their small children to attend for a while, they should consider hiring a sitter who looks after them at the reception and can take them home if they become tired and cranky. Children who are six and older should be able to eat and behave without constant supervision, enabling their parents to dance and socialize with other guests. Hope that your fiancé will agree that these are reasonable compromises and that he will be able to convince his family to act accordingly so that everyone will have a wonderful time.

*My fiancé and I have everything set for our wedding and just realized that because our families do not speak the same language, they will have a problem understanding the wedding service. I am Mexican and he is Chinese. His mother speaks only Chinese, as do the relatives from her side of the family. My mother and her relatives speak only Spanish. Our wedding party and most of the guests speak only English. What can we do so that everyone understands the wedding ceremony?*

To help overcome the language barrier at your wedding, I suggest that you conduct the ceremony in English and provide printed programs with the content of the service translated into Chinese and Spanish. (See "Personalizing Your Service" on page 91.) You might also each appoint a family member or friend who understands English and speaks the other language to cue guests into the ceremony sequence as they follow along in the program. If you do the latter, invite those two people to attend the rehearsal to discuss the procedure with the officiant.

*I am white and my fiancé is black. We are paying for our own wedding, and we would like to have a formal celebration with family and friends present. My parents are not excited about our plans, to say the least. We know that it is difficult for interracial couples, but we are committed to each other and want our families to share our happiness. My parents would prefer that we marry quietly and informally. Are we wrong to want a traditional celebration and to hope that my parents will come around?*

What you want is not wrong, and what you hope is reasonable, but probably not realistic. Unfortunately, you are not likely to be able to change your parents' lack of enthusiasm about the wedding you envision. But you and your fiancé need not let that keep you from making whatever arrangements you desire. Family and friends who are concerned only with your happiness will attend. Others will not, and you will have to be prepared for that. Try to locate other interracial couples who have had similar experiences to see what recommendations they might have to help you plan what you have in mind without running into too much disappointment. (See *Resources* under "Different Cultures.")

*I am from the Northeast and was raised a Catholic by my European mother. I now live in the Southeast, am a born-again Christian, and am engaged to a conservative Baptist, whose family roots date back to the Civil War. The customary wedding reception in my family is a sit-down dinner with an open bar and dancing all night long. In his family, it is an hors d'oeuvre buffet, fruit punch, and the cake-cutting ceremony. Obviously, because of his religious beliefs, alcohol and dancing would not do at all. How can I merge what each family expects?*

You cannot! I suggest you have your wedding in the South where you are living followed by a reception in keeping with your fiancé's family background and your own beliefs. This is also the path you have chosen, and your plans should reflect that. Tell your family what to expect, so they will not be surprised or disappointed because it is not what they are used to. If they are not comfortable attending such a celebration, they will have the opportunity to regret.

# Ethnic Traditions and Customs

*My fiancé's family lives in Italy. They will be traveling here for the wedding. I want them to feel comfortable at our celebration. What traditions are a must?*

Candy-covered almonds to symbolize the bitter and the sweet of marriage are presented to guests; sometimes, sugared almonds, called *confetti,* are tossed at the couple. A *busta* or wedding bag is carried by the bride for gifts of money. The *Tarantella* is a traditional wedding circle dance everyone takes part in at the reception. Italian wedding parties are large, and children are often in the wedding party and at the reception. Wedding feasts are sumptuous. (See *Resources* under "Ethnic Customs.")

*I come from the Philippines where it is traditional for guests to tap their cham-*
*pagne glasses with their fork or spoon, producing a clinking sound that is a sig-*
*nal for the bride and groom to kiss. Is it all right to have this at our wedding in*
*the United States?*

The custom you refer to is not limited to Philippine tradition. Italians do it
as well, and it has found its way into many American wedding receptions.

*We are perplexed about the "dollar dance." My fiancé and I always have thought*
*of it as tacky! Our friends and family have encouraged us to have it, saying cou-*
*ples net as much as $1,000 toward their honeymoon. I am planning a very elegant*
*affair. I do not want to cheapen our day by doing something gauche. What is the*
*origin of this custom?*

This is a Puerto Rican custom in which money is pinned to the bride's dress
by each man who dances with her. Because the United States is so ethnically
diverse, others have assimilated this custom into their own wedding celebrations.
If it is practiced among your family and friends, there is no reason not to do it.
But, if you and your fiancé do not feel it belongs at the type of celebration you
are planning, do not consider it.

*My fiancé is Irish, and I would like to have something truly representative of his*
*background in our wedding. Do you have any suggestions?*

You might choose an Irish linen wedding dress or have Irish bagpipers. Also
in Irish tradition, during the dancing at the reception, the groom is lifted in a
"jaunting car" (chair) to present him as a married man. You might want to
include traditional foods such as ham and cabbage in your menu. Most endearing, however, is the *Claddagh,* a wedding ring fashioned with two hands holding
a heart with a crown above it; when hands are worn facing in, the bride is married. Another idea: Purchase crystal toasting glasses with *Claddagh* etched on
them (Irish crystal, of course!).

*We are African-Americans, and we would like to have the custom of "jumping*
*the broom" in our wedding, but do not know much about it. What does it*
*involve?*

Dating back to the late 1600s, "jumping the broom" was created by the
slaves because they were not permitted to have recognized religious ceremonies.
More than hopping over a broomstick, it consists of an initial ribbon-tying ritual and six principles of the broom. Danita Roundree Green has written a book,
*Broom Jumping: A Celebration of Love,* with step-by-step instructions as well as a
complete guide to keeping African-American traditions alive. (See *Resources*
under "Ethnic Customs.")

# Participation of Loved Ones with a Disability

*My father would like to escort me down the aisle, but he cannot walk for more than a few steps without the aid of crutches. He has a wheelchair, but our cere-mony will be in a garden with a stone walk that is long and not very wide. What do you suggest?*

When the groom and best man enter from the side, the best man could wheel your father to his place on the aisle of the first row, left side. You could walk in alone or with your mother and take your dad's hand when you reach him, so he can respond when the officiant asks, "Who presents this woman...?" Then your groom steps forward to take your arm.

*My father's leg was amputated, and he must use a quad cane. My mother is con-fined to a wheelchair. I do not know what to do about walking down the aisle, the receiving line, or the dances at the reception. What do you recommend?*

The wedding ceremony should be handled as any other. Your mother is wheeled down the aisle to the front, left side, by an usher just before the pro-cessional begins, unless she would prefer to come in from the side at that time. Your dad walks with you, if that is what he wants to do. It may take a little longer, but so what? That trip down the aisle should be slow and savored. If your dad would prefer to come in from the side and wait for you at the head of the aisle, you would walk down the aisle alone to take his hand and proceed as sug-gested in my response to the previous question. During the receiving line, fathers usually circulate among guests. Your dad can stand or sit wherever he is comfortable chatting with guests after they come through the line. Your mom may be first in the receiving line in the wheelchair, following the usual proce-dure. If your dad wants to have the father and daughter dance, work with him to make it happen. If not, simply skip that. Instead, after your first dance with your groom, have the master of ceremonies invite the wedding party to join in, then all the guests.

*My fiancé has a younger brother who will be his best man. His only sister is 15 years old. She has a disability and must use a walker. I would like her to have a role in the wedding, but feel being a bridesmaid might be difficult for her. Is there something else she can do to be actively involved?*

First, invite your future sister-in-law to be a bridesmaid. If she accepts, she can either walk down the aisle with her walker slowly, or on the arm of an usher, or she may come in from a side door and wait to join the wedding party. If she does not want to do that, she may prefer to take charge of the guest book, in which case she would wear a corsage and be prominently seated near the door to the reception area where guests sign in as they enter.

# Combining Another Family Milestone with Your Wedding

*My parents will be celebrating their 30th anniversary on the day of our wedding. We have arranged a special dance for them at the reception, but we would like to do something more. Do you have any suggestions?*

Speak with your officiant about mentioning your parents' anniversary during the service. He may offer a blessing in honor of the occasion. Certainly, your choosing to marry on this date is a significant tribute to their years together and a good omen for the future of your own happy marriage. You might also want to create an anniversary montage, from photos of their wedding, to be mounted on an easel at the reception.

*My fiancé's father's birthday is the day of our wedding. What can we do to celebrate this without interrupting the mood of the wedding?*

During the reception, the bandleader should extend a birthday greeting to your new father-in-law and play happy birthday for all to join in wishing him well.

*Our wedding takes place very near my parents' 40th anniversary and my fiancé's parents' 35th anniversary. We would like to surprise our parents by recognizing these special occasions at our reception, but worry that it would cause confusion among the guests because more than one event is being celebrated. Would it be appropriate? If so, should we have two smaller wedding cakes for our parents?*

It is a tribute to the loving relationship you and your fiancé have with your parents that you are willing to share your day and make their special anniversaries part of the celebration. Rather than detract from your ceremony or confuse your guests, recognition of their anniversaries will reinforce the strong sense of unity present in your families. Have the officiant reveal the triple celebration from the pulpit. One cake for the anniversary celebrants in addition to the wedding cake is enough. It should be on a separate table, so that the two couples, taking turns or together, can be photographed cutting the cake. You and your fiancé should propose a toast to your respective parents after which each couple should be invited to dance to their favorite song. It would also be fun to have at least one photograph of them at their own wedding on display somewhere.

*Our wedding day is also my fiancé's birthday. I would like to do something very special for him in recognition of this, but I am not sure what to do or when to do it. Any ideas?*

Write a poem or essay just for him, and read it aloud at the reception and/or give him a special gift engraved with his birthdate and the wedding date. Of course, have the band strike up happy birthday. You might even have a "groom's cake" complete with birthday candles presented to him.

# Conflicting Wedding Dates

*I have been planning my wedding for a year, and everything is set. My sister just recently became engaged and has now scheduled her wedding three months prior to mine. She is also planning to have the same basic color scheme I have dreamed of having all my life, as well as some of the same food. I am upset and hurt, and feel this is very rude and inconsiderate. What are the rules about doing such a thoughtless thing?*

There are no rules about timing of weddings within a family. It is a personal decision. While consideration for others who already have confirmed plans is reasonable to expect, there is nothing you can do if your sister does not want to be influenced by that. As troubled and hurt as you are about this (with good reason), I urge you to try not to worry about comparisons or to dwell on her inconsideration. Remember, after her wedding is over, you will still have yours to look forward to!

*We are both 30 years old and are being married after 14 years of mutual friendship and love. Our families are extremely happy and supportive. The problem is my fiancé's brother who, though married, began an affair with a woman at his office. He then divorced his wife and became engaged shortly before we did. They planned an April wedding. Our wedding is scheduled six months later on October 2. Subsequently, his brother and fiancée postponed their wedding. When they began to consider another date, my fiancé made it very clear to his brother that he would be extremely disappointed if they were to choose an October date. (They will be each other's best man.) One week later, they set their October 23d date. Since then, my fiancé and I have been upset and concerned about the impact this will have not only on ourselves and our guests, but also on our relationship with his brother and future wife. Are we out of line to think of their actions as insensitive, selfish, and perhaps even jealous?*

It is the height of inconsideration for your fiancé's brother to place this strain on you two as well as on the family and friends that the two men share. In this case, fortunately, your wedding is first. If your fiancé is unable to be in his brother's wedding because you are on your honeymoon, that is the consequence of making plans that are stressful and inconvenient for others. You are certainly not out of line in your thoughts. However, you are in a position to carry on with your arrangements and let the other couple worry about the conflicts.

# Remembering Deceased Relatives

*I have always planned to be married on my parents' anniversary. Even though my father passed away four years ago, our wedding will take place on their anniversary. I would like to do something special in remembrance of my father, but do not know exactly what. I have thought about putting pictures together from their wedding day, including subsequent special events in their lives, then videotaping them and playing the video sometime during the reception. Do you think this is a good idea and, if not, do you have any other suggestions?*

Your intention to remember your father in some special way at your wedding is thoughtful, but it would not be appropriate to do what you have in mind. His memory will be in your heart and in the hearts of those who knew him. It would be sufficient for the officiant to briefly mention how pleased and proud your father would have been on this occasion. Anything more would be sorrowful and would probably make an emotionally trying time for your mother even more difficult. Another way to honor your dad is to print and distribute a wedding program with the names and roles of your attendants, the order of the service, musical selections, readings, etc., and include a written tribute in that. For example: "We have chosen this day for our wedding because it is the same date Jodi's parents wed in _____. Though Jodi's father passed away in _____, his love and commitment to her mother and their family will always be an inspiration to us."

*I was very close to my brother, who would have played a major role in our wedding. Sadly, he passed away. Of course, he will be with me spiritually, but I would also like to dedicate a song to him at our reception. I have chosen "Wind Beneath My Wings." I do not want to cast a pall over the celebration, but it would mean a great deal to me to be able to acknowledge him with just a brief comment and the song. May I do this?*

Your intention and your selection are appropriate. Make arrangements in advance with the bandleader to include it in the sequence of events.

*My 7-year-old niece, who would have been in our wedding, passed away after a lengthy illness. We would like to remember her at the wedding, but without causing more sadness. What is suitable?*

As mentioned previously, the printed wedding program is an ideal way to acknowledge a dear one without overtly calling up sorrowful memories. You might say: "We lovingly remember our niece, _____ _____, who was so much a part of our wedding plans and will always be present in our hearts."

*My mother passed away just five months before our wedding date. Our family encouraged me to go ahead with it as planned because we know that is what my mom would have wanted. It is going to be difficult for all of us, so we do not want to dwell on the loss, but we do want to include Mom somehow. We plan to light a candle during the ceremony with a special blessing in her honor. Is there some way we could include her name on the wedding invitations as well?*

I have always said no, because it is not possible for someone who has passed away to issue an invitation to anything. I still advise against it. But well-known etiquette expert Elizabeth Post published a suggestion for handling that situation submitted by a bride in similar circumstances. She worded her invitations:

*Together with their families*
*Mary Ann Smith*
*daughter of Robert Benton Smith and the late Margaret Elizabeth Smith*
*and*
*Francis Allan Jones*
*son of Mr. and Mrs. William Edward Jones*
*request the honour of your presence*
*at their marriage*
*etc.*

This is a major departure from traditional guidelines and invitation wording, but if it means that much to you, it is an option you may follow.

# Alcoholism

*My father is an alcoholic who refuses to recognize this or get any help. Now that I am engaged and planning to be married in a year and a half, I wonder if I should have my father walk me down the aisle. He has said many hateful things to me, and I am afraid that allowing him to attend at all will be a dreadful experience for everyone. What should I do?*

You have considerable time before the wedding to determine whether or not your father should be walking with you, so there is no need to worry about that question now. The answer will come as a result of his behavior pattern during the intervening time. If he does not seek treatment for his alcoholism, and if he is verbally abusive, expecting him to fill the traditional role of father of the bride is unrealistic and could be devastating. I suggest you find counseling for yourself with Al-Anon. Share your concerns with counselors there, and they will help you decide how best to deal with your father's affliction as it affects your life in general and his place at your wedding in particular. If it is not possible to have him escort you, there are other options noted in "Escorting the Bride" on page 93.

*My fiancé has a stepbrother and sister-in-law who are very embarrassing. She is an alcoholic, and the family just looks the other way when she becomes drunk and obnoxious. I have confronted her about this, and we had bitter words. Because of distance, my family and my future in-laws will be meeting for the first time at our wedding. My fiancé and I do not have anything to do with the couple now, and I do not want to invite them to the wedding because she is uncontrollable when she is drinking. He does not want to either, but he is concerned about how his family will react. We will have a cocktail hour for our guests and champagne during dinner. I have thought about telling the bartender to cut her off after two drinks, but my fiancé says that will cause a scene. What should we do?*

An alcoholic cannot be trusted to behave responsibly where liquor is being served. To knowingly invite someone who has a history of antisocial behavior is asking for trouble. Your fiancé should tell his family that they may be able to look the other way, but he cannot, and strangers should not have to!

# Other Quandaries

*My fiancé is divorced, but still on very friendly terms with his ex-wife. She and I get along, too. However, I would prefer that she not attend our wedding because it would make me and my parents feel uncomfortable. He wants to extend an invitation and let her decide. Should I allow that?*

As noted in *Invitations & Announcements,* an ex-spouse is usually not invited. The fact that you are uncomfortable with the possibility that she might attend confirms that this is a wise guideline to follow. She would probably feel the same way and might feel obligated to come if she received an invitation. Tell your fiancé his ex should not be on the guest list.

*My fiancé and the mother of my best friend had a falling out. We have not been to her house since then. When my friend and her mother ask why, I make up excuses. I have been close to the woman since I was a child and, of course, she is on my guest list. My fiancé does not want her to attend and threatens to make a scene if she does. If I do not send her an invitation when I send one to her daughter, my friend will think it is an error and ask me about it. What do I say, "Your mom is not welcome because . . ."?*

A successful marriage requires respect for the partner's past friendships. Your fiancé might not like your friend's mother, but she is an important person in your life and should be invited to the wedding.

***We planned to be married last year, then cancelled the wedding. Now our wedding is rescheduled for next year, and I want it to be smaller than what we originally planned. That means fewer attendants. How can I handle this without hurting the feelings of those I need to eliminate?***

Explain to them that in the process of re-planning, you are going to have a smaller wedding, therefore fewer attendants walking in the wedding party. Invite them to be honorary bridesmaids with special up-front seating, a corsage, and an opportunity to have a great time without the expense required to purchase attire, etc.

***I had a high school friend whose mother I adored. Our families became friends and remain so. Following graduation, we drifted apart. When she announced her engagement, she invited me to be her maid of honor. I helped in every way possible to the point of undermining my own health. Nothing I did was satisfactory. She was rude to me at the reception and has not contacted me since then. Her wedding was a great expense for me, financially and emotionally. Even so, I have tried to keep in touch by sending cards on holidays. Now I am planning my wedding, and I would like to invite her mom and brother, but I do not feel comfortable about my fiancé's insistence that I do not invite her. I am worried that her mother will be hurt if she is not invited. What should I do?***

Your fiancé is obviously concerned about your being hurt further by this woman's inconsiderate behavior. By her lack of appreciation for the many things you did to make her wedding successful and her refusal to respond to your communications, she, not you, has ended the relationship. Invite her mother and brother, but do not send her an invitation because she might come and ruin your special day.

# ❧ QUICK TIPS FOR THE MODERN BRIDE ❧
## *Handling Special Situations*

- If you are concerned about how to include divorced parents, remember that the most important thing to consider is *your* relationship with each parent.

- If a parent has remarried and you are inviting that parent, the new spouse should also be invited, regardless of your relationship with him or her.

- Try to work out any family differences before the wedding—be realistic in your assessments of others' behavior. Do not allow anyone to ruin your day.

- If your families have different cultural backgrounds, try to work in some traditions from each so that both families will feel represented.

- If you do not wish to serve alcohol for whatever reason, you should not feel pressured to do so. It is perfectly correct to forgo even champagne if that is what you prefer.

# CHAPTER 15

# Your Honeymoon

## Where to Go

*My fiancé would like to plan our honeymoon and then surprise me once he has made all the arrangements. I am concerned that he might think I am going to like some things that really do not appeal to me. For example, if he chooses a condo where we can be away from the hub of activity, but have to do our own house-keeping, I will be crazed. What can I do to avoid this without making him feel I am ungrateful for what I am sure he believes is really a gift of time and initiative?*

Thank him for the thoughtful gesture, but explain that selecting your dream trip requires a discussion about what will please you both. No matter how well a couple thinks they know each other, there are always surprises. If the two of you plan the trip and something does not go as expected—which often happens at some point—no one will be at fault, and you can laugh about it together. Here are some questions you may want to ask each other: How do we want to spend our days? What do we want to do in the evenings? Do we want to be iso-lated or more centrally located? Is a foreign culture intriguing? What is our ideal honeymoon setting? What is our budget and how can we allocate that to best advantage? Tell your fiancé that helping him plan the honeymoon is part of the fun, and I am sure he will be happy to work with you. Once you have answered those questions, a travel agent is the best person to help make your honeymoon dream a reality.

*We can get away for only a week. Should the limited time affect our choice of a honeymoon destination? Can we still go some place exotic?*

After the hectic wedding planning, you want to have time to unwind, settle in, and really enjoy being at your honeymoon destination. You will be able to do this better if you choose a place that can be reached in five hours or less by plane. Be assured, there are plenty of exciting and exotic destinations within a few hours flying time. For those who have two weeks and will be traveling farther, it is wise to plan on having a day or two at home upon return to unpack, organize, and reacclimate before heading back to work.

**My parents love Spain's Costa del Sol and think we should honeymoon there; our best friends loved their honeymoon in Jamaica. Which place should we choose?**

A honeymoon is somewhat like a wedding gown: Unless you have very similar tastes, someone else's probably will not do. Find out *why* your parents are so keen on Costa del Sol and get the same details about Jamaica from your friends. Then, list what you and your fiancé want on this trip of trips. Do either of these places meet *your* requirements? Read the honeymoon travel sections of bridal magazines and send for their brochures. You may find another destination even more attractive. (If you want to go skiing or hiking, or be near a bustling city, neither would be your choice.) Or, after comparing your list of priorities with the comments from your parents and friends, you will see which of the two places is for you. The point is, no one can or should *tell* you where to go. Only you two can make that decision.

# How to Plan

**We have not done any traveling until now, so we do not know a travel agent. How can we find a good one?**

Ask family and friends for their recommendations. A happy customer is the best assurance that you will be, too. If you do not have such a resource, you will find agents specializing in honeymoons or leisure travel listed in the *Yellow Pages*. Those belonging to ASTA (American Society of Travel Agents) must meet certain financial and ethical standards. CTCs (Certified Travel Counselors) have advanced training and five or more years of experience. Most important, an agent must be responsive to you, and you must feel comfortable with him or her. A good agent will ask you questions about your priorities and see to it that the destination you choose lives up to your expectations.

**We established a savings bank account just to pay for our honeymoon. We are both contributing to it and know just how much we can budget using those funds. Should we go for a more expensive honeymoon anticipating that we will get money as wedding gifts?**

You might factor in a certain amount more based on the gift-giving patterns of those invited to your wedding. But I caution a conservative approach, so you will not have to worry about how you are going to cover the costs when you should be enjoying your honeymoon to the max!

*Our travel agent has suggested we take a package tour because it is less expensive, but we are afraid that "you get what you pay for," and we do not want to skimp on our honeymoon. How can the prices be so much lower?*

Many hotels and resorts offer honeymoon packages, either directly or through a tour operator. Hotels recognize that a honeymoon is an important trip and want to help make it special. (Happy honeymooners tell their engaged friends about a wonderful experience and often return for anniversaries, so honeymoon packages that deliver the promise are good business!) Designed for lovers, the packages often provide upgraded rooms, a bottle of champagne, a special gift, or extras such as a sunset cruise or romantic dinner. (If you do not select a honeymoon package, still let the hotel know in advance that you are honeymooners, so you do not miss a treat or two.) With more potential savings, but also greater "risk" (if the company goes out of business) are the land/air package plans from wholesalers who contract in bulk for rooms, airfare, and other features. The savings that result from this volume purchasing are passed on to you. Bear in mind, the best prices are often based on ROH (run of house) rooms that may not have a view. Be sure to inquire about this, and specify the hotel and room type and size of bed you want. Your travel agent should confirm—in writing—all of these details as well as what is and is not included, and advise you about the reliability of the tour operator. Your travel agent also can help you compare prices among tour operators with the cost of independent arrangements to see your savings. Surcharges, taxes, and service charges add up if not included in the package. Be cautious because an unbelievable deal may become a disappointing reality.

*A couple we know made their honeymoon arrangements with a tour operator who has gone into bankruptcy. They are not sure they will get their money back, and it is very stressful for them. How can we protect ourselves from such an experience?*

Before booking, ask how long the firm has been in business. Is it bonded? What kind of assurances do they offer? (Members of USTOA, the U.S. Tour Operators Association, must meet standards of reliability and participate in a consumer protection plan.) Does your money go into an escrow account until your trip? If you buy trip cancellation insurance, does it cover you if the company ceases to operate? (Other unforeseen crises might require a couple to postpone, cut short, or cancel a prepaid trip. Attorney Less Abromovitz, author of

*Family Insurance Handbook,* advises that you consider trip cancellation/interruption coverage.) (See *Resources* under "Your Honeymoon.")

**Our wedding is in August, and we are thinking of going to Mexico or the Caribbean. But we are concerned about the possibility of hurricanes at that time of year. Do you think we should head in another direction?**

The advantage of going to either of those destinations in the summer is the off-season rates, which represent quite a savings over high season. The disadvantage is the uncertainty of the weather. Chances are you will have no problem, but if worrying about the weather during your honeymoon causes undue stress, you would be wise to select a place that is not so vulnerable.

**We want to travel light. What is your advice about what to take to a tropical destination?**

The answer to that depends on the resort. Some are very formal and require men to wear jackets and ties for dinner every night. Most, however, never require anything more dressy than slacks and a sport shirt for men and a sundress for women. Do bring a sweater or jacket for air conditioning. Pack two bathing suits, so one is always dry. A cover-up can double as a lounging robe. (Some resorts provide robes for their guests.) Linens, cottons, and silks are the most comfortable fabrics to wear in the tropics. Depending on where you are headed, you might want to take just a few outfits and shop for unusual styles and bargains once you arrive. It is fun to put together a new wardrobe on your honeymoon—clothes that will bring back fond memories each time you wear them. Ask your travel agent to advise you about the dress at the resort you choose and the shopping possibilities.

**We are getting married in December and plan to honeymoon in Australia. What will the weather be like?**

When it is winter in the northern hemisphere, it is summer in Australia. It should be beautiful at that time except in the north, around Darwin, where it is the rainy season. To find out weather for other destinations, call their tourist office or check a guidebook.

**We are going to England on our honeymoon. Do we need to change our money before we leave?**

It is not wise to carry much cash. You should purchase travelers' checks in $50 and $100 denominations and exchange them for foreign currency as you need it. You will want to convert about $50 into pounds sterling before leaving home or at the airport in England for cab fare and tipping on arrival. You pay a commission fee whenever you exchange currency, so try not to convert more than you plan to spend. Banks offer the best exchange rates, but in a pinch you can convert money at larger hotels and stores.

### *We are going to Greece on our honeymoon. I have a passport in my maiden name. Will it be valid, or do I need to get a new one in my married name?*

You cannot get a passport in your married name until after the wedding, so it is wise to make your airline reservations in your maiden name (even though it is less romantic). Your passport is valid with your maiden name. If you want to make reservations in your married name, be sure to bring a copy of your marriage certificate with you on your honeymoon. Because the marriage certificate must be mailed by the officiant to the state for the official seal and subsequently sent back to you, your best man needs to find a convenient place to stop by and make the photocopy before returning the original to the officiant. Following your honeymoon, you may have your passport amended by filling out a form (DSP19), available at your local post office. Send the form, your passport, and a copy of your marriage certificate to the passport agency nearest you. There is no fee. For details, contact the Office of Passport Services. (See *Resources* under "Your Honeymoon.")

### *My fiancé and I are not sure about who should be tipped and how much is expected. Can you give us some guidelines?*

You need between $10 and $20 in single dollars always handy for out-of-pocket tipping (unless you are at an all-inclusive resort, where *absolutely everything* is in your package price). Customs vary in different countries, so it is wise to inquire at the tourist board before you leave. Tips should be based on the quality of service. If someone does not do the job expected, less or perhaps no tip is warranted. By the same token, someone who is extraordinarily helpful deserves more. The following suggestions are based on common practice in the United States: taxi, 15 to 20 percent of the fare, plus 25 cents to 50 cents per bag; hotel limousine driver, 10 to 15 percent of fare or 50 cents to $1 per bag for complimentary service; private limousine, 15 percent of fare; porters, $1 per bag; bus driver/tour guide, $4 per couple for the guide and $2 per couple for the driver; train sleeping-car attendants, $1 per day. Cruise service tips vary for individual cruise ship lines and are listed on the back of their brochures. They range from $3 to $5 per couple, per service provided, for cabin steward, night steward, dining room waiter, dining room captain; half that amount for a bus boy, and at your discretion for special services. For more information call Cruise Lines International Association (CLIA). (See *Resources* under "Your Honeymoon.") Guidelines for hotel personnel are: bellhop, 75 cents to $1 per bag; doorman,

75 cents to $1 for hailing a cab; parking attendant, $1; room service, 15 percent of the bill; waiter (on meal plan), $4 per couple per day; beach/pool attendant, $1 per couple per day; maid, $2 per couple per day. At restaurants a waiter/waitress receives 15 to 20 percent of the bill; wine steward, 5 percent of wine cost; maitre d' or captain, $5 to $15, if you request special treatment; coat check, $1. If you take a sightseeing tour, plan to give the guide between $2 and $5 for a full day. Whenever you are signing for meal charges, check carefully to see if the service charge is included. If it is, no more is required unless you feel so inclined.

## ৯৯৯ QUICK TIPS FOR THE MODERN BRIDE ৯৯৯
# *Honeymoon Hints*

- The groom traditionally planned and paid for the honeymoon on his own, but most couples today now choose to make those choices together.

- Consider what you both want for your honeymoon *before* you pick a destination.

- As with your other resources, plan ahead to get the best value for your money.

- Remember to consider honeymoon costs when planning your budget.

- Investigate the area you are thinking about—check into the weather at that time of year, money exchange if any, clothes you will need, tipping practices, and local laws. The fewer surprises in these practical matters, the better.

# CHAPTER 16
# *Wedding Stress*

## *When Enough Is Enough!*

*On the one hand, weddings can be so beautiful, but on the other hand, they can be a big hassle. My fiancé and I are mature adults carefully thinking through the details of our planning. Believing that weddings are a family affair, I have tried to keep my family informed of our decisions. In return, I am continually criticized about these plans. I have reached the point where I want to keep everything a secret. Is it practical for me to do this?*

If your family is paying for all or part of the celebration, discussions about everyone's expectations are appropriate and their wishes should be taken into consideration, but compromise should be in your favor. It is not wise to keep your plans a secret from them. In fact, that will more likely result in unpleasant confrontations at the last minute when you certainly do not need the stress. Tell them you value their opinions, and will bear their suggestions in mind, but that the final decisions will be made by you and your fiancé.

*Planning my wedding and reception is exciting, but also extremely stressful. My father is in business with his brother, but my mother and I do not even speak to my uncle's wife. She has been very cruel and demeaning to our family, especially to my dad. Neither my aunt nor uncle has said one nice thing to me or about me since birth. She is rude, obnoxious, and the last person I want at my wedding. Of course, I know I cannot invite my uncle without her, and I really do not want him either. My father feels they must be invited. What can I do?*

Speak privately with your father about why you do not want to invite his brother and sister-in-law. Given that unpleasant history, you should not have to include such insensitive and hurtful people at your wedding. Although it might be difficult for your father to deal with his brother if they are omitted, his relationship with the man cannot be much worse than what you describe it to be already. A wedding is a time to reinforce loving family relationships. Whatever pressure they might exert on your father day in and day out cannot be reason enough to have them in attendance. I hope he will have the strength to make that decision and stick with it.

*My parents were divorced when my sister and I were very young. Our mother raised us and we three are close. My father remarried and never was in touch. My mom's brother has been like a father to me, and I asked him to walk down the aisle with me. When I told my father, he hung up the phone, then wrote me a letter about how devastated he is. I am now getting nasty calls from his mother and other members of his family, people who have not bothered to contact me in 15 years. I dread answering the phone and resent the stress I feel because of this. I also do not intend to have my father's name on the invitations as my mother, uncle, fiancé, and I are hosting the wedding. I was going to invite my father, his wife, and members of his immediate family before this happened. Am I obligated to do so now?*

Under the circumstances, you certainly are not obligated to include your father on the invitation or invite his side of the family. His behavior is manipulative and irresponsible. The meddlesome relatives are insensitive and unrealistic. You do not owe them an explanation or an invitation if they bring you nothing but grief.

# Give Yourselves a Break

*We are planning a long-distance wedding. Our families come from very different backgrounds, and we are taking that into consideration as we firm up the arrangements. We have a lot to deal with, but we knew that we would and felt we could handle it. I still think we can, but we are arguing about things that would never faze us before. I feel very bad when that happens and cry a lot. What can we do to get back on track?*

Stick to your original plan. Do not let any external influences deter you from doing what you both want to do. Plan some time away from each other, either to be alone or to do something with friends to take your mind off the all-consuming wedding plans. Arrange special activities or a weekend trip away together during which you promise not to talk about the wedding, but rather about your relationship and the love that binds you. Join an exercise class or schedule some other regular vigorous activity to work out your frustrations. If you are having a religious ceremony, your officiant may expect you to attend marriage preparation sessions, which will help you to cope with some of these stresses. Make the date now. If there is no such program available, look into attending one at a local college or university or check with marriage and family services available in your community listed in the *Yellow Pages*. Not only will you learn a lot about how to handle your anxieties, but you will take comfort in knowing that the stresses you are experiencing are quite common.

*I have a demanding job and am attending graduate school at night. My fiancé works six days a week and occasionally even seven days. We both are exhausted and fight all the time. We really love each other and want to get on with the plans to marry, but the stress of it all is overwhelming. At this point, I do not know whether to break it off or rush ahead. Any advice?*

Yes, do not rush ahead, but rather *think* ahead. Consider just how compatible you are. You may not know each other as well as you believe you do. There are ways to check on that. Seeking out a religious, family service, or private psychological counseling program is one way. Another is to avail yourselves of the compatibility inventory analysis programs recently developed to help couples identify their personality traits and the effect they will have on the success or failure of their marriage. (See *Resources* under "Marriage Preparation.") Even though your main stress comes from too much to do and not enough time to do it, you can do the analysis gradually and the results will help you determine what other factors in your lives are affecting your ability to deal constructively with the pressures. With this information, you will be able to decide on the next step. Remember, many of these stresses will continue to be present in your lives after the wedding, so learning how to handle them now will be beneficial throughout your future.

## ❧ QUICK TIPS FOR THE MODERN BRIDE ❧
### *Keeping Stress to a Minimum*

- Listen to well-meaning advice, but make it clear from the start that you and your fiancé are to make all final decisions.

- *Do not* listen to advice that is not well meant.

- Do not feel obligated to invite anyone who has been unkind or unsupportive in the past. It is your day, and you should invite only those people who are important to you.

- Consider counseling to resolve stress between you and your fiancé now—it may help you more effectively deal with such issues after the wedding as well.

# CHAPTER 17

# *Your New Life*

## *The Name Question*

***I am planning to retain my family name. How do I make that known?***

You may enclose a printed card in your invitations and announcements stating: "Alice Smith will retain her surname after marriage." The newspaper announcement should also mention: "The bride will retain her name."

***After I get married, I will continue to use my maiden name professionally. I intend to hyphenate that name with my husband's last name legally to avoid confusion when we have children. What initials should I use as my stationery monogram for thank-you notes I will use to acknowledge wedding gifts? Is it acceptable to combine our initials so that we both can write thank-you notes on the same stationery?***

You have a number of options. Have stationery printed with your name and stationery printed with your husband's name. When you write thank-you notes, you mention, "Kenneth and I" or "Kenneth joins me..." He includes you in a similar manner in his notes. You may also select notepaper with a monogram that combines all the initials: your first name initial small, two hyphenated initials for your new last name large, his first name initial small. Or print "Mary and Kenneth Jones-Smith" at the head of the stationery.

*When we marry, I will take my husband's last name. But I have a slight problem. I am a college professor with a Ph.D. All of my students and colleagues know me as "Dr. Anderson." When I get married, will I automatically become "Dr. Jamieson" or will I need to hyphenate my name? Since my degree was granted in my maiden name, would suddenly becoming "Dr. Jamieson" be legal?*

Your marriage certificate will make the Jamieson name legal, but you will have to notify the following to change your name on their records: Social Security Administration, Bureau of Motor Vehicles, the human resources department where you are employed, the checking/savings department of your bank, and the stores and banks where you have a credit card. The degree remains in your maiden name, and there is no need to hyphenate unless you want to do that. Simply inform colleagues and students of your marriage and your desire to be addressed by your married name, "Dr. Jamieson."

*My groom and I are both physicians, and I am retaining my name. How should we be introduced when we make our entrance at the reception?*

Although you will be using your title of Dr. in your professional life, it is not necessary to use it among family and friends. At the reception you may be introduced as "the bride, Susan Grey, and the groom, Jim Hanson." However, if you both prefer, you may be announced as "the bride and groom, Dr. Susan Grey and Dr. Jim Hanson."

*I am currently in medical school and have always wanted to retain my last name in my future career. However, my fiancé recently revealed that he had always assumed I would adopt his last name after our wedding. Although he was obviously hurt when I told him of my intentions, he graciously assented to my decision. I realize that my having his last name means a great deal to him, and I am considering adding his last name to my entire name, but I do not wish to hyphenate into Mine-His. I would like to be addressed professionally as Dr.-my-name at the hospital and in my practice, and as Mrs.-his-name on social occasions, such as when we vacation together and at PTA meetings. Is this possible or will I run into significant legal and/or social name problems in the future?*

It is not a problem to retain your maiden name professionally and legally and to use your husband's name in social situations. Do not change your name on any records, and sign it as you always have done. Inform friends and relatives of your wish to use your husband's name for social occasions, and introduce yourself with his name when you meet people on your vacations. Just be sure to remember that, if you travel internationally, your airline ticket must bear the same name as is on your passport. Hotels also will expect the name on your reservation to match the one on the passport.

# Premarital Agreement

*My fiancé and I each have a career and have accumulated numerous assets. When we marry, we will merge everything, but I think we ought to have a premarital agreement, just in case the marriage is not the success we hope it will be. He thinks that it is unnecessary and feels it indicates a lack of trust on my part. How can I convince him that is not the case?*

One of the best reasons for considering a premarital agreement is the discussion facilitated between the couple drafting the agreement. There is nothing to indicate a lack of trust when couples plan their lives together in a practical way. In fact, it is just the opposite when a couple feels comfortable enough with each other to draw up such a document. Marriage is an emotional *and* a business partnership. Many couples feel added confidence and security about their decision to marry after they have developed a premarital contract together in consultation with a lawyer representing each of them. Often automatic expiration dates or conditions for reevaluation are incorporated into their contracts to allow periodic updating to accommodate changing family and financial circumstances. Even if you ultimately decide not to have a premarital contract, the discussion about it is truly worthwhile. Couples with few assets certainly do not need a premarital agreement. But couples like you two and those who are remarrying and have children should definitely explore the possibility of drawing up such a contract. Every state has its own laws governing the rights and responsibilities of marriage partners, the welfare of children, the accumulation and maintenance of property, and the distribution of that property in the event of divorce or death. Only a premarital contract or will assures that your wishes will supersede statutory rights of inheritance under state law. (For "Your Legal Guide to Marriage and Other Relationships," see *Resources.*)

# Living with Parents

*Jack has his own small apartment, and I plan to move in after we are married. But it is much too tiny for us to live there comfortably for very long. My parents have a large home, and my siblings are no longer there. They offered to let us move in with them until we save enough for a down payment on our own home. I want to do it, but Jack has reservations about it. He says that the statistics on the success of those arrangements are not good. Is he right?*

Indeed, he has a good point. It is difficult enough for parents to let go of their children, and when you are living in *their* house, you still have to abide by their rules. The best situation is when common living quarters are not shared and there is a separate entrance. It is far from an ideal situation, but it can certainly be practical in the short term if it enables you to accumulate the money for your own home purchase. Some other tips to a constructive arrangement are: Meet at the beginning to set the terms of financial and domestic responsibilities; agree to respect each other's rights to privacy; and vow to keep your personal matters private. It is also important to have some time frame in mind for moving out.

## Money: Mine, Yours, Ours!

*We have both been on our own for many years. I am used to controlling my checking account, and the same is true for my fiancé. What is the best way for us to deal with who is handling what financial expenses when we marry?*

You need to draw up a monthly budget by estimating your yearly expenses. In doing that, you will know what are your fixed costs and which are flexible. The latter can be adapted to cover the former. You will both probably be most comfortable having separate checking accounts, but they should be in both your names: Mary Smith *or* John Smith. You never need to write a check from the other account, but it gives either of you immediate access in the event of some unforeseen crisis that requires it. Often one partner is more responsible about paying bills than the other. Assigning fixed expense payments to that person makes sense. More of your pooled income should go into the account from which those payments are made. Common sense and objective discussion about practical ways to handle your money will keep it from becoming a problem. As long as each of you has some "mad" money available to use at your discretion, the rest should be handled in the manner of a business partnership. If neither of you is good at financial planning, you should engage a professional who can help you allocate your earnings for cash flow and, most important, for savings and investment toward future security.

## You Work, He Works, Who Does the Housework?

*My fiancé is a neat freak! I have to be so organized in my job that the last thing I am concerned about is pristine order where I live. We both work long hours. I am really concerned about how we are going to manage the day-to-day home care responsibilities. What do other couples do about this?*

The smart ones talk it over *before* they get married. What you describe is more common than ever before, and with the traditional homemaking role gone the way of the dinosaur, it is something most couples have to address. In my opinion, the worst thing you can do is make rigid assignments; rather, keep it flexible so that you each do what you are best at. Make a schedule that takes into consideration all of the hours and responsibilities you both have outside your home. That gives you something to shoot for, but if something unexpected, either business or social, comes up, agree that you can postpone the housework and/or help the other out with it when needed. Putting things away and keeping things neat on a daily basis goes a long way to maintaining the peace in a situation like yours. If you can retrain yourself to do that, then I am sure your future husband will be able to live a little longer with some dust or wait for the laundry or whatever. Or maybe he will take responsibility for the cleaning, if you do the cooking. Of course, the best deal of all is to hire someone to come in regularly to clean, then share the marketing, cooking, and laundry chores as they appeal to your mood and fit into your schedules.

## QUICK TIPS FOR THE MODERN BRIDE
### *Your New Life Together*

- Discuss the name question well in advance of the wedding. Inform friends, family, and colleagues of your decision.

- If one or both of you has significant assets, consider a premarital agreement. It is very common these days, and is often a very good idea.

- Plan ahead on how you will handle money—cut down on later arguments by being clear on this.

- If you will both work after the wedding, plan to divide tasks according to preference and aptitude. Be sure to talk before the wedding about your expectations on such points as tidiness, meals, etc.

# CHAPTER 18
# Groom's Questions

## Taking the Initiative

*Among our friends, most couples have dated a long time and gradually agreed they would marry. Often the couple shopped for the ring together. My significant other and I are now talking about the probability of marriage. I would like to ask her soon, but wonder about a number of things: Should I surprise her with a ring? What if she does not like it? Does she need to have a ring to be officially engaged? We need time to save money for everything associated with getting married and setting up a home. Is two or three years too long for an engagement?*

Guys who select an engagement ring on their own usually have a pretty good idea of what their intended wants, probably from window shopping, perhaps from identifying photos in magazines and catalogs, etc. There are some women who love to be surprised in matters of the heart, and if your lady is one of those, there is your answer. Many others prefer to share in the selection of something so special, and it is fun to shop together to watch her try on the different possibilities. If you want to play it safe and not worry about whether your choice is what she wants, that is the way to go. However, she does not have to have a ring to be "officially" engaged. That happens whenever you ask her to marry you, and she accepts. You may give her the ring at any time during your engagement or even years later when you can afford something *extraordinaire!* A two- or three-year engagement is not unusual these days. In fact the average length is 15 months, and many couples just like you two are saving for years to pay for some, most, or all of their wedding.

*I would like to have my fraternity buddies attend the wedding. I am not that close to all of them, but I think it would be fun to invite them by putting an open invitation up on the bulletin board at the fraternity house. My fiancée turned green when I suggested that. Is this really as off the wall as she thinks it is?*

Yes! A wedding is not just another "blast." If there are good friends among the brothers, by all means send them their own invitation. But deep-six the bulletin board idea.

*I cannot decide whether to have a very close brother or my dearest friend as the best man. I really do not want to have to choose one over the other. I know the bride may have a maid of honor and a matron of honor. Can something like this be applied to the groom?*

Trouble yourself no longer. Just invite them both to stand up with you as best men. If you are having a double ring exchange, one takes charge of your ring and the other has your bride's ring. Together they can plan a great bachelor bash, and with two good men at your side, there is no excuse for being late to anything!

# Not Just a Prop

*We have secured the church, and my fiancée has selected her dress. The plans are moving along well, but I want to be part of all the decisions, including discussing the bridesmaids' dresses, selecting the tuxedos, and all the other details. Everyone is telling me not to get involved because it is **her** wedding day and not mine. I do not want to feel like a rent-a-groom. Is there anything wrong with my taking an active part in planning **our** wedding day?*

Certainly, not. In fact, your fiancée is fortunate that you care so much about all the elements that go into organizing a wedding. You should both feel comfortable about discussing every aspect of the day and predicate your decisions on the style of wedding that is mutually desirable. It is most definitely your day, too! Anyone who tells you otherwise is not living in the real world.

*I want to make all the gift registry selections with my fiancée. Her mother does not understand this. She went with her own mother to do that years ago, and she thinks the procedure has not changed. I am sure there are a lot of mothers and daughters who still do that, but it is not what I want for the two of us. My fiancée agrees with me, but does not know how to tell her mother for fear of hurting her feelings. Any suggestions?*

Your inclusion in gift registry selection need not be at the exclusion of your future mother-in-law. Your fiancée needs to take her mom to lunch or arrange some other special time together to explain that, today, the groom-to-be takes a much more active part in first-home planning. She should assure her mother that just because you are doing this does not mean that she cannot accompany you when it is convenient. It is a great way to bring you all closer together (providing mom knows how to keep any conflicting opinions to herself). Daughter has to make that clear when she extends the invitation. It is a good test to establish her independence as a woman whose first priority is the happiness of her marriage.

*I love to cook and know a lot about good food and dining. I want to have a major role in determining the caterer chosen for our wedding as well as the food selection. My future in-laws are paying for the entire wedding and seem to think that this is presumptuous. My fiancée feels caught in the middle because she understands my frustration, but she does not want to offend her parents. Should I just drop it?*

Not at all. This is your opportunity to invite your future in-laws to dinner at one of the places you think is terrific. When they have the chance to see and hear you in your "element," they will likely begin to understand what an advantage it is to have you so interested in working with them to plan a wedding reception meal that impresses everyone.

*My mother is upset that I will be dancing with the bride's mother before I dance with her. She says it does not make sense and wants me to change the sequence. Should I bring this up with my fiancée?*

No. Sounds like the green-eyed monster rearing its ugly head. There is no reason to change established procedure and upset your fiancée because your mother is feeling insecure. This is a good time to establish *your* independence from attempts at maternal manipulation and control. Tell her you are following the traditional dance sequence and expect no further discussion about it.

*I get along very well with my future father-in-law. Unlike most of the men in the world, we are really enjoying the wedding planning. Fortunately, my bride-to-be and her mother find it a relief because they both have jobs and time-consuming responsibilities. There is only one area where I am getting some resistance. I want to help her find her wedding dress, and she thinks it would be awkward. Is she right?*

To a certain degree she is. That is because most bridal shops are not as forward thinking as you might expect. Fiancés and fathers who accompany the brides-to-be are still few and far between; therefore, the consultants become flustered because they do not know where to put the men during the lengthy try-on process. With this in mind, your fiancée should let the shop know in advance that you will be coming with her, so the logistics of working with her can be determined ahead, and your presence will not throw the consultants and the other customers into a frenzy. That is also the case if her dad wants to accompany her to the final fitting. It is a great idea to do this because it helps to condition him to the realization that his little girl is about to become your wife. It takes the edge off the sense of loss and the extremely emotional experience of seeing her as a bride for the first time just before walking down the aisle. I am sure that many brides still believe that allowing anyone but their mom and the female attendants to see their wedding dress is bad luck. But I think of a bride's sharing this key part of the wedding planning with her dad and, perhaps, her fiancé as a good omen representative of the sharing and caring that will always be a part of their family life.

***Traditionally, the groom is supposed to pay for the honeymoon. I am comfortable with that, but my fiancée says that is no longer true. Is it still a consideration?***

As with everything else associated with a wedding today, personal circumstances rather than rigid rules determine who pays for the honeymoon. For example: Established career couples may choose to share the cost. In some cases, when a couple is paying for their entire wedding, the bride's and/or groom's parents may present them with the money for their honeymoon. Or, when the groom's parents have little or no other expense connected with the wedding, the honeymoon is their gift to the couple. And there are still some grooms-to-be, just like you, who welcome the chance to have one clearly defined area of responsibility to plan and pay for. (For more on honeymoon planning, see *Your Honeymoon*.)

***I would like to select the formalwear for myself and my attendants. My fiancée insists we leave it up to the formalwear specialist. Why is his choice more important than mine?***

It is not. He is there to show you what is traditional and what is currently chic. The time of day and degree of formality that you and your bride-to-be have chosen for your wedding should influence your selection and, with these parameters in mind, your preference should be the deciding factor. (For more details, see "The Groom's Attire" on page 64.)

## ❧❧❧ QUICK TIPS FOR THE MODERN BRIDE ❧❧❧
### *Hints for the Groom*

- Take part in the wedding planning. You will enjoy the event much more if you have been in on the decisions.

- Traditionally, the groom was expected to take care of picking out and paying for the engagement ring and the honeymoon with little input from the bride, while the bride handled such things as the registry and the reception. Some still choose to divide tasks this way, but it is more common today for couples to share these decisions. There is no one right or wrong way—go with what fits your relationship.

- Remember that, despite what many say, this is not just the bride's day, but yours as a couple.

# RESOURCES

## CHAPTER 1

### The Ring

*Engagement & Wedding Rings: The Definitive Buying Guide for People in Love,* by Antoinette Matlins, Antonnio Bonanno, and Jan Crystal. (S. Woodstock, VT: Gemstone Press, 1990).

For a free 4 c's buyers guide to a diamond's quality and value, call:
Designs by D'Annunzio and Company
(800) 742-8146

For information about gems, gold, and platinum, contact:
American Gem Society
Dept. MB
5901 West Third Street
Los Angeles, CA 90036
(800) 346-8485

International Gemological Institute
580 Fifth Avenue, Suite 620
New York, NY 10036
(212) 398-1700

## CHAPTER 2

### Stretching Your Wedding Dollars

*How to Have a Big Wedding on a Small Budget,* by Diane Warner. (Cincinnati, OH: Writer's Digest Books, 1990).

*Affordable Weddings,* by Leta Clark. (New York, NY: Simon & Schuster, 1989).

For an at-home wedding video, send $19.95 to:
*Do Your Own Wedding*
117 Caldwell Street, P.O. Box 125
Auburn, KY 42206
(800) 282-1996

### Hiring a Wedding Consultant

For a list of registered bridal consultants in your area, contact:
National Bridal Service
3122 West Cary Street
Richmond, VA 23221
(804) 355-6945

For a list of wedding coordinators in your area, contact:
Weddings Beautiful Certified Wedding Specialist
3122 West Cary Street
Richmond, VA 23221
(804) 358-9241

For a list of its members in your area, write:
Association of Bridal Consultants
200 Chestnutland Road
New Milford, CT 06776
(900) WED-N-DAY

For consultants trained by June Wedding, Inc., contact:
Robbie Ernst
325 Roosevelt Way
San Francisco, CA 94114
(415) 252-9195

CHAPTER 3

## Deciding on Wedding Style

*Modern Bride Wedding Celebrations,* by Cele G. Lalli and Stephanie H. Dahl. (New York, NY: John Wiley & Sons, 1992).

*Emily Post's Complete Wedding,* by Elizabeth L. Post. (New York, NY: HarperCollins, 1991).

*The New Etiquette,* by Marjabelle Young Stewart. (New York, NY: St. Martin's Press, 1989).

*Planning a Wedding to Remember,* by Beverly Clark. (Long Beach, CA: Wilshire Publications, 1986).


CHAPTER 6

## The Bride's Attire

*Dressing the Bride,* by Larry Goldman. (New York, NY: Crown Publishers, Inc., 1993).

## Special Size Resources

Manufacturers:
  .Alfred Angelo (petites 3 to 11; plus sizes 38 to 44)
  601 Davisville Road
  Willow Grove, PA 19090
  (215) 659-8700

  Priscilla (petites 0 to 15)
  40 Cambridge Street
  Charleston, MA 02129
  (617) 242-2677

  Bianchi (petites 3 to 13)
  293A Street
  Boston, MA 02210
  (617) 482-5450

Fink Brothers (petites 5 to 15)
1385 Broadway
New York, NY 10018
(212) 921-5683

Mori Lee (plus size 44)
498 Seventh Avenue
New York, NY 10018
(212) 947-3490

Lili Designer Wedding Gowns (four styles to plus 44)
1117 East Main Street
Alhambra, CA 91801
(818) 282-4326

Bridal Originals (plus sizes to 30)
1385 Broadway
New York, NY 10018
(212) 921-1190

## Men's Attire

"Formalwear Guide," available for $1 and a SASE from:
  International Formalwear Association
  401 North Michigan Avenue
  Chicago, IL 60611


CHAPTER 7

## Photography and Videography

For a brochure, "What Every Bride Should Know About Wedding Photography," and a list of professional photographers and videographers in your area, send a SASE to:
  Professional Photographers of America
  Membership Department
  1090 Executive Way
  Des Plaines, IL 60018

## Music

*The Essential Wedding,* arranged by Jerry Ray, and *Classical Music for the Wedding Service,* edited by Maurice Hinson, available for $6.95 each from:

Alfred Publishing Co., Inc.
P.O. Box 10003
Van Nuys, CA 91410-0003
(818) 891-5999

*The Bridal Guide,* 5th ed., by Pamela Thomas (440 musical selections), available for $12.95 through:

The American Guild of Organists
475 Riverside Drive
New York, NY 10115
(212) 870-2310

*Celebrating Marriage: Preparing the Wedding Liturgy,* by Paul Corvino, Ed., available for $5.95 from:

National Association of Pastoral Musicians
Pastoral Press
225 Sheridan Street West
Washington, DC 20011
(202) 723-1254
(202) 723-2262 (fax)

"The Wedding Album," by RCA Victor, a collection of wedding music, available in music stores or by calling (800) 221-8180

## Flowers

*Wedding Flowers,* by Fiona Barnett. (New York, NY: Grove Weidenfelf, 1990).

Ask to see *Wedding Album* at Teleflora member florists, or for other brochures and information, contact:

Teleflora
12233 West Olympic Boulevard, Suite 140
Los Angeles, CA 90064
(310) 826-5253

## Transportation

For referrals to limousine companies in your area, call:

National Limousine Association
(800) NLA-7007

## CHAPTER 9

## The Ceremony

*The Catholic Wedding,* by Molly Stein and William Graham. (New York, NY: Paulist Press, 1988).

*The Jewish Wedding Book,* by Rabbi Daniel B. Syme. (New York, NY: Pharos Books, 1991).

## Personalizing Your Service

*Weddings from the Heart,* by Daphne Rose Kingma. (Berkely, CA: Conari Press, 1991).

*With These Words...I Thee Wed: Contemporary Wedding Vows for Today's Couples,* by Barbara Eklof. (Holbrook, MA: Bob Adams, Inc., 1989).

*Wedding Vows,* by Peg Kehret. (Colorado Springs, CO: Meriwether Publishing Ltd., 1989).

*Words of Love and Poems of Love,* (New York, NY: St. Martin's Press, 1991).

For information about printing a wedding program, write:

Johnston Press
1741 Stanford Lane
Sarasota, FL 34231
(813) 923-9699

## Interfaith Marriage

*Modern Bride Wedding Celebrations,* by Cele G. Lalli and Stephanie H. Dahl. (New York, NY: John Wiley & Sons, 1992).

*The Intermarriage Handbook,* by Judy Petsonk and Jim Remsen. (New York, NY: William Morrow/Quill Paperbacks, 1988).

*Mixed Blessings: Marriage Between Jews and Christians,* by Paul Cowan with Rachel Cowan. (New York, NY: Doubleday, 1987).

*Intermarriage,* by Susan Weidman. (New York, NY: Free Press, 1989).

For referrals to rabbis who will marry interfaith couples, contact:

Rabbinic Center for Research and Counseling
128 East Dudley Avenue
Westfield, NJ 07090
(201) 233-0419

For officiants for interfaith couples from local societies, contact:

Clergy for Ethical Culture
(212) 873-6500

For *Dovetail,* a bimonthly newsletter addressing the issues and challenges faced by interfaith couples, send $19.99 for six issues to:

Dovetail Publishing
3014A Folsom Street

Boulder, CO 80304
(303) 444-8713

## CHAPTER 10

## Reception Locations

*Places: A Directory of Public Places for Private Events and Private Places for Public Functions,* by Hannelore Hahn and Tatiana Stoumen. Available from:

Tenth House Enterprises, Inc.
Caller Box 810, Gracie Station
New York, NY 10028
(212) 737-7563

*The Down the Aisle Directory*—The New York Metropolitan, Tri-State Area, (New York, NY: MRS Publications).

For a romantic Southwest wedding location, write:

W. J. Marsh House/Snyder Cottage
Huning Highlands Historic District
301 Edith Southeast
Albuquerque, NM 87102
(305) 247-1001

## Toasting

*Can You Say a Few Words? How to Prepare and Deliver Wedding, Birthday, Anniversary Toasts,* by Joan Detz. (New York, NY: St. Martin's Press, 1991).

*Toasts,* by Paul Dickson. (New York, NY: Crown Publishers, 1991).

*How to Plan Your Wedding Reception— The Party of Your Life,* a Tott's and *Modern Bride* video. To order with a credit card, call (800) 358-7790.

## Wedding Cakes

*Colette's Cakes—The Art of Cake Decorating,* by Colette Peters. (Boston, MA: Little Brown & Co. 1991).

## CHAPTER 11

## Destination Weddings

For help in arranging your wedding at a honeymoon destination or abroad, contact:

> Weddings Around the World
> 5944 Luther Lane, Suite 302
> Dallas, TX 75225
> (800) 648-7000

> Far Away Weddings Incorporated
> 4516 Lovers Lane, Suite 178
> Dallas, TX 75225
> (800) 882-WEDS

## Remarriage

*Emily Post on Second Weddings,* by Elizabeth Post. (New York, NY: HarperCollins, 1991).

For premarital preparation program, contact:

> Prepare MC (married with children)
> P.O. Box 190
> Minneapolis, MN 55440
> (800) 331-1661

For counseling, membership, newsletter, and resources in your area, contact:

> The Stepfamily Foundation, Inc.
> National Headquarters
> 333 West End Avenue
> New York, NY 10023
> (218) 877-3244

For information on the special ceremony, "Celebrating the New Family," and the Family Medallion, write to:

> Reverend Roger Coleman
> Clergy Services
> 706 West 42nd Street
> Kansas City, MO 64111

## Military Weddings

*Service Etiquette,* 4th ed., by Oretha D. Swartz. (Annapolis, MD: Naval Institute Press, 1988).

## Marrying Abroad

The embassy or tourist information bureau of the country in which the marriage is to be performed is the best source of information about marriage in that country. American embassies and consulates abroad frequently have information about marriage in the country in which they are located. For some general information on marriage in a limited number of countries, contact:

> Office of Citizens Consular Services
> Room 4817
> U.S. Department of State
> Washington, DC 20520
> (202) 514-2000

Information on obtaining a visa for a foreign spouse may be obtained from any office of the Immigration and Naturalization Service, U.S. embassies and consulates abroad, or contact:

> Department of State Visa Office
> Washington, DC 20520-0113
> (202) 663-1225

## Holiday and Theme Weddings

*Wedding Plans: 50 Unique Themes for the Wedding of Your Dreams,* by Sharon Dlugosch. (New Brighton, MN: Brighton Publications, Inc. 1989).

*Your Victorian Wedding,* by Georgene Lockwood. (New York, NY: Prentice Hall, 1992).

## Reaffirmation

For reprint of article, write:
  Editorial Department
  *Modern Bride*
  249 West 17th Street
  New York, NY 10011

## CHAPTER 12

## Showers and Parties

*Games for Wedding Shower Fun,* by Sharon Dlugosch. (New Brighton, MN: Brighton Publications, 1987).

*Showers,* by Beverly Clark. (Los Angeles, CA: Wilshire Publications, 1989).

*Wedding Occasions: 101 Party Themes for Wedding Showers, Rehearsal Dinners, Engagement Parties and More!* by Cynthia Lueck Sowden. (Brighton, MN: Brighton Publications, Inc., 1990).

*The Best Party Book—1001 Creative Ideas for Fun Parties,* by Penny Warner. (New York, NY: Simon & Schuster, 1992).

## CHAPTER 13

## All About Gifts

*In the Tiffany Style: Gift-Giving for All Occasions,* by Nancy Tuckerman. (New York, NY: Doubleday, 1990).

## CHAPTER 14

## Handling Divorced Parents

*Planning a Wedding with Divorced Parents,* by Cindy Moore and Tricia Windom. (New York, NY: Crown, 1992).

## Different Cultures

*Modern Bride Wedding Celebrations,* by Cele G. Lalli and Stephanie H. Dahl. (New York, NY: John Wiley & Sons, 1992).

For interracial couples:
  New People Magazine
  P.O. Box 47490
  Oak Park, MI 48237

## Ethnic Customs

For further research and information on their traveling exhibit, "Ethnic Weddings in America," contact:
  The Balch Institute for Ethnic Studies
  18 South Seventh Street
  Philadelphia, PA 19106
  (215) 925-8090

*Broom Jumping: A Celebration of Love,* by Danita Roundree Green. (Richmond, VA: Entertaining Ideas, Ltd., 1992).

*Jumping the Broom: The African American Wedding Planner,* by Harriette Cole. (New York, NY: Henry Holt, 1993).

## Accommodating a Disability

For interpreter service agencies in your area, write or call:
> Registry for Interpreters for the Deaf
> 8719 Colesville Road, Suite 310
> Silver Springs, MD 20910
> (301) 608-0050

## CHAPTER 15

### Your Honeymoon

For a variety of consumer pamphlets, including tips for packing and traveling abroad, send a double-stamped, self-addressed envelope to:
> American Society of Travel Agents
> Dept. FC
> 1101 King Street
> Alexandria, VA 22314
> (703) 739-2782

For a brochure, "Cruising—Answers to Your Most Asked Questions," send a double-stamped, self-addressed envelope to:
> CLIA (Cruise Lines International Association)
> 500 Fifth Avenue
> New York, NY 10110
> (212) 921-0066

For information from American Hawaii Cruises, call:
> (800) 765-7000

For quality-rated small bed and breakfast inns inspected by AAA, Mobil, and the Independent Innkeepers Association, call: (800) 344-5244 or American B & B Association, (804) 379-2222

For questions about changing your maiden name to your married name on your passport, contact:
> Office of Passport Services
> 1425 K Street, NW
> Washington, DC 20524-0002
> (202) 647-0518

Details about trip cancellation/interruption insurance are in the *Family Insurance Handbook,* by Les Abromovitz. (New York, NY: Tab Books, 1991).

## CHAPTER 16

### Marriage Preparation

For information about premarital inventory test programs, write:
> Myers-Briggs Type Indicator
> "Relationship Report"
> Consulting Psychologists Press
> 3803 East Bayshore Road
> Palo Alto, CA 94303
> (800) 624-1765

> FOCCUS (Facilitating Open Couple Communication, Understanding & Study)
> The Archdiocese of Omaha Nebraska, Family Life Office
> 3241 North 60th Street
> Omaha, NE 68104
> (402) 551-9003

PMI Profile
Intercommunications Publishing, Inc.
52-A Dogwood Acres Drive
Chapel Hill, NC 27516
(800) 999-0680

PREPARE (Premarital Personal and Relationship Evaluation)
Prepare-Enrich, Inc.
P.O. Box 190
Minneapolis, MN 55440-0190
(800) 331-1661

*Please Understand Me: Character and Temperament Types,* by David Keirsey and Marilyn Bates, available for $11.95 plus $2 shipping from:
INTJ Books
2153 DeMayo Road
Del Mar, CA 92014
(619) 481-0576

CHAPTER 17

## Premarital Agreement

For a booklet, "Your Legal Guide to Marriage and Other Relationships" (publication #235-005; cost $2.50 plus $1 shipping and handling), call or write:
American Bar Association
Order Fulfillment
750 North Lake Shore Drive
Chicago, IL 60611
(312) 988-5000

CHAPTER 18

## Groom's Questions

*The Groom's Survival Manual,* by Michael R. Perry. (New York, NY: Pocket Books, 1991).

# INDEX

Abromovitz, Less, 175–76
Accessories, 12, 16, 59–62
Accommodations, 13–14, 40–41
  guidelines, 87
  and long-distance weddings,
    122–23
  for outdoor weddings, 123–24
  for out-of-town guests, 83–87
African-Americans
  broom jumping, 163
  and interracial marriages, 161–62
Age
  teen marriages, 159
Alcohol, 78–80, 105–7
  and alcoholism, 168–69
  and cultural differences, 160, 162
American Society of Travel Agents
  (ASTA), 174
Angelo, Alfred
Anniversaries, 165–66
Announcements, 1, 4–5, 10
  guidelines for, 38
  of postponements, 7–9
  sending, 36–37
  wording of, 36–37
  See also Invitations
Army weddings
  See Military weddings
Attendants, 39–53
  accommodations for, 83–87
  attire fittings, 45, 48
  candlelighting, 99–100
  children as, 49–51
  with disabilities, 164–65
  expenses of, 40–41
  flower girl, 40, 43, 50, 53, 148
  gifts for, 146–48

  guidelines for, 53
  number of, 39–40, 42
  pregnant, 51–52
  processional, 95–97
  for reaffirmations, 130
  recessional, 95–97
  ring bearer, 40, 49–50, 53
  selecting, 41–42
  traveling, 43
  ushers, 40
  See also Best man; Bridesmaids;
    Groomsmen; Maid of honor;
    Matron of honor; Ushers
Attire
  See Dressing
Australia, 176

Babysitters, 49–50, 86, 87, 160–61
Bachelor party, 49, 137, 142
Band
  feeding, 105
  leader, 110
  legal issues concerning, 80
  selecting, 73–76
  size of, 74
  vs. disc jockey, 75
Bartender, 106
  and alcoholics, 169
  tipping, 116
Better Business Bureau, 79, 81
Best man, 48–49, 192
  bachelor party, 137
  child as, 121
  duties of, 49
  gifts for, 147
  and rings, 92, 192
  See also Attendants; Groomsmen

Birdseed, throwing, 101, 104
Birthdays, 165–66
Black Tie, 67
Blusher, 60
Bouquet, 77
Bridal gift registry, 136, 143–44
Bridal luncheon, 136
Bridal shops, 16–17, 55–56, 80
Bride
    accessories, 59–62
    attire for, 55–64, 68, 198
    brother of, 94
    changing her name, 185–86
    dress
        cost, 16–17, 40–41, 58–59
        handling, 60
        preserving, 64
        rental, 63
        selection, 55–57, 193–94
    escorting, 93–95, 154–56, 168–69
    father's attire, 67, 93
    fittings for, 55–56, 62–63
    full-figured, 62–63, 198
    gifts for, 148
    luncheon for, 136
    mother's dress, 66–67
    parents of
        expenses, 11–13, 23, 72, 76–77
        gifts, 148
        on invitation, 29–30
    petite, 6, 198
    pregnant, 158
    and remarriage, 119–21
    resources for, 198
    stand-in for, 139–40
    teen, 159
    and thank-you notes, 149
Bridesmaids
    accommodations for, 13–14, 40–41
    accessories for, 147
    attire, 44–46, 68
    children as, 121
    duties of, 46–47
    expenses of, 40–41
    full-figured, 62–63
    gifts for, 146–47
    invitations for, 34
    junior, 41, 50–51
    pregnant, 51–52
    selecting, 41–43
    *See also* Attendants; Maid of honor
Broom jumping, 163
*Broom Jumping: A Celebration of Love,*
    163
Brunch, 14, 20
    *See also* Buffet; Caterers; Food;
        Luncheons; Menu
Budgeting, 11–18
    allocating expenses, 12–14
    and bride's parents, 11–13, 23
    and groom's parents, 12–14, 23
    guidelines, 18
    resources, 197
    for honeymoon, 174–75
Buffet, 109–10
    *See also* Brunch; Caterers; Food;
        Luncheons; Menu
Buses, 79, 84
Butler, 106, 109–10

Cake, 110–12, 116
    and anniversaries, 165
    and double marriages, 125
    groom's, 111–12
    resources, 201
    types of, 111
Candlelight, 99–100
Caribbean, 174, 176
Caterers
    establishments, 104–5
    legal issues concerning, 80, 105
    selecting, 23, 105–7, 193
    *See also* Food; Menu
Catholic weddings, 89–90, 157–58
    scheduling, 90
Centerpieces, 113

"Celebrating the New Family," 121
Ceremony, 89–101
  and candlelight, 99–100
  Christian, 96–99, 157–58
  and Christmas theme, 127–28
  church, 89–101
  civil, 3–4, 97–98, 157–58
  cultural and ethnic differences,
    159–63
  finding an officiant, 89–91
  interfaith, 97–99, 157–58, 162
  invitation to, 35
  Jewish, 94, 96–99, 101–2, 156
  planning, 101
  processional, 95–97
  programs for, 91
  recessional, 95–97
  resources for, 199–200
  seating during, 92–93
Certified Travel Counselors (CTC),
  174
Charities
  donations to, 145
Checklist, 122
Children, 28, 41, 43, 49–51
  accommodations for, 86
  as attendants, 49
  as best man, 121
  babysitters for, 49–50, 86, 87,
    160–61
  and cultural differences, 160–61
  as candlelighters, 99
  and premarital agreements, 187
  of previous marriages, 121
Christmas weddings, 19, 115, 126–28
Churches, 89–101
  layout of, 93, 125
  seating in, 92–93
Civil Weddings, 3–4, 90–91, 97–98,
  157–58
  and reaffirmations, 129–30
Claddagh, 163
Clergy

  *See* Officiant
Cocktails, 109–10, 169
Coleman, Roger, 121
Coloriffics, 61
Community Christian Church, 121
Computer Theme, 128
Consultant, 55–56
  duties of, 22, 81
  fees, 15–16
  hiring, 15–16
  for outdoor weddings, 123–24
  during reception, 110
  resources, 197
Costs
  *See* Budgeting; Expenses
Country-and-Western Theme, 61
Coworkers
  inviting, 26–27
Cruise Lines International
  Association, 118, 177
Cruises, 118, 177
Cultural differences, 159–63
  and alcohol, 160, 162
  children at wedding, 160–61
  Greek Orthodox, 157–58
  interfaith, 89–91, 97–99, 157–58,
    162
  interracial, 161–62
  Italian, 124, 145, 162
  Jewish, 90, 96–98, 101–2, 156
  language issues, 159–61
  resources for, 202
  *See also* Ethnic differences

Dancing, 114
  cultural differences, 160, 162
  at double marriages, 125
  groom and mother of the bride,
    193
Dates
  conflicting, 166–67
  *See also* Scheduling
Deceased relatives, 167–68

Destination weddings, 117–19
  resources for, 201
Disabilities, 164–65
  resources for accommodating, 203
Disc Jockey, 75, 81, 110, 116
Divorce
  on invitation, 31–32
  and inviting ex-spouses, 169
  parents, 5, 31–32, 93, 153–56
  in newspaper announcements, 5
  seating, 93
Dollar dance, 114, 163
Double weddings, 124–25
Dressing, 55–70
  accessories, 59–62
  all white, 127
  bride's attire, 55–64, 68, 193–94
  cost of bride's dress, 16–17, 40–41,
    58–59
  bridesmaids, 44–46, 68
  for double weddings, 124–25
  expense of, 12–13
  fittings, 45, 48, 55
  groom's attire, 64–66, 69, 194
  guests' attire, 67–70
  father's attire, 67, 69
  for military weddings, 121–23
  mother's dress, 66–67, 69
  pregnant attendants, 51–52
  at reception, 113–14
  and remarriage, 119–20
  resources for, 198
  styles of, 20–21, 59–70
Drinks, 78–80, 105–7, 116
Dyeables, 61

Elopement, 21, 141
Engagement, 1–10
  announcing, 1, 4, 10
  broken, 8–9
  dinner, 5
  guidelines, 10
  in Holland, 2–3

newspaper announcements, 1, 4–5
  length of, 3–4
  presents, 5–7
  parties, 1, 5–7
  postponing, 8–9
  proposals, 1
  and reengagements, 9
  rings, 2–3
England, 176–77
Ethnic differences, 162–63
  resources, 202–3
  *See also* Cultural differences
Ex-spouses
  inviting, 27–28
Expenses, 11–18
  allocating, 12–14, 23
  for bride's parents, 11–13, 23, 72,
    76–77
  for bridesmaids, 40–41, 43
  dressing, 12–13, 16–17
  flowers, 76–77
  gifts, 145
  for groom's parents, 12–13, 23, 72,
    76–77
  guidelines, 18
  honeymoon, 174–75
  reception, 14

Family
  as attendants, 42, 44, 48
  attire, 66–70
  changing names, 185–86
  and conflicting dates, 166–67
  counseling, 3
  cultural differences between, 159–63
  deceased relatives, 167–68
  delegating to, 22–24
  with disabilities, 164–65
  divorced parents, 153–56, 182
  ethnic, 162–63
  and guest lists, 25–28
  handling disagreements, 20–22, 27,
    43, 154–58, 168–71, 182–83

living with, 187–88
milestones of, 165–66
in receiving line, 108
seating at reception, 108–9
and small weddings, 27
stress, 181–83
*See also* Bride; Groom
*Family Insurance Handbook*, 175–76
Family Medallion, 121
Favors, guest, 111–12
Floral designer, 77
Florists
    alternatives to, 115
    as groom's expense, 76–77
    legal issues concerning, 80
    selecting, 76–77, 199
Flower girl, 40, 43, 53, 121
    gifts for, 148
    seating for, 109
    *See also* Attendants
Flowers
    expense of, 12–13
    selecting, 76–77
    resources, 199
Food, 107–8, 116
    ethnic, 163
    selecting, 23, 193
    *See also* Brunch; Buffet; Caterer;
        Luncheons
Foreign Countries
    resources for marriage in, 201
    travel to, 174–177, 179
    weddings in, 124, 140
Formalwear
    *See* Groom, attire; Groomsmen,
        attire
Fourth of July wedding, 127

Games
    at reception, 113
    at shower, 133–34
Garden weddings, 103–4
Garters, 114

Gifts, 143–51
    alternatives, 145–46
    and announcements, 36
    for attendants, 146–48
    between bride and groom, 148
    and broken engagements, 8–9
    discouraging, 7
    displaying, 144–45
    donation to charities, 145
    engagement, 5–7, 10
    expense of, 12–13, 133–34,
        194–95
    money as, 135, 145–46
    for parents, 148
    opening, 7, 116
    for reaffirmations, 129–30
    registry, 136, 143–44
    resources for, 204
    sending, 145
    shower, 134–36
    thank-you notes for, 7, 149–50
Gloves, 61
Gown, *See* Dressing
Grandparents, 94
Greece, 177
Greek Orthodox weddings, 98,
    157–58
Green, Dania Roundree, 163
Groom
    attire, 64–66, 69, 194, 198
    bachelor party, 49, 137, 192
    father's attire, 67, 69
    friends of, 192
    gifts for, 148
    mother's dress, 66–67
    parents' expense, 12–13, 76–77
    parents' gifts, 148
    participation in planning, 192–95
    hints for, 195, 198
    and honeymoon, 194
    in prison, 156
    questions of, 191–95
    resources for, 198

and ring, 191
and thank-you notes, 149, 151
tuxedo vs. morning suit, 65–66
and the wedding dress, 56, 58, 72
Groom's cake, 111–12, 166
Groomsmen, 47–49
  attire, 48, 194
  accommodations of, 13–14, 47–48
  duties of, 48–49
  gifts for, 147
  invitations for, 34
  *See also* Attendants; Best man;
    Ushers
Guest book, 42–43, 110
Guests
  accommodations for, 83–87
  attire, 67–70
  with disabilities, 164
  divorced parents, 154–58, 182
  entertainment for, 114
  ex-spouse, 169
  favors for, 111–12
  compiling list of, 25–28
  out of town, 83–87
  for rehearsal dinner, 138–39
  and rescheduling, 170
  for shower, 134–35

Hairdressers, 60
Halloween wedding, 127–28
Headpieces, 12, 16, 59–62
  for attendants, 46
Heirlooms, 60
  dresses as, 56, 58–59
  preserving, 64
History themes, 128
Holiday weddings, 126–28
  *See also* Christmas weddings;
    Theme weddings
Honeymoon, 173–79
  budgeting for, 174–75
  changing money for, 176
  destinations, 117–19, 173–74

as groom's expense, 194
limited time for, 173–74
marriage during, 117
packing for, 176
passports for, 177
planning, 49, 173–79
postponing, 19–20
resources for, 203
scheduling, 19–20
tipping, 177–78
tours, 175–76
travel agents, 174–75
and thank-you notes, 150
and weather, 176
Honor attendants
  gifts for, 146–47
  parents as, 46
  pregnant, 51
  in processional, 97
  *See also* Attendants; Best man; Maid
    of honor; Matron of honor
Hosiery, 61–62
Hotels, 104–5
  *See also* Accommodations
Housework, 188–90

Immigration and Naturalization
  Service, U.S., 124
Interfaith marriages, 89–91, 97–99,
  157–58, 162
  resource for planning, 200
Interracial marriages, 161–62
Invitations, 25–37
  addressing, 33–37
  and bride's parents, 29–32
  to ceremony only, 35
  compiling guest list, 25–28
  computer-generated, 29, 128
  and deceased relatives, 167–68
  and divorced parents, 154–56, 182
  elopement and reception, 141
  form of address on, 29–35, 186
  guidelines for, 38

and menus, 107–8
and nicknames, 29
for reaffirmation, 129–30
to reception only, 35
to rehearsal dinner, 138–39
for remarriage, 120–21
response to, 28–29
selecting, 28–29
style of, 21, 29
Ireland, 140
traditions of, 163
Italy, 162
sending gifts to, 145
weddings in, 124

Jack and Jill Parties, 134, 137
Jamaica, 174
Jewish weddings, 94, 96–99, 101–2, 156
Junior bridesmaids, 41, 50–51, 121

Kissing
at the reception, 113, 163

Language issues, 159–61
*See also* Cultural differences
Legal Issues
alcohol, 78–80
bridal shops, 79
caterers, 80
florists, 80
and marriage abroad, 124
musicians, 80
names, 186
premarital agreements, 187
photographers, 80
Limousines, 78
*See also* Transportation
Liquor
*See* Alcohol
Lodges, 84
*See also* Accommodations
Long-distance weddings, 122–23

Luncheons, 136
*See also* Brunch; Buffet; Food; Menu

Maid of honor, 39
attire, 44–45
duties of, 46–47
groom's equivalent, 192
pregnant, 51–52
selecting, 39
and shower, 134–35
*See also* Attendants; Bridesmaids
Marionat, 61
Master of ceremonies, 116
*See also* Band; Disc jockey
Matron of honor, 39, 47, 51
groom's equivalent, 192
*See also* Attendants; Bridesmaids
Menu, 107–8, 193
*See also* Brunch; Buffet; Food; Luncheons
Mexico, 176
Military weddings, 121–22
resources for, 201
*Modern Bride*
children's gifts from, 148
checklist, 122
department store shows, 143
Money
as gift, 135, 145–46
premarital agreements, 187–88
sharing, 188, 190
*See also* Budgeting; Expenses; Gifts, money as
Money tree, 146
Music
for ceremony, 73–74
cultural differences, 160
dancing, 114
disc jockey, 75
expense of, 12–13
for reception, 11–12, 74–76
*See also* Bands

Name changing, 185–86
Name tags, 109
National Limousine Association, 78
Navy weddings
   *See* Military weddings
Newspaper announcements, 1, 4–5,
   10
   of broken engagements, 8–9
   and deceased parents, 4
   and divorced parents, 5
   and professional degrees, 30
   and remarried parents, 5
   and stepparents, 5
   timing of, 5–6

Office of Passport Services, 177
Officiant, 89–101
   Catholic, 89–90
   finding, 89–91
   Jewish, 90
   and pregnant bride, 158
   and vows, 91

Parents
   anniversary of, 165
   as attendants, 46
   cohost wedding, 32–35
   disagreements with, 20–22, 27
   divorced, 5, 31–32, 93, 153–56
   expenses of, 11–13, 23, 72, 76–77
   father's attire, 67
   living with, 187–88
   mother's attire, 66–67
   object to marriage, 156–58
   seating, 93
   transportation to ceremony, 78
Parking, 85–86
Parties
   bachelor, 49, 137
   bridal luncheons, 136
   engagement, 1, 5–7
   etiquette, 142
   gifts for, 134–36

   guest list, 7, 44, 133–35
   hosting, 6–7
   informality of, 6–7
   invitations, 6
   post-wedding reception, 140–41
   pre-wedding reception, 140–41
   rehearsal, 138–40
   resources for, 202–3
   showers, 47, 133–36
   *See also* Gifts; Reception
Passports, 177
Pastor
   meeting with, 89–91
   *See also* Officiant
Pearls, 62
Perfume, 112
Philippines
   traditions of, 163
Photographers
   feeding, 105
   during ceremony, 101
   legal issues concerning, 80
   at post-wedding reception, 140
   selecting, 71–73
   resources, 198
Photographs
   expense of, 72
   and announcements, 4
   and divorced parents, 156
   and pregnant attendants, 52
   restricting, 72–73
   scheduling, 72
   in thank-you notes, 149
Piccione, Michele, 62
Post-wedding receptions, 140–41
Pregnancy, 158
Premarital agreement, 187, 190
   resources for, 204
Pre-wedding reception, 140–41
Prison, 158
Processional
   order of, 95–97
   for double marriages, 125

for remarriage, 119
*See also* Bride, escorting
Professionals
listing degrees on invitations, 30
and name changing, 186
forms of address for, 33–34
Programs
for ceremony, 91
Proposals, 1
Protestant weddings, 98
*See also* Ceremony, Christian
Puerto Rico
customs of, 163

Reaffirmations, 128–30
celebrations for, 128–29
gifts for, 129–30
invitations for, 129–30
and religious services, 129
resources for, 202
rings for, 129
Reception, 103–16
alcohol at, 106–7
allergies at, 112
budgeting for, 14
cake, 111
caterer for, 105–7
entertainment at, 114
ethnic, 162–63
essentials, 110
expenses of, 11–14
guests, 14
invitations to, 35
location of, 103–4
menu for, 107–8
multiple, 140–41
post-wedding, 140–42
pre-wedding, 140–41
quandaries at, 112–15
receiving line, 108
resources, 200
scheduling, 19–20, 110–11
seating, 108–9

smoking at, 112
in separate place from ceremony, 37
style of, 20–21
Recessional
for double marriages, 125
order of, 97
Registry, 136, 143–44
and groom, 192–93
Rehearsal festivities, 138–40
and divorced parents, 154
invitations to, 138–39
seating for, 138
stand-ins for, 139–40
Remarriage, 119–21
resources for, 201
Renewal celebration, 3
Resources, 197–204
for bride's attire, 198
on budgeting, 197
on ceremony, 199–200
cultural differences, 202
destination weddings, 201
divorced parents, 202
ethnic customs, 202–3
flowers, 199
gifts, 202
for groom's attire, 198
guests with disabilities, 203
guidelines for, 81
holiday weddings, 202
honeymoon, 203
interfaith marriages, 200
marrying abroad, 201
military weddings, 201
music, 199
parties, 202
photographers, 198
preparations, 203–4
premarital agreements, 204
reaffirmation, 202
for reception, 103–8, 200–201
remarriage, 201

on rings, 197
showers, 202
selecting, 71–81
theme weddings, 202
toasting, 200
transportation, 199
videographers, 198
wedding cakes, 201
on wedding consultants, 197
on wedding style, 198
Rice throwing, 101, 114
Ring bearer, 40, 49–40, 53, 92
gifts for, 148
seating for, 109
*See also* Attendants
Rings
and broken engagements, 8–9
choice of, 2
Claddagh, 163
engagement, 2, 10, 92
etiquette of, 92
expense of, 2
and gems, 2
and groom, 191
handling, 92
for reaffirmations, 129
resources, 197
wedding bands, 2

Schedules
choosing a date, 19–20, 89
conflicting dates, 166–67
engagement, 3–4, 10
of ceremony, 4, 20, 90
of honeymoon, 19–20
of photographs, 72
planning, 4, 103, 183
reception, 110–11
and resources, 81
selecting a gown, 56–57
and stress, 181–83
Seasons, 45, 56, 59, 103
Seating

at ceremony, 92–93
for double marriages, 125
at reception, 108–9, 116
for rehearsal dinner, 138
Shoes, 61
Showers, 47, 133–36, 142
games, 133–34
gifts, 134–36
guest list for, 134–35
for remarriage, 120
resources for, 202–3
Singing
at reception, 113
Spain, 174
Special situations, 153–71
alcoholism, 168–69
attendants with disabilities, 164–65
conflicting dates, 166–67
cultural differences, 159–62
deceased relatives, 167–68
divorced parents, 153–56
divorces, 169
ethnic traditions, 162–63
family milestones, 165–66
interfaith, 89–91, 97–99, 157–58, 162
interracial, 161–62
inviting guests, 170–71
objections to marriage, 256–58
personality conflicts, 169–70
postponing weddings, 170
pregnant bride, 158
prison, 158
teen marriage, 159
Specialty weddings
*See* Weddings, specialty
Stress, 181–83
*See also* Family, handling disagreements; Therapists

Tents, 123–24
Teenage marriage, 159
Thank-you notes, 149–51

Theme weddings, 126–28
  Christmas, 126–27
  computers, 128
  ethnic, 162–63
  and family milestones, 165–66
  Fourth of July, 127
  Halloween, 127
  history, 128
  resources for, 202
  *See also* Weddings, specialty
Therapists, 3, 156–57
  resources for, 203–4
Tipping
  bartender, 116
  during honeymoon, 177–78
Toasting, 110, 137–40
  resources for, 200
Transportation
  and alcohol, 78–80
  buses, 79, 84
  limousine services, 78, 199
  for out of town guests, 83–87
  resources, 199
  *See also* Travel
Travel
  of attendants, 43, 47–48
  accommodations, 13–14, 40–41,
    83–87
  and dress fittings, 45
  honeymoon planning, 173–79
  and long-distance weddings,
    122–23, 182–83
  reception in distant place, 37,
    140–41
  and travel agents, 173–76
  wedding in distant place, 117–19
  *See also* Honeymoon; Transportation
Travel agents, 173–76
Tuxedos, 64–67
  *See also* Dressing
U.S. Tour Operators Association
  (USTOA), 175–76
Unity Candle, 100

Ushers, 40, 47–49
  gifts for, 147
  junior, 51
  and seating, 92–93
  *See also* Attendants; Groomsmen

Veils, 12, 16, 59–62
Videographers
  feeding, 105
  during ceremony, 72–73, 101
  resources, 198
  selecting, 71–73
Videotapes, 71–73, 81
  restricting, 72–73
Vows
  writing your own, 91

Weather, 103–4, 123–24, 126
Wedding cake
  *See* Cake
*Wedding Celebrations,* 97
Wedding consultant
  *See* Consultant
Wedding dress, 55–64, 68, 193–94
  cost of, 16–17
  *See also* Accessories; Bride, attire;
    Dressing, bride's attire
Weddings
  abroad, 124
  Christian, 95–99, 157–58
  civil, 3–4, 90, 97
  Catholic, 89–90, 157–58
  conflicting dates for, 166–67
  destination, 117–19
  double, 124–26
  ethnic, 162–63
  garden, 103–4, 123–24
  Greek Orthodox, 98, 157–58
  holiday, 126–28
  home, 123–24
  interfaith, 89–91, 97–99, 157–58,
    162
  interracial, 16–62

Jewish, 90, 96–98, 101–2, 156
long-distance, 122–23, 182–83
military, 121–22
outdoor, 103–4
Protestant, 98
reaffirmation, 128–30
and remarriage, 119–21

rescheduled, 170
specialty, 117–31
stress, 181–83
themes, 126–28
Wishing wells, 133–34
Work
  inviting friends from, 26–27

# About the Author

**Cele Goldsmith Lalli,** Editor-in-Chief of *Modern Bride* magazine, is a nationally recognized authority on the American bridal market, wedding planning, and etiquette, and the changing needs of today's bride. She travels throughout the country speaking with brides and grooms about all aspects of wedding, honeymoon, and first-home planning. She writes a wedding etiquette column in *Modern Bride* and is a frequent guest on television and radio shows.

Mrs. Lalli, who began her publishing career in science fiction and then moved into the women's service field, has been an editor with *Modern Bride* since 1965. She was appointed editor-in-chief in 1980. A graduate of Vassar College, she lives in Connecticut, with her husband, Michael. They are the parents of two daughters.

She is also the co-author of *Modern Bride Wedding Celebrations: The Complete Wedding Planner for Today's Bride.*